Sixty Years of Light Work

EXIT

Sixty Years of Light Work

Fred Bentham

Strand Lighting Limited, 1992

First Edition

A *LIGHTS!* publication.
Strand Lighting
Grant Way
Syon Lane
Isleworth
Middlesex TW7 5QD
United Kingdom

ISBN: 0 902277 02 2

Designed and produced by Barrie James West Associates Limited

The frontispiece shows those present at the final Sales conference as Strand Electric, held at 29 King Street London in January 1968. Those present were: Messrs. Ashwell, Avison, Baker, Bear, Bentham, Biddle, Birch, Bond, K. Bourke, Bristow, Britten, Brown, Buck, Burroughs, Church, Clarke, Cohen, Collingwood, Coppendale, Corne, Corry, Day, Davis, Fenner, Fitzwater, French, Gatfield, Gibson, Hearn, Heath, Hughes, H.O. Jordan, L. Jordan, Lang, Legge, LeSueur, Madre, Magnus, Martin, McKenzie, Morgan, Mould, Payne, Regester, Rose, P.R. Sheridan, Smythe, Walker, Watling, Watson, Webb, Weston, Wood, Wooderson, Woolnough.

CONTENTS

INTRODUCTION:

Give my address as 29 Shaftesbury Avenue and there is an awe-struck but not really surprised gasp. On the other hand, 15 Crownhill Road would not mean a thing to anyone, and this in spite of the fact that there is a Bentham stone* there carved by my sculptor brother, Philip. To initiates, Shaftesbury Avenue means theatres and for someone who, like myself, has spent sixty years working one way and another for theatre, a penthouse or at any rate a tiny office in one of the six theatres in that avenue is not all that improbable. Until, that is, one remembers that for forty years I worked for Strand Electric - a firm where the rates of pay would never stretch to such luxury. It is my career in that firm which makes me use the preposition 'for' instead of 'in' above. Our work involved us very closely in theatre in those days and "Strand Electric" was a password at almost any stage door. It is also a famous name in the history of theatre and I have to add that my own name did also become well known in the arcane circles within which we worked - stage lighting.

The chapters which follow deal with the rise and fall of that firm from the very personal viewpoint of one who was playing a role of one kind and another in its cast. Rise is easily understood but by 'fall' I mean the loss of control over lighting control in the late 1960s due to our inability to keep up with technology appropriate to the time. At which point the Rank Organisation literally, if unwittingly, came to our rescue. Strand began as a private firm in 1914, became a public company in 1936 and, in my opinion, expired when the premises in Covent Garden, the heart of London's theatreland, were vacated and in consequence I decided on premature retirement. Since then Strand, or rather Rank Strand, and latterly Strand Lighting, has had a mixture of good and bad years; which means that their balance sheet has looked good or looked bad. This is the only way a taken-over firm can talk to it's organisation's Führer. This is not a good word; for although it may evoke the atmosphere, the chairman and his board cannot lead in the true sense of the word, or in my own interpretation of the word. A leader must know the ground and the people on it. There is little logic in people's enthusiasms for engineering equipment; in this field which is so closely related to art at any rate. My own guiding principle seems to have

*Contrary to expectations, it does not record "Benthams lived here" but is a foundation stone for an extension to the Keeble School!

been that it was inconceivable that I could be the only one as crazy as I was over stage lighting. In pursuing what I did over the years I not only gathered up the 'as crazies' but seem to have infected borderline cases.

Strand Electric is a good example of the small specialist firms in our time and back in history in which two or three people originally got together to promote some enthusiasm or other - even just the making of money. I have never been able to understand that; it doesn't grip me, so lets stick to engineering. On only two occasions in my career has personal financial gain motivated any important action of mine; "and more fool you" many people will probably say. My trouble was that I was so keen on the things I wanted to get done, that the fact that my employer could be persuaded to make them at all was the best reward I could envisage at the time. However, the reader can gather whether this was really true or not.

Another thing does stick out, which is I could not bear to separate myself from the things which originally drew me to stage lighting. To sit behind a desk and organise people so that they had all the fun was not for me. Thus demonstrating the equipment, playing with the light itself, and therefore lecturing and writing about it, has always been something to enjoy. An example of this kind of thing is the Dolmetsch family firm of Haselmere (founded by Arnold and carried on ever since by his son Carl). They made, and get made, 'ancient' instruments and they also play them in public. Excepting that their main aim has been backwards in time, whereas mine had to be forwards, there are distinct parallels. Carl Dolmetsch and I are the same age, and like me he is a past-master of The Art Workers' Guild, and our fathers were members of that guild of craftsmen and artists.

In 1976 when revising my *The Art of Stage Lighting* so that Pitman could publish it in an enlarged more glamorous format (marketing up to its pranks?) I found myself getting them to print this dedication: "To the members of my department over the years, without whom Strand Electric and the 'I' of this book could not have done what we did." This I repeat here but it will become apparent, when reading my story, that there were other *key* figures, both inside and outside the firm - indeed there were!

Finally I must remark that although I had completed what I thought of as my Auto-Bio, I had not taken any real steps to get it published. In the financial Gloom of the present, it seemed unlikely that anyone would consider sixty years of light work a proposition. So except for extracts as "Archival Nostalgia" in *Sightline,* or "I was there" in *TABS,* there it lay in my filing cabinet. At which point enter Andy Collier and it is thanks to his drive and his friend 'Mac' together with the wonders of printing in this post-Hot Metal era, the book is here.

I: CROWNHILL ROAD
St. Matthew, St. Paul & Aeschylus 1911-29

Number 15 Crownhill Road Harlesden was where I was born on October 23rd 1911. It was in Middlesex, but the postal code was London N.W.10. A number of the principal characters in these chapters were born in the following year; but except that Captain Scott made second place to the South Pole, nothing much seems to have happened in mine. Father, although the eldest son of a bank cashier, was a sculptor. Mother was the daughter of a chemist. Grandfather, John Kingdom Hobbs was a qualified pharmacist who had originally a shop in the High Street; but when the road had to be widened for the electric trams, he built himself a chemist's shop with a house alongside and there it was that first myself, then my brother Philip (a year and eight months later) were born. In those days birth in hospital was rare in middle class homes. The family doctor always 'did it' at home. I don't know who the doctor was who delivered me but I do know who christened me. It was the Rev. Noel Bonavia Hunt, the curate at St. Matthew's, Harlesden. He was an organ enthusiast who not only designed the specification of the 3-manual instrument in that church but became quite a name in the organ building world. Since I was to hear that instrument regularly for some sixteen years, its quality may have had much to do with my addiction to organ music and organ consoles ever since.

When in 1928 my sister Celia (named after Mother) showed signs of imminent arrival I was packed off to the house of a school friend ten minute's walk away. The journey was done in our car. Since those were still the days where people walked, this needs explanation; especially as the walk to 'our' garage was almost as long as that to my friend's house. It was one of a set in a converted mews originally used for stabling horses. The relatively few owners of cars then, did not park them on the kerbside overnight. The car was used because, unbelievably, my model theatre had to go with me! So there it was perched up on the back seat of our open-top bull-nosed Morris Cowley.

This was not because at the age of seventeen I could not bear to be parted from it even for one week, it was because my friend's parents thought it would be a good idea for me to put on a colour-music show for some of their friends while I was there. In theatre parlance this was my first touring date! I know it happened, but as I type these words I find it difficult to believe them. My model theatre was never at any time simple and for the majority of its existence had a small room to itself at the back of no. 15, en suite with my bedroom. This makes our home sound rather grand, but it was a typical London plan house of before the first World War. Were it not for the need of a shop alongside, it would probably have been a terrace house. To the East it was semi-detached but not in the normal meaning of the word. Next door was smaller in every dimension and it sort of leaned up against us: the party wall was so thick that no sounds got through. The house on the far side of the shop was the first of a terrace and did not overlook our garden at all. Backing on to the garden was the boys' playground of the Keeble school (C. of E.) and on the far side of that was the Convent of Jesus and Mary set in large grounds amid some trees.

Many, many years later a certain Mary O'Malley attended this convent school and later wrote "Once A Catholic" (which I much enjoyed at Wyndhams Theatre London in October 1977). Mother too was an 'old' Convent girl. Although at no time a Catholic, she had been very happy there, so for both Phil and I it was our first school: the nuns took on couple of dozen boys till the age of nine. In other words it was a mixed school for the 'safe period', though I must confess I can still remember being somewhat fascinated by a quiet girl in my class with a red sash around her gym tunic. Not that I ever spoke to her or any girl there. Her name was Gardiner and the red sash meant she was a border. Why did we not go to the Keeble school immediately next door? They were too 'common' and we simply did not mix or even speak to them or they to us - not even when they climbed our fence during their breaks to gaze at what we were doing. And why should they find our play so interesting? The answer lay in our Bassett-Lowke model railway, which was gauge 1 (1³/4-ins) and ran round our small garden; but this is to anticipate. The playground was only used during school hours and the geography of house and garden gave an unusual degree of seclusion for such a built-up area. There were no young children nearby with whom we could associate and playing in the street was something we did not need to do. Except for scooting along with Mother to the shops and to Roundwood Park we did not play outside the house. The local shops were either for *them* or for *us*. Some were for them and us; but even then there could be a hint of division. Hersant the butcher in the High Street near the Jubilee clock was a good example. Inside to the left was imported meat; to the right was the fresh meat. Separation was by an impressive wood cash-kiosk. Mother always went right, but this time they were not able to provide the size of joint she needed. Whereupon young Hersant dropped his voice to say that they had some New Zealand which he could recommend. Consent obtained, he stole round the back of the kiosk. There hanging on the left he saw *the* joint. This he sneaked back and exposed to Mother. I have a feeling that New Zealand lamb figured often in our menus so long as it was obtained the *right* way. Fresh meat really was fresh meat. One could encounter animals being herded up the High Street, among the traffic, to the slaughter-house at the back of Hersants. Almost next door was 'The Crown' with that long surviving class-distinction of Public and Private bars.

(I think what we are dealing with here is habit rather than snobbery. Where do we feel *relaxed*?). Phil and I were thrown very much together, and although he was to join the tennis club when he grew up, I became something of a recluse due to my devotion by then to my model theatre and to reading.

Mother did not get out and about all that much either. It was Father who shot off to the studio all days of the week and sometimes Sundays as well. As an artist he enjoyed his work and the socialising it involved. Except for the fact that he had a very outgoing personality, his attitude to work was to become mine. His influence on me was by deeds rather than words, I could see for myself that work could be fun. How can a child who grows up in that atmosphere be the same as one in a family where work was work; something to earn money to use to do things you would like? It was certainly not the case that the nature of my future work became clear early on. My brother may have had his eye on the studio in Chelsea, but I did not; although we both enjoyed our days-out there and the chance to do some modelling in clay, to see plaster casting or whatever.

In the 1920s Father could be very busy at times with a number of craftsmen in his employ. His studio was one of a cluster alongside Stamford Bridge railway station on the opposite side of the Fulham Road to the football ground. Two sets of white footprints (sculpture is a very dirty-clean craft) identified the entrance doorway. One set wheeled round to the adjacent railway station, where Father had the use of their telephone (Putney 22). Incoming calls meant the porter would rush round to the studio's entrance and shout. The second set of footprints went across to the 'Rising Sun' and was used by 'his man' young Wood for jug-traffic. The football ground, especially on a cup-final afternoon, could create a lot of annoying noise. The studio block was far from glamorous; but handy for Father as he could rent one or two more of them depending on the amount of work in hand. Often it was war memorials, with a life-size or larger statue of a soldier with his rifle in some pose or other, but always with long lists of casualties to be cut in wood or stone; or cast, as bronze panels were in demand. This could be followed by work on new buildings such as the P & O's head office in the City. Father's range was wide indeed; not only in application but in style. He was equally at home with classic, medieval, or art deco; but he did not approve of Epstein's "Night and Day" on St. James' Park station office block, and that kind of thing. It is strange to see in the Tate the modern 'Art' exhibits of bricks, pebbles or tortured metal and remind oneself that Father had much to do in the Duveen galleries. Above all he was a practical man in the crafts required by a sculptor. Later with the decline in the amount of decoration on buildings, and the slump in general, times got hard. So much so that the acceptance of a teaching post offered by Johannesburg University was seriously considered. My story, had that happened, is beyond imagination: especially if it is realised that I turned down an invitation to take part in a theatre conference in South Africa in 1974 with the remark that there was a risk that I might say something which could give offence.

When young, Phil and I were expected to go to church on Sundays. There was a children's Eucharist at 10-o'clock, for which a special small altar was lifted out and put immediately below the chancel arch to make the service intimate. This was in the 1920s, so it was very advanced for the time. The church was "St Matthew, St Mary's Road, Harlesden, 1902, by Caroe," to quote the single line given it by Pevsner*. At the time it seemed to me unlike other churches resembling neither the Gothic ones nor those of the Wren ilk. The day would come when I was to find myself, as an elderly man, selling sherry every fortnight beneath W.D. Caroe's name in guilt letters; but that venture belongs to my last chapter.

St Matthew's was high on incense, vestments, ritual and music. It must have been the theatre in it all that which got me as a boy. The vicar and two curates looked after the parish, and memory suggests that attendances at services were good: two sometimes three houses for early morning communion. As High Church, Phil and I were confirmed very early: I would be twelve and he ten-plus. A big hurdle was confession a day or two before the monthly communion, at which we went up to the high altar to eat the body and drink the blood of Christ. And that was what we did, our belief was absolute. Because of this 'fact', no food was permitted before these early morning services, so it is hardly surprising that on the odd occasion the very tall candlesticks wobbled and I nearly fainted.

To help us find some sins to confess, there was a printed check list, and only three presented any difficulty. The key adjective in each case was "impure". The sins were: impure words, impure deeds and impure *thoughts*. This last strikes me as particularly unfair because any resolute behaviour was bound sooner or later to be undone by a vivid wet dream. Our priest, Father Davis, was a jolly chap who became a great friend of the family and coached me in mathematics. He also enjoyed a drop of scotch with my father†. There was no concealment behind a grille as in Roman Catholic practice; there he and you were, out in the open and about to say that you had had impure thoughts and maybe worse - once again. Nevertheless my addiction to the Faith and its rituals persisted and I even saw myself taking holy orders and, like a number of others, becoming a celibate schoolmaster (though not of course at the Keeble school!). To achieve this meant continuing to take Greek as well as the normal Latin - this first at Colet Court, the preparatory school for St. Paul's School immediately opposite on the Hammersmith Road. The skyline to the West of the

* *The Buildings of England,* by Nickolas Pevsner.

† I took Fr. Davis to his studio in Gunter Grove one morning; we had just passed the 'Gunter Arms' and were walking down the road, when out of 8a popped Wood and the empty jug. Sighting me and the dog-collar alongside, he tried to hide it behind his back. Needless to say, once inside the studio we all had a jolly good laugh!

Colet Court playground and playing field was dominated by the silhouette of the King's Theatre Hammersmith. By Sprague, it was a real theatre outline with the stage tower to the right and the upward sweep of the roof over the circles and front of house on the left.

The interior of the 1,566 seater King's Theatre was familiar, for that was where we were taken by Father and Mother to see Frank Benson's company touring Shakespeare, Fred Terry in *The Scarlet Pimpernel*, and much else including pantomime. It was our local theatre, though it was 45-minutes by tram from home. Our true 'local' was the Willesden Hippodrome (1907-1927), a large Variety house by Frank Matcham. It was only a short walk away but we didn't go to that type of show. Any variety acts in our life were to be seen on the stage of the 3,000 seater Shepherds Bush Pavilion (later the Gaumont and still later the Odeon) a Davis house by Frank Verity. Mother never went to the Willesden Hip' but Father occasionally used to take Phil and me to its first house when there was a play he knew we would like - such as *Alf's Button*, *The Flag Lieutenant,* and *The Ringer* by Edgar Wallace. We sat in the front in what I am sure must have been called the fauteuils, a term which lingered on in some Variety houses. It was certainly in use at the Chiswick Empire until it was pulled down in 1959.

The Willesden Hip' was always crowded, and it was very impressive to emerge from the centre vomitory (an unusual means of stalls access) and see all those people massed up behind. The end of the show was equally awe-inspiring with the audience noisily pouring out, and the masses waiting to get in during the quick change from one house to the other. It was destroyed by a bomb in 1940 and the King's Theatre was demolished in 1963. The interior of the most influential entertainment building in my early life, the Shepherds Bush Pavilion, was, as I indignantly put it in my *Builder* article of September 2nd 1932, "vandalised" by W. E. Trent, but that bit was censored. In more recent times it has become far more mucked about. First, in the interests of twinning and now, seemingly, of BINGO. What did survive well into the 1980s was the Coliseum cinema Harlesden, just round the corner from where we lived. It was well described by David Atwell* as an "amusingly claustrophobic little auditorium with a tiny balcony hardly changed at all since 1912." That balcony was where Mother would take us after Convent school to see *The Whip*, *King Solomon's Mines*, *Mutt and Jeff*, and *The Kid*. There were also some New Era war films (*Mons*, *Ypres*, and the *Coronel and Falkland Isles*) though I think they must have been Father's choice and he would have taken us instead. With *The Covered Wagon* in 1923, our allegiance was transferred to the brand-new Pavilion - even though it was a tram-ride away. Rather nearer was Sydney Bernstein's Empire Willesden (later to

* *Cathedrals of the Movies,* The Architectural Press 1980

become the Granada) where the cinema organ console made its first impact on me, as I saw the small 3-manual Christie came up, spotlit, on its lift. Cheap matinees in the school holidays were to see me alone in the front row balcony watching the organist accompany the second feature - the gestation years for my Light Console had begun.

It is difficult for me to recall road transport in the early 1920s. The trouble is that I was a railway not a car enthusiast. At our local station, Willesden Junction, there was only one taxi (run and owned by a Mr. Reid). Our first private car ride is memorable. Harry Hill, an acquaintance of Father's, picked us up at home one Sunday morning and drove via Wembley and Harrow Weald to Stanmore common. The car was an enormous Daracq with big brass acetylene headlamps. I rather think the thing had solid tyres; anyway it would be a treasured antique now. That grassy patch amid the overgrown scenery at Stanmore is still there, seemingly unchanged as we pass it from time to time. Private cars were not much in evidence in the suburbs. Our first car, the bull-nosed Morris Cowley, was second-hand and had belonged to the architect Professor (later Sir Albert) Richardson. Father did a lot of work for him both at University College and his church jobs in Bedfordshire and elsewhere. On Sunday, the car was used for picnic outings more often than not to Aldbury, near Berkhamstead common. Mother's picnics were elaborate affairs needing a lot of preparation on her part. Fog could engender a real crawl, often with us walking as guides. Those were the days without any of the white line guidance we take as a matter of course. It was a real relief to reach the tram-lines down the middle of the road. No roundabouts and to encounter a traffic-light was a rare event indeed. Policemen were very much in evidence; both strolling along the pavement or controlling a busy crossing. The road to Brighton, our nearest seaside (and great-aunt!) could be jammed with cars. Lorries were not so much in evidence; but on the railways there were lots of 4-wheel privately owned trucks clanging up and down. Shunting was real fun to watch for us as schoolboys; so was the unloading of cars at Addison Road station for the Olympia Motor Shows.

A thing that sticks out is the amount of walking everyone took for granted during my school days. To get to Colet Court school meant a walk up the road, down the High street, past the Jubilee clock and All Souls' church along Acton Lane to Willesden Junction station. Even then there was quite a walk along the length of the low level platforms and up the stairs to the high level and across a footbridge to our three coach 'pretty-train' waiting on its siding. Both LNWR[*] electrics and the LCC[†] trams were known to us as 'pretty' due to their smart livery of chocolate and spilt-milk. In due course LMS[††] red took over. The 9:04 train was cutting it a bit fine; we

[*] London and North Western Railway
[†] London County Council
[††] London Midland and Scottish

really ought to have caught the crowded 'ten to' but seldom managed that. There were three stations - St. Quentin's Park, Shepherds Bush, and Addison Road where we left the train to go on and terminate at Earls Court. For us there was quite a walk: first up over the long footbridge (Addison Road was quite a large station then) and out into Blythe Road round the back of Olympia and onto Hammersmith Road past Lyons Cadby Hall with its smell of chocolate; then while St. Paul's bell was tolling (there is no other word for it) rush into Colet Court just in time for prayers in hall - except when we weren't.

Chocolate was not the only smell around, especially some Mondays. A particularly nasty smell would hang about all morning. This we attributed to the salt-beef for lunch which we loathed and never had at home. The real source was said to be a saccharine factory; on reflection could it have been the brewery down by the Thames when the wind was in a certain direction? Lunch was at 1 o'clock and lasted twenty minutes, which left over an hour - a long time when young - to be spent shut out in the playground whatever the weather. The half-hour before the meal was OK, we could spend it in hall leaning up against the radiators or reading; it was afterwards that was so terrible for non ball-game enthusiasts such as me. Unlike those who went home to 'dinner' we were not allowed to sneak out and go for a walk - though one did when older. An ice cream in Cadby Hall was nicer than anything in the school tuck shop. The assumption that 'every boy this day did his sport' was worse still in St. Paul's where I arrived in the Lent term of 1924, after having passed the common entrance exam - not the slightest hope of a scholarship for me.

I can only wonder what made Father and Mother choose Colet Court and St. Paul's for Phil and me. It must have imposed a great financial burden; so much so that it was surely a relief when Phil failed his exam and it was decided that a career in the Studio and training at the Central School of Arts and Crafts in Bloomsbury would suit him better. In one way the education I got at St. Paul's was a nonsense. Art-school was used as a punishment; imposed automatically for being late, or doled out; "Take five art schools," for some offence or the other, like accidentally wearing odd socks (*both* had to be black). Real crime (impure deeds?) meant you were art-schooled for a whole term; i.e. you did an hour after school each evening - except on your games afternoon. Cricket was compulsory in the Summer term and rugger in the Autumn and Lent terms. Arriving a week late through illness, in January, I was tipped-off by another ex-Colet Court boy from Harlesden, Guy Evans, that if one joined the OTC (Officer Training Corps) there were no compulsory games in the Lent term and no compulsory lunch-time PT (Physical Training) in any term: so I signed on as a cadet there and then. This was no case of the war-time spirit but opting for the lesser of two evils - a decision equally as hasty and ill-considered as Eden's *Suez* or Thatcher's *Falklands*, maybe!

A redeeming feature in the OTC must have been, as in religion, the ritual. Some of this ceremonial was familiar, thanks to our annual visits to the Royal Tournament at Olympia and the searchlight tattoos at Wembley stadium. I would feel stupid doing PT in little white shorts; but the fact that a young schoolboy like me, in OTC khaki, sometimes with full Webb equipment and pack, striding through High Street Harlesden might look funny to some 'common' men had yet to be brought home to me. And that equipment and brass buttons took a devil of a lot of cleaning on my part, whereas the cotton PT shorts would have been a job for Mother on wash-days. Apart from the two parades a week, there was a field-day each term in Richmond Park where we fired five blanks in our short Lee-Enfield rifles. If you were not careful, a pair of you could get landed with the role of Lewis gunners, which meant a feeble wooden dummy and a police rattle to wave around. In the Easter holidays there was an optional visit to Bisley to fire real rounds and in the Summer holidays there were visits to Camp. I never went to Bisley or spent much time in the rifle range in the school basement. The idea of just shooting did not appeal; but I did go to two camps, one at Tidworth on Salisbury Plain and the next at Strensall near York. York Minster was my real target; but I was also bowled over by the walk along the city wall.

Salisbury Plain was familiar to us because Father had been stationed there for the mid-war years and we small boys had lodged with Mother in a tiny cottage over the hill, whose owner kept a lot of chickens. The hen house and the 'toilet' were one and the same shed, and for us the real terror of that war was the daily visit to use the facilities. The famous daylight raid on London, during which we saw and heard planes shooting it out overhead from our garden at no. 15 (until Mother persuaded us to come inside), had been great fun; but those 'free-range' birds flapping about under the roof and dropping their missiles were another matter! Though we did not know it, things were moving to a dramatic climax for Mother. Father, then in the Royal Field Artillery, was under orders to leave for France. His brother (our uncle Jack Bentham) always revelled in that kind of call, and his long life was punctuated, wherever opportunity served, by great chunks of that sort of activity in the RNVR*, the RFC†, and the RAF†† (rising to Wing Commander), and it continued even in his 91st year with a trip across the channel to revisit the battlefields. As for Father, it was discovered at the last moment that he had heart trouble and so he, the artist, was allowed to take over as a camouflage officer.

Before long we found ourselves living on Hayling Island, just down the lane from the little wooden railway halt at North Hayling, and we enjoyed that wonderful single track line at the most active time of its whole existence. With troops stationed at South Hayling (the officers' mess was the Royal Hotel) the traffic on the line in those 'pre-car' days can only be imagined. One unhappy memory remains: lunch with the C.O. -

* Royal Navy Volunteer Reserve
† Royal Flying Corps
†† Royal Air Force

Colonel whoever. Phil and I were quite unprepared for the parting at lunchtime to join the children in the nursery - the first and last time ever. Some of the 'children' seemed quite grown-up and, presumably while the port was on its rounds, we were taken out on the beach to see sand-yachting. This vision remains stuck in my mind; as does the sight and smell of the van with a gas balloon on top which gave us our daily bread; or the hanging around in the front garden on Monday washdays (while our play-shed was in use for that purpose) waiting for the girl on a bike to deliver our *Rainbow* comic (Mother had already taught me to read). However, these are peripheral to my aim in these pages and we must leave the scene with two small boys gazing, one morning, in amazement at our 'elderly' landlord who had suddenly gone mad and slung his cap high into the air - while all hell was let loose, across Langstone harbour, in Portsmouth. It was the eleventh hour of the eleventh day of the eleventh month of 1918.

The atmosphere of that war tended to cling to the St. Paul's OTC and our officers, being masters in disguise, went on parade wearing their old uniforms and Sam Browne belts. Relics of the War we had sometimes played with at home. Uncle Jack Bentham used to talk vaguely about the next war being against the French; but it was not until I had left school, that the shape of the real menace began to surface. Although always a man of peace (I was mistakenly to welcome Munich) I could not stand the Nazis. I could not take the sight of those tall bullying young louts in uniform standing over the be-whiskered and be-hatted old Jews; nor the burning of the books. These things must have been in the cinema newsreels, as *Picture Post* did not appear until October 1st 1938. Mussolini never made any real impact; he was altogether too comic as he shouted and strutted about. It was *The Shape of Things to Come* which put on the screen exactly what I expected the next war to be like. I also fell for the post-war scientific-socialist clean-up in the film. I was a sucker for that side of H.G. Wells between the wars and for some time afterwards.

Serving in our OTC, the peak each year was the Summer term Inspection and March-past. Our band used to emerge at the rehearsal parades, only to be replaced (in desperation?) on the day itself by the real thing: the band of the Grenadier Guards. This was the regiment to which we were "attached" and a high officer of the Grenadiers would take the salute. All this was followed by a special tea in the great dining room way up under our roof. Other good things were the death of a master, since this meant we had to stand at the end of morning Preces while Handel's *Dead March in Saul* was played on our 3-manual Father Willis organ. There were also occasional addresses by a Bishop in order that he could ask the High Master (the redoubtable and remote Dr. Hilliard) for a "remedy" - a one-day holiday. By tradition only a bishop could ask for this and it was saved officially for an annual day-off at Henley.

Tradition and ritual were around in large doses during that period of my life. We had a King - George V - who looked exactly right in the part, as did his Queen Mary with her head crowned by a tall toque. HRH Edward Prince of Wales was a particular hero of mine and I looked forward to his reign as a good thing. But I was unaware of what he thought of Hitler and above all, of the part really impure deeds played in his life and that of his grandfather's. For myself, I still firmly believed in the power of prayer and would unhitch my mind from impure thoughts, in order to pray fervently for fog on Thursdays in the Autumn term. This was the only thing to put a stop to the compulsory rugger afternoon. Apart from this practical use, fogs were so dense as to be great fun for us boys to find our way around in. Each Autumn they were fairly frequent; but there were five school days a week and the problem was that they did not necessarily turn up on the correct day. And they had to be very dense indeed: the fact that you could not see all the playing field was not enough to veto an afternoon of healthy sport in the open air. With coal burning fires all around us, these fogs were black pea-soupers: nothing would be done about it until after the Great Smog of 1952.

It must appear that my parents made the considerable financial sacrifice in sending me to St. Paul's in vain. On reflection I do not think this was so. The fact that the curriculum was not much good for me was undoubtedly my own fault. Although having passed the common entrance exam at first go, I was soon out of my depth. However, I might have been more successful had I not stuck to the classical side of the school curriculum; and that arose from *my* pursuit of the ideal of taking Holy Orders. This still overwhelmed any engineering talent which was beginning to surface. What I did get out of St. Paul's owes much to the building itself. I am not, of course, referring to their present home down by the River Thames at Barnes, in a series of prefabrications on the CLASP system - whatever that may be! The school moved there in 1968. The building which welcomed F.P. Bentham, canes at the ready, was of "Purple brick and orange terra-cotta." Pevsner continues: "Prim Early Gothic, terribly like a North German *Gymnasium*. The front is symmetrical, the back of a looser, only general, symmetry. As in all Waterhouse's buildings there appears an odd inability to age gracefully." Built 1881-5 it had its own generating system for the electric light, which was just as well since the majority of the classrooms faced North onto the Hammersmith Road and never got any sunlight. Not a building to love, one might think; but to me it was great Theatre. To walk about was a dramatic experience: the changes of light through the windows; the lines of Roman emperors 'busting' on top of each row of our lockers lining the corridors, or the Laocoon group with its fig-leafed figures struggling in serpentine embrace at the head of the stairs. All this fully countered the waste of time represented by half of the curriculum imposed on the masters. Whose stupidity was it that decided Art School would make an excellent punishment? Theatrical performances in the great hall were restricted to once a year at Apposition - the annual prize-giving at the end of the Summer term. The play was usually by Aristophanes, a great comic writer; though the laughter from the audience of 700 or so was infrequent, since the plays were always performed in their Classical Greek. For scenery there was the show-pipework of the organ and for lighting they decided on what the Deity provided via the stained-glass windows that particular afternoon. One thing to be said in favour of CLASP village is that they do have facilities for staging theatre - thanks to someone's choice of Tim Foster as architect for that bit.

My building has long since been demolished; but Colet Court opposite, "less scholastic in appearance and no more attractive." remains; albeit converted to offices. The best known Waterhouse survivor is the Natural History museum in South Kensington. Although Pevsner never seems to have had a good word to say for Waterhouse, I don't think anyone will dare to demolish that one. Walking recently from Olympia along Hammersmith Road to the Broadway past my old school's site, I found myself entering to sit in the forecourt with the 'drive' curving round the neglected lawn, the centre feature of which used to be the Colet Monument of 1900 - "a good seated figure with two kneeling scholars l. and r., bronze, under a graceful iron canopy; one of Thornycroft's most appealing works" - which is now down in the CLASP village. Before me was that lawn. Suddenly, I rose up and deliberately walked across it to the other side. Behold, in my eightieth year there was no one to award me an art school, or a week of them, for my crime!

Colet Court was dead right for Phil and me in the climate of the time. Even the relatively long daily journey from home was a good thing and Mr. Bewsher, the son of the founder, was a superb headmaster. I did well in exams there - coming top in Divinity and good at English brought me out in the first three (if I recall aright) in spite of having to take Greek on board for the last year and being no good at French. Over the road all that was to change. I did very well for a start in the Classical Third, as the lowest class was called, and I was moved up two forms on my exam results. At this point the divine prop was kicked away and Divinity became Greek testament. The language of the Authorised version, which I was adept in, was confined to St. Matthew's on Sunday. Even the twice daily school assembly for prayers had become Preces in Latin and Greek out of a small book going back to the days of Dean Colet, whose portrait by Holbein was reproduced as the frontispiece. Most of my other work was so non-bright that one master accused me of getting Father to do my weekend homework essay for me. A nice touch when it is realised that he used to ask me to check and polish his drafts for his after-dinner speeches, as president of the Master Carvers Association, for example.

Although Father Davis coached me in maths for the London University matriculation exam, religion had already been supplanted by the call of stage lighting. By then he was living at Colindale (near Edgware) and this involved a long tram ride, but it signalled my 'successful' exit from St. Paul's. Maybe it was that Greek testament which was at the bottom of my falling out of love with religion; perhaps I had been confirmed too early. In any case that two hour confirmation service which I looked forward to so much had turned out to be a visit to purgatory: I can still remember the agony of it. The service was at 6pm and after tea I had taken the usual precaution of a trip to the toilet. We had to be in our pews up-front well before the congregation arrived, and by the time St. Matthew's filled-up I wanted to go again, but there was no question of leaving my place and trying to find *it* if, being a church, there was one anyway? It became a matter of hanging-on and praying not to disgrace myself. And that became my exclusive preoccupation until hours later when we arrived home. I managed: but it is hardly surprising that my confirmation did not take, as they say in medical circles.

What triggered any engineering in me? I think the answer has to be Meccano. We began, when small, with a number 2 set and in time this became no.6 plus the Meccano Electric set, which was as far as one could go. As it was then, the various parts and components were not in different colours. They were also basic, which meant ingenuity and some skill were needed in assembly; especially as we tended to devise our own creations rather than rely on those in the instruction book. The electric power came from a small 4-volt accumulator. A radio shed at the bottom of a garden nearby provided a re-charge service. This was a common practice as the valve-amplifier emerged from the crystal-set/headphone radio age. In due course a DC power unit, known as an eliminator, became available for use on AC; but this was no good to us as our neighbourhood did not have any electricity mains: the Gas Light and Coke Company reigned supreme.

The story of how model theatres came to dominate my youthful life could take a lot of space. Suffice it to say that by the time mains electricity was brought to Crownhill Road and we could use a transformer instead of accumulators, the model and its lighting had become fairly elaborate. The complication was that I needed not only a proscenium to frame the stage, but also a chunk of auditorium which went as far as the beginning of the circle as well in order to express my lighting ideas. There were three such auditoria, the first had colour-change laylights I made myself using cardboard plus some wood and Meccano. The second and third were made in plaster sections at the Studio to my designs, as was the 'great' cylindrical cyclorama to encompass a large part of the stage. There was no trace of Matcham anywhere. Cinema-theatre was the influence, especially in the last one, which was to lead to my temple to Colour Music in 1939. Another advantage electricity brought was the replacement of the His Master's Voice clockwork acoustic-gramophone by an all-electric one. A 3-valve radio set could also be assembled, thanks to sets of parts by Mullard or Cossor complete with instructions.

How were my model theatres lit? The lamps were 3.5 volt MES torch-bulbs. There was only one size. I lacquered them in 3 colours, plus white. They were assembled in rows, each of four circuits to form footlights or overhead battens. Luckily there were available small brass castings carrying four MES holders at a time. They came from Grafton Electric as did much else. Goodness knows what their real purpose was, but they suited me fine to make up my battens and auditorium colour lighting. What lacquer colours were needed? The answer was the three-primaries (Red, Blue and Yellow) so that they could be mixed to form secondaries using dimmers. What to use as dimmers? That was easy; there were all sorts of small variable rheostats with rotary knobs available in 6, 15 and 30 ohms. This made it more or less possible to match them to the load. Connected up on my stage, I started to colour-mix; all was as expected until I put blue and yellow full-up. Instead of green, it was near-white. No mixing produced Green. My switchboards had 2-way and off switches above each dimmer for mastering. The last was out-front and had its own in-built lighting *with dimmer*. All wiring was done in double cotton-covered bell-wire.

So far so good if all one wanted was washes of light. Here bus-conductors enter our model scene. The open upper-decks needed a local light to see where to bell-punch the destination hole in the ticket. So a small torch with a lens and hook to hang it in his lapel, with flex to a battery in his pocket was available. Ideal, I threaded them onto Meccano strips as overhead acting area lights and also fixed them up aloft left and right as side lighting. This localised lighting meant that I was able to 'sack' brother Phil, whose job it had been to speak-for and push-on lead figures. From now on, it was up to music and light to tell the tale.

Early in 1928 Mother and I went to see Galsworthy's *Escape* at the Memorial Hall, Acton Lane. The amateur company was the Aeschylus Repertory and they did five productions a year. Mother decided there and then that they needed her son's lighting talents and saw to it that I joined their scenery section in time for the next production *Paul I* by D. Merejovsky. A visit to my model theatre by A. Gardner Davies, who ran the Aeschylus, followed and I became "Lighting Manager" with the prefix "Scenic and... " added for the last couple of years or so. From now on a reversal took place: at St. Paul's in time I gravitated from the top three to the bottom three in class, which meant that often I was not moved up into the next form, and consequently found myself among mainly younger boys. In fact I never got beyond "the Remove" into Senior school. In contrast, at night and at weekends at the Aeschylus I was a schoolboy, the only one, listening to talk about their real jobs by members of 'my' scenery team. And our scenery was *real* scenery, mainly box sets. We made all our own in a slum mews just behind All Souls church. People actually lived there and one of the two WCs they all had to share was immediately outside our door. We occupied a two-floor ex-stable, one of a row. The smell and flies in warm weather we attributed to that WC, which we took good care not to need, until by chance, looking over the unfilled gable in the party wall, one of us located the real source. Our neighbour used his stable to hang rabbit skins and left them to dry-out over each weekend. Row upon row of eviscerated rabbits hung up there while we breathed their last!

The Aeschylus Rep. in Harlesden had built their own 'portable' switchboard sometime before I had joined them. Whoever it was that did the job, must have got the circuit out of Harold Ridge's *Stage Lighting for Little Theatres* (published 1925). The Aeschylus board had, if I remember correctly, a group of 5 circuits on the left and a similar group on the right with master blackouts between the two. At each end there stood a dimmer, making a total of just two. The individual circuits could be switched directly to the mains or to 'their' dimmer. The dimmer was of course an earthenware drainpipe filled with a solution of water and washing soda, the strength of which would depend on the load. Into this mix one plunged a rod with an electrode on the end. The supply was DC and an insulated handle was fitted, an ingenious use of the china chain-pull handle then common in WCs. There was no provision for holding the thing at check. The whole lot had to be rigged for each production in the tiny Prompt-side so-called dressing room at a lower level than the stage and without any view of it. However it did provide a good, if distracting, view of certain still memorable quick costume changes. In spite of this, for Galsworthy's *The Roof* I moved the switchboard up-stage OP to give me a better view of the flame effects I was vamping by waggling the dimmers, since the hire of optical effects was out of the question. Even this locale was not without distraction: at dress-rehearsal during the final scene, when the heroine had to slide down an escape-shoot over the roof parapet, her skirt rode right up as she emerged. My awe-struck teen-age gaze made this into a real dress-rehearsal for her, and the camiknickers were replaced by camibockers (a garment associated with the Charleston) at the subsequent performances.

The Memorial Hall Acton Lane Harlesden was an excellent training ground. In design it had almost every conceivable fault. Four hundred or so seats on a flat floor, which had to be cleared for other activities. They faced a high stage with a tiny 'dressing room' at hall floor level with a WC either side. As their walls encroached on the stage immediately behind the house tabs, there was no wing space at all. This meant that the Male room had to be used as an off-stage assembly area and the men had to use a committee-room, which was only accessible down an outside flight of emergency iron steps and around a path in the rain. There was no real height above the wide proscenium opening and the roof was of course a hipped one, the same as the rest of hall. Not only that but the up-stage area had a low flat roof because it had been added as a low cost box-like extension by the Baker Perkins firm, to create enough floor area to get the chorus on for their annual Gilbert & Sullivan.

The Roof

In that stage extension there was a mains switch which could be used to feed our temporary board; but the hall's own stage lighting consisting of open-type footlight and batten (2 circuits each) was switched only; perversely, the one from the PS and the other from the OP. Obviously they had to be diverted to our board which was another rigging complication. Get-in and rigging of everything was on Monday evening. Dress rehearsal on Tuesday, with a chance to modify and polish on Wednesday provided we left the tabs closed and kept to quiet jobs. This was due to a regular let to the local branch of the Womens' League of Health and Beauty each week. Their activities were decidedly noisy at times and resulted in a certain amount of peering round the tabs. First night was Thursday with get-out immediately after the Saturday night show. There were five productions a year. Big scene changes were complicated by the fact that the only place to store anything not in use was out in the open under the stage extension with access only via the emergency steps. On one occasion the top of a very large table stored half-way in and out of the doorway, bit through our temporary power cable with a loud bang and flash. Not only did we lose lights for a bit, but we lost our stage manager who rushed out of the building and was seen no more that performance. He was a case of "shell shock" as it was known after the first world war; no doubt it now goes under some medico-scientific title. Once Gardner Davies departed to direct professionally, our Rep. folded in 1931 after a couple of productions.

The big difficulty in being an active member of this amateur dramatic society was reconciling each production-week with the claims of school homework. Some of this could be done at St. Paul's in hall during the 1pm to 3pm lunch-break; but the rest had to be covered by devising ingenious excuses - a good training for the real world outside. I was caught out in hall on one of my lies, by chance, and caned for it - a strange sacrifice in the pursuit of a career in stage lighting! I also failed in an OTC 'Cert. A' test, through not only not knowing "How many miles can an army march in an hour?" but also for making such a shy exhibit of myself while not knowing. 'Cert. A' was the certificate to ensure an early death as an officer in the next war. At about the same time, any remaining faith that there was anywhere exciting for me to go to, in the event of an early death, also evaporated.

I avidly read and collected the tiny volumes in the 'Thinker's Library'. *Religion without Revelation* by Julian Huxley was one and *Humanity's Gain from Unbelief* by Charles Bradlaugh was another. Then there was J.B.S. Haldane and above all Joseph McCabe, who had been shut up in a monastery for about the same number of years as Edmond Dantes in the Chateau d'If, before escaping. Both my strict agnosticism and my love of fine church buildings has remained with me ever since. Overall, the question must be how far that early, largely self-imposed religious discipline has influenced my real life or, more relevant in the context of this book, my career? Christianity never helped me to love my neighbour; the class structure of this England was and is too strong. The Keeble boys and girls were 'working class' and our grandfathers, the Bentham one a bank cashier and the Hobbs one a pharmacist, did not belong to that. On the other hand, financially they were hardly any better off, if at all. It was the way any money was spent that might differ. Owing to the early deaths of our grandparents, we only ever knew Grandpa (Fred) Bentham. The other three were just faded photographs. There was, however, a formidable childless lady known to us all as "The Mater". She was Grandpa Bentham's second wife; the first having died while still young of tuberculosis, having given birth to four children.

Servants never really figured in our young lives. I think one maid lived-in, using the room my model theatre was to occupy years later, before the 1914 war. During our schooldays there was sometimes a 'daily' who lived out. When at last I went to work, there was, for a short time, one who arrived early enough to serve me breakfast in the front room before the others were down, so I could get to Kingsway by 9 o'clock. She would have departed by evening. A memorable daily as small boys was Mary, who married a milkman, though not ours. It was she who, after our repeated requests, pulled up her skirt to display her bloomers. Not long afterwards, with our curiosity satisfied, Father Davis turned up one morning to discuss something private with her; but I think we can take it that any sin she needed his celibate advice on was nothing to do with us. For most of the time it was not even a daily but a 'woman' for a morning once or twice a week. And it always seemed to me that her help was somewhat negated by the amount of tidying-up that had to go on before she arrived!

It has been a feature of my life that I find myself retracing my steps. I was born in the London postal district of NW10. When at last the family did move, it was only to Harrow on the same compass bearing. My marriage to one of the few citizens of the Free State of Danzig only caused me to move slightly westwards to Ealing W13, and years later to Norwood Green still in the London Borough of Ealing. Work ensured that I was based in the Covent Garden area and for the larger part of that time the Strand Electric factory was either in Gunnersbury or West Ealing. Crossing the river into deep South London has always been an adventure therefore. In old age, using the top deck of the buses to explore, so to speak, one is surprised at how much has survived the raids of the War and the ravages of Developers. The top deck view, of course, lessens the impact of shop-fronts and fascias. The moment one descends to road level it all becomes so undisciplined. I am sure London even in its poorer parts, and Harlesden certainly had many of those, was tidier. Everything is so filthy; in spite of the fact that we have had clean, as distinct from polluted air, free of pea-soup for decades.

Instead of 'love' what my Christian phase may have left, has been a desire to see fair play for most fellow mortals - socialism without the bondage of Unions or of Communism. And outrage at what those with money or title have taken for granted. I remember the General Strike of 1926; but did not understand it at the time. What it did mean was that the bull-nosed Morris Cowley, we had by then, was used to drop us and some friends at school on the way to the studio; but there had to be some very long walks back home. Some of the Fifth formers (there was no Sixth at St. Paul's) from the OTC became special constables, and Uncle Jack Bentham drove a train on the Inner Circle underground. He had as much fun, in other words, as my use of our canal cruiser 'Peter Sam' to get from home to Regents Park; to use it there as a base during the transport strike of the 1980s. With the Thatcher/Scargill years behind one and higher unemployment in 1992 than when I first went to work in 1929, what can one believe in as a target except fairplay; but go on to say that in a world-wide view there is little more evidence of fairplay now than in the 1920s.

II: KINGSWAY
Picture Palaces 1929-32

Sometime in November 1929 I got off the bus from Euston and with Bush House looming up on my left and the ornate facade of the Stoll Opera House behind me, I crossed Kingsway to Clare House - the great unknown. Some three weeks earlier I had been interviewed there by Mr. F. W. Winstanley, one of the G.E.C directors, and obtained my first real job. Not much of a one - a kind of assistant junior draughtsman, who they had nowhere to put, at a salary of one guinea per week. The Fittings Drawing Office was on the sixth floor, and its windows on my side overlooked the main Ladies' toilet block of the adjacent Magnet House across a white-tiled well. I wasn't working near any window so although for quite a lot of the time I had nothing much to do, I was unable to indulge in any regular mass-observation which might lead to statistical evidence of frequency or duration. Nevertheless, I remain convinced to this day that such provision as is stipulated in regulations for Places of Public Entertainment is hopelessly inadequate for the other sex*. They were obviously drawn up in the days before the adoption of the word "loo" made it respectable to admit to what was then regarded as an impolite weakness.

Much of my time was spent in browsing through a set of superbly illustrated large volumes published by *Country Life* or *Batsford* and devoted to the great houses. Pay at the door access was very rare in those days and these books were a revelation to me: they did much to wean me from Gothic as God's own architecture. My classical education had given me a love of Greek and Roman history but when attempting to design a complete Acropolis or Roman forum on my model theatre, it was difficult avoiding tedious repetition. Buildings were either large or small with more or less columns, so to speak. Nothing to be compared with the variety to be found in the cathedrals!

The possession of such works of reference was logical in this drawing office since variants on 'Period' lighting fittings still constituted a large part of the work. These were specials - just a few off - for particular clients. "Mr. Chancellor of Frank

* LCC regulation 62 (1939): "For females: one WC for the first 100 or part thereof; two WCs for 100-250; three for 250-500; and an additional one for every 400 or part thereof over 500." But a 1991 committee has found that females need four times as long as males.

Matcham wants to know when..." is the only one to echo over the intervening fifty years. First there would be a colour sketch on stiff grey or black paper in which the draughtsman conveyed the feel of the metal, copper, bronze, gilt, silver or whatever. Some were very skilful indeed at this. There followed the drawings from which the thing had to be made. Then it was that I learnt that the policy was never to give the job to Whitton - the GEC's own works in Birmingham. There were a number of very small firms in our own neighbourhood, more or less. Depending whether the stuff was for a cinema or a bank, so to speak, and on the style, there was an appropriate specialist firm. One that sticks in my head was Assersohn near Holborn Viaduct. I was often sent there and he was not far from Snow Hill where my first humiliating introduction to the facts of life had taken place.

That was where my very first 'card' had had to be picked up, lunch time on my second day - from the Labour Exchange! To an ex-public schoolboy at eighteen this seemed the very end. The taint of 'worker' hung heavily about the place; it positively oozed from the brickwork - only one stage removed from the workhouse! Of course, the real cloud in 1929 was lack of work - unemployment was 1.25 million and by 1932, 2.8 million. It was thirteen months before my cousin Donald got any work after leaving university and he was one of the lucky ones because he could read and read. One of my uncles had to wait for the outbreak of war really to solve this problem for him. Did I but realise it, I was lucky to be able to go to collect my card rather than to sign on. My immediate problems also arose from the 'disease' that I had caught from my Father. He was a sculptor and self-employed. Working at something just for the money had no place in his philosophy and this runs right through my own career and explains both the joys and the mistakes in it.

But to get back to the cards. There were two and the second, the Medical one, had to be taken to the agent of a Friendly Society - I have never understood why. Anyway, he promptly sold one a Life Insurance policy, for £50 in my case. It was thanks to Father that I had a job at all. He had already made one abortive shot via an architect friend. We went along to a firm called Higgins & Griffith, electrical contractors of some repute who occupied the sort of dark and dingy premises they always occupy. This must be qualified immediately because before long another such firm, Troughton & Young, were to make the feature pages of the architectural press with their Bauhaus style conversion of their own offices and showroom in Knightsbridge. When Mr Higgins emerged into the gloom at last, he didn't think that I would do and he was right. It was not wiring that called me but light, and his firm obviously didn't go in for that. Father then took me to the Art Workers Guild to listen to a talk and in the interval introduced me and my problem to Oliver Bernard. This was acutely embarrassing as I had to shout through dry lips at the great man. Bernard had been deafened at the Battle of Zeebrugge - the model one in the Admiralty theatre at the Wembley Empire Exhibition, that is. Originally a scene designer, he was then at the height of his fame as an architectural designer with a penchant for novel lighting effects. His Tottenham Court Road Corner House for J. Lyons had been a sensation and he was at work on the Strand Palace and the Cumberland hotels for them. The GEC were doing most of his lighting hence my interview with Winstanley.

That GEC must not be identified with the Weinstock one of today, it was a relaxed friendly affair. Sir Hugo (later Lord) Hirst at the top had begun it all and had served behind his own trade counter in Queen Victoria Street in the City. Out at Wembley in the new research laboratories, the well-known Dr. Clifford Paterson reigned and this was the university, so to speak, where most of the elder statesmen of illuminating engineering originally studied. The GEC (not to be confused with the G.E. or General Electric in the States) prided itself on being the electrical engineer's equivalent of Harrods. The firm claimed, with justice, to supply "Everything Electrical". This it did, beginning with turbo-alternators, masts and lines for the new Grid, everything for the wiring installation right down to what we call consumer goods - cookers, kettles, lamps and the like. Not that they were consumed: except for lamps, everything lasted for ever - it was real quality stuff. Staff purchases were a good buy indeed. We got at least 60% off lamps and just before I left I stocked up with 3.5W MES torch bulbs for my model theatre. I had so many that ten years later (during the war) I was able to donate sufficient of that by then rare commodity to complete the Great White Way backcloth for one of Robert Nesbitt's revues *Best Bib and Tucker* at the London Palladium.

The sixth floor at Clare House was shared with the Illuminating Engineering (I.E) Department. The GEC never did electrical contracting, though they supplied all the requisites, but were prodigal with advice and the preparation of schemes. This was the job of I.E. Dept when it came to lighting. There were of course no fluorescent lamps and so lighting fittings fell into two classes; the utilitarian or industrial and the decorative. This distinction even applied to street lighting as one of my early jobs shows. I had to trace on linen in India ink (with the aid of a pepper-pot of French chalk) the Wembley Lantern and the Worthing Lantern. None of that 'luminaire' nonsense then! The first represented 'science' and was an efficient affair with prismatic refractor and an engineer's housing of copper spinnings. The second was much less efficient but captured exactly the refined spirit of that seaside resort then with a large egg-shaped opal globe and a copper top-knot.

The Wembley can still be seen hanging on wires over the Thames Embankment, though with discharge lamps instead of tungsten. These overhead wires are significant especially when the trams used to run along the self-same embankment. It was a rule that in Central London the street should not be disfigured with tramway wires and posts. In consequence change-over stops ambushed the inward journeys, the overhead trolley was docked and a man with a giant pair of tongs trundled a pick-up exactly resembling a plough into position behind the trailing end of one of the bogies. This took next to no time, the real expense was the vast complication that the conduit represented to house a live rail safely under the road. Those overhead wires and posts for lighting signalled a decline in standards, but we could not guess then that one day the London Building Act, which before the war restricted architects to eighty feet, would disappear and with it London's skyline and building scale. This act kept developers in some order as can be seen in the office building which overlooks the Embankment Gardens and for which the heart of the Adam brothers Adelphi was torn out. Close examination shows this uninspired building to be the base of an American skyscraper of the period. It is a case of arrested development, as it was intended to go up and up. What was fun at that time was the re-opening, on my working door-step, of the Kingsway tunnel. It had been closed for enlargement to take double-decker trams instead of the single-deck specials of my boyhood. To sit in the front on top for the journey South to North and finally to shoot up the steep slope where the driver clapped on the brakes (holding everything and everyone at an acute angle) until the all clear was given to turn across the traffic in front of the Central School, was really something. It was as if an aircraft stopped absolutely still just after take-off! There was an underground tram station just outside Magnet House so we had better get off there now.

Floodlighting was another I.E. Dept. outdoor enterprise. There had been quite a lot of this at the Wembley Exhibition of 1924 and 1925 but it was the various temporary installations for the International Illumination Conference in 1931 which really showed what could be done with London's public buildings and monuments. GEC engineers' calculated approach caused them to look down upon the try-it-and-see lighting rehearsal habits of Strand Electric who had been allocated the National Gallery and St. Martin in the Fields and had captured considerable press acclaim. It was the theatre influence in them no doubt. It must not be thought that GEC had it all their own way, there was competition from other big boys like BTH, Ediswan, Crompton and Philips.

When it came to lamps these companies had everything neatly sewn up in the ELMA* lamp 'Ring'. This outfit functioned complete with educational booklets, demonstrations of *Better Lighting* and a lecture theatre at the top of No.2 Savoy Hill - a building vacated by the BBC when they moved to their new purpose-built Broadcasting House; a palace which still manages to conserve something of its

* Electric Lamp Manufacturers' Association. This was a price-fixing cartel which controlled distribution and stopped low-cost entrants. Jules Thorn beat it by developing alternative distribution channels using grocery outlets to sell lamps rather than electrical stores.

authentic thirties grandeur and promise. ELMA's own display premises partook very much of the exhibition stand 'here today and gone tomorrow' cardboard architecture. As well it might, for somewhere Jules Thorn was ticking gently, away but no one had heard of him and by the time he surfaced I was already some years into my career at Strand. Think of it, no Thorn Lighting! I have to confess that when at last I had to go to Enfield, for some reason or other, I left the small but new brick building convinced of the stupidity of the little man putting himself against the mighty ring of the lamp.

In 1980, forty-five years later, at the National Illumination Conference (at the University of Kent) no less than 58 of the 244 delegates came from Thorn*. Other firms were simply nowhere; twelve Philips and four came from the GEC. Much the same applied to the speakers. Without Thorn there would have been no conference and descending to a personal level, I would have lost the opportunity to indulge in what someone described afterwards as "Vintage Bentham". How I did enjoy myself, alone but for my 'tricks', upon the stage of the Gulbenkian theatre for one whole hour!

The National Illumination Conference was an Illuminating Engineering Society function. Better known as the IES (and referred to as such in these pages) it now just manages to keep its identity as the Lighting Division of the Chartered Institution of Building Services Engineers. I am not alone in thinking that this title suggests expertise in drains and plumbing rather than lighting, or indeed, in heating and ventilation - the partner in the shot-gun marriage being the IHVE†. Economics and the D.E.S. made this match in 1976. It is impossible to overstate the importance of the role the IES has played in lighting over the years since its foundation in 1908.

The very fact that membership of the society had not been restricted to illuminating engineers as such meant that it really had been able to talk and discuss *lighting*. It is true that from the fifties there became 'professional' grades for which qualification had been tightened up over the years but it was always possible for others to make their home in the IES. In the process of lighting, the boundary between what is engineering and what is practical commonsense or even artistic inspiration is ill-defined indeed; to put it mildly. On the equipment side - what produces the light - the range is all the way from the design of the lamp and its bulb to the optical distribution of the light from a housing which is strong enough, not too

* Alas, since the death of Sir Jules, lighting has been banished from Thorn House, "One of the best office buildings of its date, 1957-9, in England." (Pevsner). Designed by Sir Basil Spence, it was once the tallest building in London. Thorn Lighting left Thorn House in Upper St. Martins Lane in December 1980. Sir Jules died on the day the company's head office staff took up their new positions at Tottenham. Thorn Lighting today is no longer a lamp manufacturer having sold those interests to GE of America.

† Institution of Heating and Ventilating Engineers

repellent in shape, gets rid of the lamp heat and costs next to nothing to make! This done, there comes photometry for accurate measurement of light distribution and colorimetry for the same in respect of colour. Thereafter the field is wide open - the wide world of the user.

After an eternity at GEC - probably two or three months - someone left and there was a real vacancy complete with drawing board and desk with a view from the windows on the other side, of the Kodak building just across the alley. I had already noticed that this building turned a lovely pink as it reflected the sunset - an effect I was to admire on the Jungfrau from Wengen one day - nevertheless I didn't want the job, I did not want to become a draughtsman. This I told Mr. Penwarden - the kindly grey, suits and all, artist who ran the office in what appeared to be an absent-minded preoccupied way. What I wanted to do was what I had already being doing for some years as an amateur: theatre lighting. This ricocheted down to Winstanley in the regions below and simultaneously luck made an entrance in a big way. A certain Basil Davis was, as part of the GEC's advisory service, about to be set up as a Theatre Consulting Engineer and in addition to a typist he needed a general factotum to hold the other end of the tape and turn the handle of the Megger, while being able to draw and literate enough to learn to write specifications. The job was made for me - it could not have been more suitable for that time. Goodness knows what caused me to turn that draughtsman's job down. I was very quiet and shy in those days and people were kind to me up in the drawing office. Indeed, except for Friday mornings when all the travellers returned and were everywhère, Clare House with its lack of bustle suited one side of my nature. Basil Davis had a very small office on the first floor of Central House overlooking the Waterman fountain pen shop and part of Kingsway. Why the building was called 'Central' is still a puzzle since it was an exact counterpart of Clare but abutting the south side of Magnet House. The latter, I looked at once again but this time across the bottom of a well. The office was tiny, I was alone, the light had to be kept on all day and the view was, to say the least, restricted since the people opposite always kept their black blinds drawn. This turned out to be the showroom full of German Schwabe stage lighting equipment for which, encouraged by Basil Dean, the GEC had a small department. The only complete job of any importance that I can remember that they did about this time was the Commodore Cinema Hammersmith. This had a large stage with a cloth cyclorama, Schwabe lighting and unusually in the U.K., a complete set of genuine Schwabe vertical-commutator tapped-resistances tracker-wire operated from a standard German regulator. Appropriately, H. Lester Groom who ran this short-lived GEC adventure had been educated at Heidelburg and bore the obligatory scar as proof.

Basil Davis seemed to prefer Strand Electric stage lighting and in any case the terms of the free consultancy we offered only went as far as giving GEC a chance to quote for "Everything Electrical" on the job. It was rather complicated because the equipment was part of the competitive tenders of a number of electrical contractors keenly after the wiring installation. GEC not unnaturally never did any of this wiring themselves. (One of the objections sometimes voiced about Strand Electric was that they both made equipment and competed for the wiring installations for which it was specified.) It was the drawing up and detailing of complete installation specifications which was our main job. I had not only never done anything of the sort but I didn't even know that such things existed. Within a few days all became clear and taking an earlier example as a model, I was happily writing away and marking up the 1/8th scale plans with symbols to indicate primary and secondary maintained lighting points, socket-outlets and the rest. Two most valued works of reference were the IEE Regs and the LCC Regs - it is still amazing what they managed to contain in a small space*. Basil Davis was an ideal instructor. He really knew his stuff and could convey it and yet he expected, rightly, a lot of initiative on my part. Apart from anything else he was out for a lot of the time - one could not sit around and wait for him to come up with the solution to a problem and there was no one to ask or discuss it with. I remember he asked me to go to the site of the new Savoy Cinema in North Acton and find out who the supply company was. So off I went by Central London tube from the long since disused British Museum station. When I arrived at last at North Acton I combed the immediate neighbourhood until I found a large excavation surrounded by a hoarding and boards proclaiming it to be the new super cinema. What next? I had never been on a building site before, there was no bell and the occasional rough worker simply kicked with a vast muddy boot until part of the hoarding was dragged open with a string of oaths. I think that must have been the first time in my life that I heard the word which began with an "F" and although it was repeated several times I had no idea what it meant, especially as the men using it did not seem to be angry. Another circumnavigation of the hoardings widdershins followed and as no opening presented itself I adopted a different tactic. The site was on one corner of the junction of three roads, each of which bore a nameplate. Three boroughs were represented - Acton, Willesden and Hammersmith. At that time it was still common for a borough to run its own electricity supply and a public call box nearby, complete with telephone directory, enabled me to find out that the new cinema would be in the area of Hammersmith. Note the fact that there *was* a directory - it all went in one volume. Nowadays with four, even one would come as a surprise. Anyway back to Central House in triumph. These small independent authorities did mean that it was often possible to have a secondary supply without use of a battery in cinemas. Even gas might be used. The Palladium had gas as secondary lighting until long after the war - it added a component to the characteristic smell of the place.

* Until the 'Europeanised' 15th Edition of the IEE Regulations of 1983!

Most theatres have, or anyway used to have, their own smell. At Drury Lane it was a mixture of size and oranges while the Coliseum evoked for me - elephants! No one has agreed about this and of course there is no logic to the idea, and I am not sure that I know what an elephant really smells like anyway.

Cinema projection rooms used to smell of ozone - something one used to smell on the Central London tube where they had their own distinctive *Ozonaire* system. Other tubes did not seem to have any ventilation and smelt of warm wet cardboard. It was the carbon arcs burning away hour after hour which made ventilation of the projection room important and one could see the garishly-lit muck shooting out to be caught in the exhaust cowl. There was none of the long spool automation which can run the whole show on one reel. Change-overs came every ten minutes or so and the second machine had to be started and run to speed, arc struck and dowser operated on cue. On shut down of the first machine, off came the spool to be taken away and rewound while the new reel was threaded. Basil Davis knew this work intimately since he had served in all the important departments of the theatres his father* ran. One of his ideas at this time was to collect all the various push buttons and switches and duplicate them to the right of each set of projection ports. Hitherto the curtain controls, house lights, arc controls and so forth had been scattered about in the various metal boxes supplied by the manufacturers. The theatre was to take ages to get the idea that some integration on the same lines in the prompt corner might be a good thing! The principal ingredient in these panels was a series of switches to step up the current to the arc. It gives an idea of the state of the art when it is realised that these switches were direct-operated, with the current carrying wiring flushed into the wall. Mr Barsdorf of E.L.S. dept. actually designed a special switch for 'us' which the GEC made - at Whitton!

The panels at the new Trocadero Elephant and Castle gave trouble in the first weeks which defied diagnosis. The screen tabs from time to time decided to close in the middle of the film. While it was easy to open them again, the veil drawn over the picture hardly accorded with the image Messrs. H & G (Hyams and Gale) cinemas wished to present. The teething trouble turned out to be located in the backside! The bulging hip pocket of a certain projectionist came in contact with the 'close' button as he stooped to thread the bottom (no pun intended) spool box. Thereafter a guard rail or plate was fitted. This cinema, much trumpeted as the largest with a capacity of six thousand, had been in trouble on its opening night. The members of the audience, including both members of our office, each arrived with a contribution of London 'pea-soup' fog in their lungs. The second feature, which as usual came first, was impossible to see. The projector's rays had not only to travel through fog to the screen but back through it to our eyes. Only white or near white objects could

* Israel Davis was a pioneer in building a circuit of super-cinemas

really be seen without strain. One of these, a nude statue labelled "Psyche", got a great laugh when the comic pulled a face at it. This I probably wouldn't have seen to this day, had not Basil Davis's secretary Kathleen, alongside, ejaculated "fishy"!

The turn came of the 4-manual Wurlitzer to rise and *turn* (this was a new gimmick). This really was what the publicity claimed "the largest in Europe"; the capacity of the house itself was a fiddle. The auditorium seated 3500 or thereabouts, the rest of the claim came from the large capacity for queuing inside the building instead of around the outside of it. (Places like Radio City Music Hall, New York, really do seat the six thousand or so they claim. There is a theatre in the University at Madison which I have seen and which claims six thousand and a couple of hundred odd in order to have the edge on Radio City; almost as if that was number one on the architect's brief.

A super-cinema now, like the Trocadero, demolished, whose auditorium capacity I felt first from the stage was the Davis Croydon. Gazing out from the stage awe-struck I remarked to Basil Davis that all those four thousand five hundred empty seats looked very impressive. To which he replied, "Yes, but I prefer the look of them full!" The Davis was by then the sole house which remained with the family after disposing of their circuit to Gaumont British. They kept it on as a kind of hobby. Designed by Robert Cromie it was very much in the art deco style and had colour changing lighting behind the cornices and in the fittings. Basil Davis had driven me down there in his Lagonda sports car as an initiation ceremony to his world. We looked over everything. Nothing was left out, organ chambers (a Compton 'speaking' through a grill over the pros.), switchboard on its perch (Strand bracket-handle), projection room with curious tracker wire operated Strand dimmers for the colour lighting, orchestra pit, grid and finally the roof over the stage. This last involved a climb up a vertical cat ladder - my first experience - right up the outside of the stage tower wall. The target was a large extract fan lazily idling in the breeze. There was a fine view of Croydon spread out below but the memory of shoving my foot over the parapet into it to find the rungs of that cat ladder for the return, remains vivid. And in my best suit too!

Lunch in the balcony of the Rotunda (the Davis was very spacious out-front) followed; but before it did Basil Davis spotted a queue across the marble floor below. Striding up to the head, the attendant immediately made way for us and there it was - my first glimpse of television, ever! Baird 30 lines flickering away to give an orange head and shoulders singing. The experiment used to go out using one BBC transmitter for sound and the other for vision for half an hour midday. The Davis's allowed the public in to take a look at something that was rare indeed. Like a number of their fellow exhibitors, they never missed a trick. All this excitement over the use of the foyers of our new theatre buildings would be old hat to the cinema managers of those days. One must not confuse those *palaces* with the poky 'twins' and 'triplets' of today - one girl issuing tickets with one hand and selling Mars bars with the other. To their owners the places were theatres and the stages and other facilities more than justified the use of the term. If they were large and the public loved them that way, so was the staff which waited on you. Intimate theatre in this cinema context meant the 'flea pit'. A term not always unjustly bestowed. You would be straight into the auditorium out of the street; some have lived to see their big neighbours come and go. One such was the Palladium, a tiny house sandwiched between the Shepherds Bush Empire (now the BBC theatre) and the new 3000 seater Pavilion of 1924. The latter, designed by Frank Verity for Israel Davis, was in the manner the Romans might well have used if they had had to face the problem of the super cinema. It was not just a matter of applied decoration as was to follow with many a Forum up and down the country. To look at the "restored" drawings of the Baths of Caracella in Banister Fletcher* is the best way to get the idea. Only the exterior now remains. Although hit by a doodle-bug† during the war the real destruction was by redesign. First W.E. Trent the Gaumont 'architect' had a bash at it in 1932, then Rank took charge and imposed a nondescript remodelling of the auditorium walls and ceiling, in much the same way that they later believed that a change in top management in one of their firms was an effective substitute for lack of 'product'. Finally they imposed a Bingo split so that only the Balcony lingers on as a house - and a very shoddy one too!

Leaving our tram from Harlesden and crossing the road to the Pavilion high on expectation had been a regular feature of boyhood. There it was that the great silents, *The Covered Wagon*, *The Ten Commandments* and *The Thief of Baghdad* were to be seen. The last two complete with prologues on the stage: Moses carving away at his tablets as the ten commandments appeared one by one out of the Strand Electric storm clouds; and dancing girls who probably had very little on by the standards of the time. We used to go to the 'one-and-two's in the afternoon. The continuous performance would already have started at 2pm and we would rush upstairs, ignoring the slow 'Express' lift, clatter quickly across the dance floor which formed the centre part of the restaurant/foyer and enter by the vomitory, balcony centre. Darkness and the organ made its presence felt. Immediately below the 2/4's and 3/6's stretched out and beyond lay the mystery of the downstairs where in the darkness the lit book-desk identified organist at work. Turning our backs on this and the screen we climbed as few steps as possible to take our seats while the 'eight-pennies' (afternoons only) went on climbing to the very back of the balcony. That organist and the fine 4-manual Compton were very important to me. He was Quentin Maclean and his artistry

* *A History of Architecture on the Comparative Method*

† German V2 missile used in the Second World War.

▲ Curzon Mayfair

◀ Shepherds Bush Pavilion in 1920

enabled me to enjoy, often with eyes elsewhere or closed, the love stories which the second features more often than not had to tell. After a sojourn at his Christie in the Regal Marble Arch, he it was, who came up on the Trocadero Wurlitzer a little earlier in this chapter. The organ would also accompany the *Pathe Gazette* and was superb for *Felix* or *Bonzo* - the cartoon films of the time. Coming attractions were relegated to a few slides; usually of the sort which allowed you to scratch your message on and which were, I was to learn later, known to the trade as election slides. Suddenly, there would be a change of timbre as the orchestra under Louis Levy took over. Depending on the nature of the stage show they might be on the stage itself or in the pit and of course they always accompanied the main feature. There may have been a couple of dozen players but this would be augmented when a film like *Faust* (with Emil Jannings as Mephisto) warranted it. Indeed in that particular case singers were introduced, spotlit alongside the screen, from time to time for the best known arias. The normal stage show would either consist of a famous act like Layton and Johnstone, Flotsam and Jetsam or Jack Hylton's Band, or what was called a 'musical' scena. In this last case the resident band would be on the stage and soloists would render selections from, say, *Madame Butterfly*. Sets were mainly of drapes but some scenery would be used with, of course, lighting effects; especially colour changes. This was all the rage. It was as if dimmers had just been discovered - perhaps they had! Even at Bertram Mill's Olympia Circus the colours changed gently on drapes behind the band. During the piano solo which formed part of *The Favourites* on the pier at Sandown, Isle of Wight, it went on and certainly at the Shepherds Bush Pavilion where colour lighting was housed behind the Roman cornices, laylights and in the decorative fittings out in the auditorium and across the folds of the curtains on the stage. It was there that I first saw how rich amber light from the side looked on black drapes. Something which I was to exploit to the full later. Against this early background, my life-long mania for Colour Music may become more comprehensible. This was lighting for me. I intended to do this in the cinema theatre rather than in the real theatre where, except for ballet, it would be distracting. Little did I know ballet and balletomanes then! Basil Davis, after I left him, got me to come back and do this kind of lighting change on the very special occasion of the first night of Mayfair's first cinema - the Curzon. Appropriately, the manager was the Marquis de Casa Maury and I wore white tie and tails to operate the bracket-handle board in the projection room. I also wore odd socks - one black the other coloured - a result of the rush home to change, which I did not discover until I changed trains at Queens Park.

The interior of the Curzon, by Sir John Burnet, of Tait & Lorne (not the present one), was particularly suitable; plain white with a series of coves with three-colour lighting sweeping across the ceiling. Being a small house all on one floor, everything was in view of the audience. Although the film was *Unfinished Symphony*, a continental one about the composer, what I had to accompany for an hour before the show was Jazz on records - not really my line. Usually it was the architecture that was at fault, as witness this extract from an article of mine in 1932 - my first in the technical, or any other, press and a long one.

> *Light in the theatre and the cinema (auditorium) has only been considered from the decorative point of view up to the present. Light has apparently been regarded as an addition to the already too large list of materials at the disposal of the decorator. ... When will architects realise that modern theatre design does not mean substituting polished squares and circles for gold cherubs and acanthus leaves? Take the Shakespeare Memorial Theatre - all very delightful as interiors go, but does it help bridge the innumerable gaps that Shakespeare's plays consist of, even in a theatre, where a sliding stage is installed? For a blackout, even if it only lasts for half a minute, is a definite break in the visual continuity. Atmospheric backgrounds are used for the stage proper. Why not provide the means to treat the forestage in the same manner?**

* *The Builder* 2/9/1932

Revealing stuff; what I was after was the opportunity to modulate from one scene to another using light much as incidental music had been used. Little did I envisage the type of production we have today! However, I did get a chance to design a small theatre to show what I was after - the blitzed Strand Electric demonstration theatre of February 1939, but that must wait its turn.

After lunch at the Davis we went into the auditorium to see the colour changes on the fifteen dimmers for the auditorium while the organist Alec Taylor played. A growing source of vexation was the random nature of the changes in relation to the music. As the film began we sneaked out and off down the road to the Croydon Empire, not for the show I must add but to survey the place for conversion to the talkies. A certain Victor Sheridan (no relation at all to the other three Sheridans who were to feature so largely in my life) had four Variety houses he wanted done as cheaply as possible. The others were the Hammersmith Palace, the Kilburn Empire (the best one) and the Islington Empire. Our search for a site for a new projection room - any existing one was virtually a cupboard - always led up stairs plastered with obviously ineffective notices "Commit no nuisance" to the Gallery. A couple of projectors suitable for both sound-on-film (Movietone) and sound-on-disc (Vitaphone) plus a Non-Sync represented the minimum. Sound-on-disc involved a large slow-running turntable, part of and driven from the projector. In those days of 78s, to see something turning so slowly was very strange and so was the effect on the screen if the pickup jumped a groove or two. The non-sync was a pair of turntables, sometimes located in the orchestra pit, used to cover intervals and the silents which were still around as second features. These places were very run down by that time and much more ought to have been done. At Croydon the electric intake was outside in a covered passage above the refuse bins. And at Kilburn, Basil Davis warned that he would not stand close as I to the curtain around the orchestra pit. If that was 'alive', then a general air of death and decay hung over the rest. Particularly moving was the occasion at the Empire Cinema Willesden (a Bernstein House, later the Granada) when the band had to play themselves out of their job by providing the accompaniment to the trailer announcing the joys of the talkies installed to begin next week. A less thick-skinned manager might have allocated that item to the organist who after all was going to stay on to provide a solo spot, continuity and standby in case the sound broke down.

If cinema musicians were out of work then cinema architects and the suppliers of the equipment for their buildings certainly were not. After a year or so I had someone to share my tiny office. Percy Newton came from the Strand Electric Contracts department. About ten years my senior he had been a wireman originally and knew the work intimately. He was also very meticulous and tidy and the frontier between our back to back desks was often violated. Nevertheless, we got on well, and soon I was not only learning more about this job but getting some information about life inside Strand as well.

The next conversion to the talkies was of two purpose-built ice rinks, one in Hove and the other in Golders Green. Although the buildings, virtually identical, were modern and the conversion was thorough, they made strange cinemas being long, low and narrow - the screen, small anyway in those days, seemed miles away from the projection room. Walking back from the Golders Green cinema behind Basil Davis, who lived at Golders Green and had not invited us to tea, we noticed our chief, whose salary at the GEC was reputedly two thousand (a magic figure then), had a hole in each of his socks. Curious, because he was always well turned out and had a neat, almost ascetic, figure. I would have liked to have seen his house because it was a new one and I had designed the large vertical stained glass window on the landing. Some time earlier he had shown me what some firm had put forward as 'modern', and would I sketch something to show what it ought to be? Intrigued, I drew it out - the leading and all - and quite enjoyed myself. I knew a little about glass from the days at the fittings drawing office. The result was very restrained, clear cathedral with the leading at right angles and three asymmetrically placed motifs in a pale straw and steel blue colour. I neither got, nor expected, anything but thanks. This was very much in character - for the both of us.

Another time the buzzer went and Davis told me that there was a scale-model of the new cinema to be built in Commercial Road (the Troxy, later the London Opera Centre) which needed some stage lighting made and would I go and see what was to be done? So a walk down to George Coles' office in Craven Street followed. On hot days the office used to resound to the clatter of washing-up through the open windows of the Strand Corner House just across the narrow road. The model proved to be a longitudinal section through the entire building - foyers and all - intended for public exhibition. The scale, recollection suggests, was 3/8ths inch to the foot. His office had done the decorative fittings very nicely themselves, but as ever, with architects, they had shied off the stage lighting and the gap had to be filled in a hurry. There was nothing for it but to make the stuff at home on the kitchen table over the weekend.

I was a card and shellac man. There was always a small bottle of artist's shellac from father's studio at home (I have a model of the 4-manual Marble Arch Christie organ before me as I write). To roughly the same scale as we are talking about, it used to come up on a lift in the centre of the orchestra pit in my model theatre upstairs, while colour changes used to go on in the kind of auditorium that ought-to-have-been-built but wasn't! The stage lighting on that model had to be practical and produce effects. For the Troxy model, scale came first so separate colour change circuits and dimmers were out of the question. A half-tone photo (from *Kine Weekly,* probably) shows three battens and two wing floods. The batten housings were made of shellacked card and the fourth side was formed of tracing linen stuck thereto. This latter was marked with the compartment battens in India ink. The alternative colours - white, red, blue and green - relied on lamp lacquer. The lamps were tiny medical ones without caps mounted as one circuit on a card strip which pushed in from the far end of the resulting tube so that withdrawal for lamp maintenance was possible. Never put your trust in lamps is an early lesson we all learn! Hanging on 12-gauge wire 'bars' suspended from their model grid they gave the right impression. Something of the sort was used for the footlights but memory does not extend to the wing floods on stands.

Percy Newton brought with him a contact which produced a job for our department - the Ambassador in Hendon Central. For some reason, probably the prima donna in him, Basil Davis seemed to resent this and always referred to it as "that lousy job." It is true that money was very tight indeed on it and Webb and Ash were not cinema architects but the place succeeded and what is more one can still pass it on the A1 out of London. Something else connected with it was also to survive for a very long time. Somehow or other I got involved with the house manager (a Mr Hutchinson, who was later to turn up in the same role at the London Palladium) who wanted an adaptable set of scenery to use with his stage drapes. The stage was 65ft wide by 24ft from the back of the safety curtain but although this could fly out in one piece there was no stage tower over the rest. The screen frame had therefore to be pushed up to the back wall to clear for stage interludes. The idea was some bits and pieces which could be stood up quickly and make a variety of designs. Racking my brains with Harold Ridge's book open at the pages which showed the Cambridge Festival theatre sets, Father looked over my shoulder and suggested that a geometric relationship might be more rewarding. The resulting design used six pairs of shapes painted black on one side and grey on the other which could be put together in various ways.

To this day I don't know whether Hendon ever used the idea but I certainly did. In one particular arrangement it was used for Colour Music and Tchaikovsky from June 16th 1935 to January 1977, and I'd use it tomorrow given the chance. It is very difficult, and perhaps a bad thing, to separate artistic invention from that involving mechanical and electrical materials, so to speak. They certainly can run close together in the theatre which is one reason why I find it so difficult to understand how so many designers are content to leave to others the fun of lighting their sets. Especially as so many are now conceived as a model rather than a drawing. Anyway, Basil Davis' department which memory suddenly suggests, out of the blue, was known as TCE (Theatre Consulting Engineers) provided an excellent training mix and it is time to introduce the Mansell clutch. Basil Davis always had an eye for the new: he himself had invented an improved circuit for charging the secondary lighting batteries in cinemas and a special mounting for motor-generator sets. These latter provided the

DC for the projector arcs and to keep current runs down, had to be located near the projection room, so noise was a constant hazard. His ingenious solution was to mount the motor-generator on a reinforced concrete raft which floated in a bed of peat. Another invention of his concerned a series of triangular ribs or flutings for lighting coves. These were geometrically drawn out so that their faces would catch the light from one side of the cove only. It was an extension of the side lighting on the folds of a curtain effect. The result, for example beyond the edges of the Davis cinema pros. arch was a pattern of stripes - garish or gentle, depending on the colour mix used - which could be made to vanish altogether with a similar mix both sides.

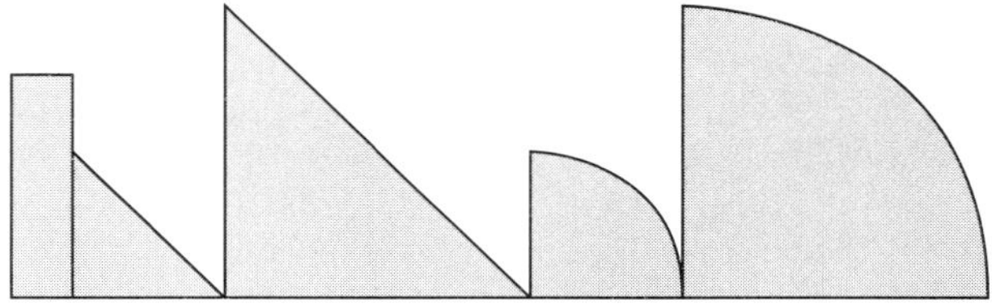

Units for shadow setting

The Mansell clutch arose out of the need for a remote control of a number of dimmers whether manually or automatically. Moss Mansell's own firm made electrical items such as resistances for cinemas and he himself had actually run a small cinema at one time - The Electric Theatre - in Notting Hill Gate. The need to be able to control dimmers both from the stage and from the projection room to fade lights automatically (and of course, mix the colours!) was peculiar to cinema work. At the Trocadero cinema the architect had had to place the axis of the auditorium diagonally across the tight site in order to get the numbers in and this made the stage a triangular affair without wings - yet live shows had to be, and were, staged. In that case Basil Davis had used a remote panel by Major which had reversing fractional-HP one-speed-only motors, driving each slider dimmer up and down by lead-screw. Mansell's clutch was a simple device in which either a pair of electro-magnets could be energised to grip an iron wheel to drive a dimmer up or down, although the shaft on which it was mounted rotated in one direction only. Thus a whole series of dimmers could be selected to move in appropriate directions using one motor only.

Basil Davis was the first to use the clutch in this field - if that is the term, since he really took the thing to sea. The venue was the ballroom of the new 'Monarch of Bermuda' - a luxury cruise liner. A panel with a map of colour lighting coves with switches located appropriately, operated resistance dimmers stowed away somewhere remote. Basil Davis departed to enjoy the commissioning trials. Two days out, a signal was received heralding disaster and was followed closely by the sender. At this distance in time one wonders why he bothered to send the radiogram. He probably thought (and rightly) that his little department was hanging on news of his adventure. Of course it was crazy to make the first use of a new device on the high seas - and on a ship which was to be based on the other side of the Atlantic too. Something of the same was to happen in Iceland twenty years or so later.

The present trouble arose from the effect of all the heat from the dimmers cooped-up in a confined space. This heat affected the limit switches which automatically cut each clutch at the end of its travel. In retrospect, I think these limit switches would have failed anyway. As we shall find in a later chapter, breaking the circuit to this clutch poses a particular problem. Anyway, here aboard there was a real disaster - the whole lot had to come out and what heatless dimmer to put in its place? The GEC's Marine Department ('Everything Electrical'!) came up with the answer to the dimming overnight - a 'negative booster'. The ship's supply was DC and this ruled out any of the more sophisticated solutions that we have become accustomed to, even if they had been around then. A negative booster worked by passing the load through a motor-generator set and controlling its field thorough a shunt regulator to cause the voltage to the lights to raise and fall as required. This was an ingenious technical solution but it involved stuffing the 'dimmer cabin' with at least three costly motor-generator sets - one per colour circuit. But it had to be, or had it?

I know what happened, but trying to analyse at a distance of sixty or so years why that young chap, myself, acted as he did is another matter. There was no reason for this. It wasn't his job and his seniors had the solution sewn up and it was going ahead at once with an urgency that seems rare in this country today. My discontent may have had an artistic base. Three sets of machinery whirring away just to blend three circuits of colour was like taking three nutcrackers to the one nut. And they weren't even going to open the nut cleanly. The shunt regulators (i.e. dimmer handles) would be set at 120° to each other in order to produce a colour cycle and driven up by a small motor geared right down to produce a slow change. This was already common practice using orthodox resistance dimmers. Such 'automatics' produced a poor cycle of colour because no two primary colours could ever be at full-on together. By the time the new colour circuit was at full its predecessor was well on the way out. Any two only met half-way on equal terms, so to speak. To hold a dimmer full-on to allow the next to catch up with it each time was an expensive mechanical complication which was out of the question in the very competitive cinema equipment industry.

In the meditative mist of that weekend the trigger must have been the words *full-on.* If lights were to be full-on what were they doing on a dimmer at that time? Likewise at the bottom end one never had a situation in which the two unwanted circuits were switched off and one could enjoy a pure third. If a circuit at full was switched over to independent to allow the next to come up and join it and switched off for that third of the cycle it was not needed then *one* dimmer could be used for three circuits. And this in the case of the negative booster was really something! Out came the squared paper, and three circles one vertically above the other repeated three times represented full on, dimmer and off periods respectively. Segments showing the active periods of each were shaded-in, using pencil. Try as I would, the result couldn't be faulted. And there was no one to show it to - my first invention! No one to try it out on. To do the automatic switching would be easy, simply make a flasher drum with the appropriate contact segments. These things were in common use for automatic displays like the 'Bovril' sign in Piccadilly Circus. Basil Davis could probably have been contacted by telephone but we did not have one then at home so I had not grown accustomed to its face. I used to be terrified in the early days when there was no one in my part of the drawing office and I had to answer it. There was a Mr Duffus of the luxurious showrooms way down in the Magnet House basement who was not content with being told the man he wanted was not there but demanded, not once but every time, to know who it was that was on the phone. My name was difficult to convey and when at last it registered, meant absolutely nothing to Duffus - or anybody else for that matter.

Monday came at last. Basil Davis must have found his assistant bubbling over on the door mat. Audience reaction left nothing to be desired. The explanation of the segments in the diagram had to be gone through two or three times, not because he was slow in the uptake, but he also thought it was too good to be true. "That's very good, very good indeed," he said with enthusiasm and rushed off to show Mr. Ellis who ran the marine department.

The opportunity to have another go at the Mansell clutch, this time nearer home, came with the new Regal Cinema Uxbridge. It had several colour lighting coves in a decorative scheme devised by Maples, a firm much better known for their furniture store at the end of Tottenham Court Road. The dimmers were selected from a series of 2-way and off switches and as a precaution the dimmer bank, although remotely controlled from a panel in the projection room, was physically accessible to it. The clutches were actually fitted with handles for manual operation - in case! The boss to which the handle fitted remained on the castings for years and years as a vestigial evidence of Basil Davis' nervousness over this, the first clutch job that worked. And work it did late in 1931. Two and a half years later the 120 dimmer ways for the Royal Opera House were operated by the Mansell clutch but its main use in the thirties was for automatic colour cycle dimmers. This type of equipment also provided plenty of opportunity for my 'drum' as the 'Monarch of Bermuda' device came to be known - the actual dimmer being of course a standard resistance one, for land based jobs.

It is quite extraordinary how far the craze for colour changing dimmers extended. For example, TCE's drawing office reference no. 181 is the wiring diagram for an automatic dimmer to control the outside lighting for Ipswich's New Electricity

Showrooms. This drawing of mine tries to remind me, with but partial success, that there were white lamps, red lamps and blue lamps in Windows, and another set in Panels. These panels separated the windows of one floor from another and I think were of opal glass, back-lit, but what on earth you lit in windows above street level must remain a question - perhaps curtains were pulled across by night. The image of the public lined-up on the pavement opposite gazing entranced at their local electricity showrooms is difficult to conjure up. The diagram of the drum contact segments shows that the odd number windows were separated from the evens and the same happened with the panels and these went through a cycle in which the colours sometimes contrasted and at others were in unison. None of this was left to chance, it being a feature of the 'drum' that the changes had to relate to the dimmer exactly as it reciprocated up and down. The display marched like a Guards regiment to regulation step. At this point I get suspicious; all this looks very much like me! In my solitude I was always devising this kind of thing. Out would come the squared paper, and away the ideas would run.

This kink of mine reached its apotheosis, as we shall see later, in the North Cascade at Glasgow where the whole hour's light entertainment could only be enjoyed if a tram broke down at the Paisley Road entrance to the exhibition and provided its top deck as a stand from which to view. The truth is that the clients and architects merely asked for changes of colour wherever it was and the 'change-ringing' came from this opportunist sitting alone in his office at the bottom of the well. This spotlights a feature of consultancy; namely the specification or the drawings or the ideas can become an aim in themselves - standing in relation to the devisor in the same way as a work of art does the artist. This shows particularly in the case of an architect but engineers and other consultants are not as far removed from it, not as objective, as they may think. Sometimes this comes up as a professional bonus, the client gets more than he has asked for; but at others, he may find that he has got more than he bargained for!

The reason for vagueness in the case of the Ipswich job is that my visual memory (the only bit that really works) never got a chance to function, as by the time the thing was completed and working I had left the GEC. This came about quite suddenly and all because I got my guinea a week back. This had been taken from me shortly after joining the firm. To lend support to the idea that they were doing something about the financial crisis, His Majesty's Government applied a 10% cut to the salaries of Civil Servants and the Judges, as an example to the Nation. Our loyal GEC board, with an Olympian fairness worthy of Margaret Thatcher, applied the 10% and a ban on any kind of salary change whatever from top to bottom. Thus my guinea had become 19 shillings per week. The sudden appearance of an extra two shillings in the wage envelope proclaimed that the ban was off, so across the polished lino passage I went to Basil Davis who admitted the justice of my claim. There had been no increase with the change from drawing office to his office nor for skills acquired over nearly three years. He went into action right away and before long called me in to tell me that there would be another 8/6d. Much as I enjoyed the work this even to me was the signal to get out.

Strand Electric was the obvious firm to try, especially as Moss Mansell, one of its three directors, had already knowledge of my prowess at automatic colour-cycle dimmers! I had visited him several times, on TCE department's work, in his tiny office in Endell Street whence he had fled after the fire which burnt out his Floral Street works. By now Mansell had taken charge of a brand new factory in Power Road Chiswick which contained both his own and Strand's factory; also from Floral Street but burst-out rather than burnt out of their premises. However, this was the engineering end of the business, and it was lighting that called, and as many can testify, its call is strong. Percy Newton thought I should make contact with Strand by going round to the Grosvenor House ice rink. This was a large hall at the back of that Park Lane hotel which was the venue for that year's CEA (Cinematograph Exhibitors Association) exhibition. An annual event then, it was a must for both exhibitors and those who had things to sell them, alike. It was fortunate that it was in London that year as it was usually in somewhere remote and difficult like Blackpool. Even more fortunately for me, Arthur Earnshaw himself was sitting on the stand and best of all, had I known it, he actually had a vacancy he needed to fill. And that vacancy was - someone to look after the new demonstration theatre and hire fittings showroom. Think of the luck, from the heart of the cinema theatre world into legitimate theatre in one move!

Of course, this didn't happen on the spot but it was arranged that I should go and see him, and before long I went into Basil Davis with a job at £3 per week under my braces (we didn't wear belts very often then and certainly not in the office), to announce that we must part. Basil Davis was clearly put out and said that I would regret it. But I never, never have regretted it. What *never?* Well, hardly ever! The fact that Davis resented my leaving him gives a clue to a master and man relationship which I doubt could exist in as large an organisation today. I worked for Basil Davis not for the GEC. I knew who my boss was, he was in the office just across the passage. On the factory floor or on a building site it would have been the foreman. At school it was the form master who would be backed by the head. At Strand I would enjoy the same personal relationship, this time with the three men who managed and owned the firm. You could see whose money you might be wasting or saving. Praise from them carried a real message.

Back to Basil Davis, he was interested in the things I did for him - at times he positively enjoyed them and equally he liked to show me what he had done and knew. The bond between that callow youth and the experienced mature engineer was the work. At his suggestion my Central School of Arts and Crafts evening classes had been given up in favour of three nights a week in Electrical Engineering at the Regent Street Polytechnic. Appropriately, the muffled strains of the Compton organ in the adjacent cinema became audible, from time to time, through a particular classroom wall. One puzzle, looking back, is where all the time came from. In addition to the Poly. homework there were the five productions for my amateur society and I also did a certain amount of 'moonlighting', as it is now called. For instance, there was the flasher hired from Strand Electric for the lighting of a stand I had designed for Powell Duffryn (coal merchants) at the Ideal Home Exhibition (in 1931 probably). The way the flasher did its automatic lighting 'cues' was all over the place. This meant a visit very early in the morning to work out and show the contractor how the cams must be reset. There was no question of stopping there in Olympia; it was a matter of seeing him start and then dash off to Clare House to clock-in by 9-o'clock. There was no clock at Central so I always had to call at Clare during my time at GEC and then out to Kingsway past Magnet House into Central's front door. The slightest irregularity, beyond five minutes grace, had to be cleared with Basil Davis' signature and the card returned to the sergeant on the door.

My work with the Aeschylus amateur dramatic society was a valuable adjunct to my training. Not only did I enjoy it but it brought me into contact with that other theatre of next to no money and where enthusiasm and ingenuity was everything. Mind you, our standards were high; we would not have dreamt of putting on a box-set without a ceiling. It simply wasn't done; although the rigging of the ceiling was the most difficult task we had to face, especially if there had to be a change of box-set under it. All this was brought home to me when seeing a revival of *Thark* at the National Theatre a few years after it had opened. The panelled set with its staircase was complete in all its three-dimensional detail; yet it had no ceiling. That ultimate piece of realism would have got in the way of all those spotlights! This society came to an end two productions into 1931. Gardner Davies, the driving force had become a professional but by then he had been responsible for my meeting Alfred Emmet of Questors, so my direct work in amateur theatre was to continue off and on for many years. I use the word 'direct' to differentiate between the advice I found myself giving to such societies as part of my job in Strand. An influence in getting that job must have been my model theatre which was still in the full flower of its creative existence.

Father and I collected, albeit with difficulty, Arthur Earnshaw from 24 Floral Street one evening for a dose of colour music and that clinched the deal. The Strand Electric (Seecol*) demonstration theatre under construction would become in effect my model theatre and that itself would no longer need to exist. The difficulty in collection that Spring evening in 1932 was due to the fact that Floral Street was

* Strand Electric and Engineering Company Limited

regarded by the market traders as one-way only, though not so signposted in those distant times. Half-way down from the Opera House stage door end we found ourselves deeply and singularly contra-flow.

Little did I think that a time would come when the great GEC would up-anchor and depart from Kingsway leaving no trace behind. For many years now a curious circular building by Richard Seifert has stood on the site of Magnet House. Its main purpose seems to have been to use up the cracked-lintels left over from Seifert's Centre Point building. Clare and Central house have vanished so has the Stoll Opera House which ran the entire length of the block opposite. There is no Kingsway theatre round the corner or Holborn Restaurant, or the Holborn Empire just up the road near the tube station. But the rest is still there including the Kodak building and what used to be Watermans fountain-pen shop.

III: FLORAL STREET
Stage Lighting 1932-35

It was exactly five minutes walk from the G.E.C head office at Magnet House Kingsway to the Strand Electric head office at 24 Floral Street in Covent Garden. Not that I ever worked in either; it was always a case of next door or over the road. My theatre and showroom were to be at number 28 opposite and before they were at all ready I was lodged in the old showroom at 19a. My early adventures in light seemed fated to start in gloom. That old showroom was indescribably dingy and dusty - worse than even Higgins and Griffiths! The June sunlight which tried to get in through the one small and dirty window - one of those which were never cleaned - only succeeded in darkening the place even more. The walls were laden with decorative fittings for hire as set dressing or props. Curious that I should start both my jobs in an ambience of period fittings. Also in both cases my job didn't really exist to begin with. The demonstration theatre was not officially opened by the impresario C.B. Cochran until ten months later. Being 'our' own job it was constantly dropped in favour of others and we simply never got round to finishing it off.

On reporting to Arthur Earnshaw, he immediately gave me a week's holiday which enabled me to establish contact with Phyllis, the girl I had my eye on, by turning up 'accidentally' on her train from Harlesden to Watford one morning. I had no means of knowing whether the architect's office where she was secretary started work at nine or ten o'clock, so this had led to my hanging about the station rather a long while. Right from inception I had realised that there was no hope for me while I was in the guinea a week stakes but as a three-pound man I could make my move. Move was the right word, for before long my family had to up sticks, 'coincidentally' when she and her family did, to take up residence in the same road in Harrow but a few doors down. The motivation came from me of course; but there had already been a gradual exodus outwards on the North West compass bearing as Harlesden slid socially. It brought the family a fine view of the church on Harrow Hill across the fields. It was this kind of London expansion which led to the establishment of the 'Green Belt' to set some limits.

The 'girlful gain' outweighed my sadness at the demolition of my model theatre for which there would be no room in the new modern house. True to tradition there were some positively the last performances of my colour music shows therein. We moved house on my brother's twenty-first birthday in June 1934 and exactly one year later the "Inaugural Recital" was played on my Strand Light Console - the last item being "Symphony No. 4 1st movement by Tchaikovsky" - so I did not have to wait long for my enduring love. However, back to that first move in the other direction: it led to an invitation, armed with my very first pair of 'briefs',* to my very first outing with a girl. And about time too! The show was Bridie's *Jonah and the Whale,* the theatre the Westminster, and the seats were balcony centre, about the third row. Amner Hall had just converted the place from a cinema and it had a shallow stage with what was then very unusual; a plaster cyclorama. Molly McArthur, the designer, made very good use of this as a background to simple but naturalistic sets. She had created quite a sensation with Bridie's previous play there, *Tobias and the Angel,* by using a Linnebach lantern to make wings grow behind Henry Ainley as the archangel Gabriel. The term 'projector' would be a misnomer since the thing is really a shadowgraph using a giant slide. The memory of Adolf Linnebach is held in such esteem in Germany that the *ring* awarded for technical innovation is named after him. The German stage has a thing about rings, of course. Instituted in 1973, the first recipient was Walter Unruh - a German theatre consultant of repute.

Anyway *Jonah* was a success both as a show and an outing except that I failed to pick up my cue when she wanted to powder her nose at the end. This caused her some physical anguish, and gave me, when I realised it, some mental anguish on the journey home. I was very raw and unversed in the ways of the world. Yet all alone I was able to make the Strand Electric showroom and demonstration theatre my kingdom and what is more, in a matter of months, expand its boundaries to include research and development - something the firm did not have at all.

Three and a half years later everything was there: new equipment like Mirror spots, Acting Areas and Pageants, the Light Console and the rest - all properly classified in my brand new 120 page case-bound catalogue of 1936. What made this possible was my relationship with my three bosses - the three directors of Strand Electric. Like Basil Davis they were not jealous of me. They saw no threat to them or the two sons, Stanley and Jack, in my work. The sons, while working for their fathers' firm, were not pursuing a career as engineers. Thus their fathers took a 'fatherly' interest in me and a pride in the bright ideas of *their* prodigy. It is inconceivable that someone could join any large organisation today and enjoy such freedom to do his own thing. Someone like that soon becomes a marked man - he has rivals at every level and the nearer he gets to the top the more likely his head will be in the firing line.

* Complimentary tickets - to avoid confusion!

Another difference is the 'job description' insisted upon by trained managers today. The whole time I was in Strand Electric we were so loosely (amateurishly?) managed that those who became the 'stars' did so because they gravitated towards what they were good at and enjoyed. For example, we shall find in a later chapter a member of the hire department (B. Bear) initiating and running a great and successful drive to sell advanced lighting controls to television studios. Furthermore, he continued for three years to use that department as a base in direct opposition, so to speak, to the two official sales departments.

Back in the thirties, the fact that I had been bad at school work and indeed at further education - the Polytechnic Engineering course would soon be given up - was an advantage because when at last I did find something I was good at there was no holding me back. Even the shyness which made me terrified of new faces (like Bill Buckle the sheet metal shop foreman), was useful. It made for a diffident approach when he had to make things for me. In consequence I got on the right side of such people in spite of my youth and public school education. Most troubles and friction in my working life have been with my contemporaries and there were none around then. Everyone was much older than I. The same had applied to the amateur dramatic society at Harlesden (The Aeschylus) when I was "Scenic and Lighting Manager". It is true in that case that the age difference was only a few years, but at that time of life every year counts.

My week's holiday had not made any difference to the condition of my ultimate destination 'across the road' so it was the old showroom in 19a for me meanwhile. How I got into it I do not know; there is no recollection of any person telling me anything - not even which of the two grimy desks was to be mine. Before long this dilemma was solved by a young Cockney lad madly rushing in and taking something out of *his* desk before dashing out again. This was my introduction to Jack Madre, whose wife had just had their first baby, and who, naturally, was not seen again that day!

Fortunately, all the male staff had to cross the showroom to get to their only lavatory, so in time I got to know some of them. Furthermore, sooner or later one of them would not want to go to the toilet and this would identify him as a customer. As to what one did with such a person time would show. It was to be hoped that he knew the routines better than the chap appointed to serve him. At that time of year there were not many visitors in search of prop fittings - except the film studios. Twickenham Studios particularly comes to mind. A Mr. Hasler would come in, glance around and literally clear a whole area of wall. These fittings were dumped on the floor to indicate reservation. This was simple enough, but it was the silk shades for the period chandeliers and brackets that were the problem. They had been packed up in boxes and left over the road until the real move took place.

Hasler knew exactly what he wanted but trying to find it in a stack of large unlabelled cardboard boxes was another matter!

When at last the move across the road was completed the more obvious gaps in the range of props had to be filled. The stock was particularly weak in modern stuff and curiously this meant wrought iron. It also meant the more obvious chromium-plated fittings with white globes or cylinders associated now with the thirties. I went around with Stanley Earnshaw who had some idea what the customer wanted to hire and where to get it. There were a number of small firms which were comparatively local who made such things in small batches on their premises. The last of these firms to survive in the district is Comyng Ching who continue in the triangle across the road from the Cambridge theatre stage door. My own taste in such things and in music was as yet naive. One of the rather expensive table lamps we bought for the showroom so appealed to me that I ordered one as a present for my parents. It was many, many years later that I learned that they hated the design. My reading became more and more Bauhaus orientated. Plain uncluttered surfaces in any case suited the idea of extracting the maximum emotional and decorative effect whether on scenery or in the auditorium by changes of light. Ketelbey was ousted by Wagner and in Adolphe Appia I found a like mind. Due to Henry Wood's playing large chunks of orchestral extracts at Monday Proms I did not realise the problem Wagnerian singers (and their props!) presented until I found myself on the new Covent Garden switchboard in 1934.

As I write, the last thing that would excite me would be the Bauhaus and any of its works. They are just as much museum pieces as the Louis and Empire gilt brackets with which that hire showroom of 1932 was so liberally bedecked. Unlike the latter, physically they did not have the seeds of survival within them either. Louis was tough and most of those fittings and the wrought irons ones went on to survive, in the showrooms of J.M.B. Hire at Shepherds Bush in the 1970's. Disenchantment with the Bauhaus style could not alter the warm glow at John English's compliment at the time of the closure by Rank of the Covent Garden premises, homes of *TABS* and the theatre, in October 1973, when he compared us to that institution. Pevsner wrote of the Bauhaus,

> *... it was to become, for more than a decade, a paramount centre of creative energy in Europe. It was at the same time a laboratory for handicraft and for standardisation; a school, and a workshop. It comprised, in an admirable community spirit, architects, master craftsmen, abstract painter, all working for a new spirit in building.*

Change the context and components of this quote to stage lighting and it does describe what we became over the years. And what is more, none of us set out to create this. It arose from doing what came naturally in a field of work to which we were attracted. You cannot organise for such a thing.

Once we had moved across Floral Street there was not much to occupy me during that summer in 1932. Theatre went quiet; it was not the tourist attraction it was to become and it was the close season for the amateur societies. I should have been very lonely but for the fact that my domain housed the staff sink. The closing of 19a had removed the male WCs except for a special directors' one on the landing and a dire affair for hire department workers in the basement.

Most of the staff preferred to use a pair of WCs set aside for them in the large but sparsely populated workshop (a leftover from the departed works) next door to me. The more hygienic of them would seek out my sink en route back to number 24 opposite. Thus a customer going up 'my' stairs could encounter a male descendent redolent of Lifebuoy soap (they did not make the toilet stuff then) with his towel slung over his shoulder. This soap was much enjoyed by the rats, so much so that we came to bait the 'break-back' traps with it. It was not surprising that in Covent Garden we should be infested with them. Rehearsing late in our theatre, as I often did, they would gradually collect and stand around like pickets outside the gates until I could stand it no longer and backed out homewards. Maybe they liked colour music?

Heating was another problem. There was no hot water, of course, and the whole showroom had to rely on one anthracite stove lit daily by the housekeeper and tea-lady, Mrs. Ventem. Anthracite was a smokeless fuel but you would never guess it at times. The result of anthracite fires, plus the all too common London pea soup fog could reduce visibility to a matter of yards. It is no exaggeration to say that it was impossible to see one end of the showroom from the other. And this vision was essential because the internal phone was sited down at the far end whilst the external G.P.O phone was nearly at the other end - a sprint of twenty yards or more.

Why such perversity? There really was some logic behind it but it is necessary to understand the geography of the showroom. My kingdom had been the sheet metal shop of the departed works and was L-shaped around two sides of a glazed well within which Windovers the famous "By Royal Warrant" coach builders (by then bespoke car bodies, of course) still functioned.* The other two sides were occupied by neighbour Frank Weston's workshop and those WCs, served by another set of stairs which continued up to the Sign department on the third floor over the lot of us. Incidentally, part of the far corner up there had been leased by Strand to the original

* The buildings and well are still there in 1992

Gate Theatre of 1929. Let no one imagine that there were not fringes long before The Fringe. Norman Marshall who worked there with Peter Godfrey evokes exactly the atmosphere "on the top floor of a ramshackle warehouse in a Covent Garden alley called Floral Street".*

Below my showroom was the Sales Counter and Stores, and across the narrow street was number 24, "a simple industrial building of 1858-9 by C.G. Searle," according to Pevsner (It was demolished in 1981). It housed accounts, theatre lighting department (TLD), hire and contracting departments. The buildings both sides were such as to warm the conservationists heart and Floral Street ran like one of the lesser Birmingham canals between them. Fortunately it wasn't a canal, for the hire department often used it to assemble their bulkier items like, spot-bars, when the police (who lived in Bow Street at the top end of the road past the stage door of the Opera House) weren't looking.

The main work of the Sign dept. above me was hire and Monday was the big change-over day for them. Their speciality was "interchangeable" signs. Large letters, seemingly held together by layers of paint, and lumps of angle iron whizzed by on the crane outside my windows; some down and some up to be slung on the wooden floor overhead with a crash and dragged into store. The bigger items in my stock, like the chandeliers, had to travel by the same crane and the opening of the large dock doors to do this effectively removed any modest supply of anthracite heat that had accumulated for some hours. Looking back the noise was awful, but they were, in a sense, necessary noises: we did not have to endure today's perpetual pop music. There were no transistors to accompany the workers where ere they worked - and there wasn't any 'musak' either!

Once up the stairs, the customer was intercepted by a desk which was not always manned, since there was only one of 'us' to begin with. To get to the demonstration theatre there was a narrow carpet running the length of the showroom which ended at a red door. This is where the logic behind the house phone at that end came in. It was a push-button intercom, and there had been only one spare button and line. It had, therefore, to serve both theatre and showroom. The GPO phone could not be there because there was no room for the desk, and the clatter of the bell would interrupt demonstrations. The house phone had a buzzer. The term 'showroom' is misleading, the place was really an old fittings warehouse round which the customer could ramble. There were large tables on which the table lamps were massed in confused ranks, shelving for even more table lamps, wooden battens on the walls to carry the lamp brackets and a couple of very large glass-fronted showcases for the smaller shades and globes. This was easier to manage than the cardboard boxes, but not all that much. Phillip Sheridan reckoned that they looked untidy right by the

* *The Other Theatre* by Norman Marshall

theatre door, and he was right, so he had the back of the glass covered with paint to give an unconvincing effect of graining. Thus one was perpetually sliding the doors to and fro to find out where the particular customer's favourites had been put. The graining and other odd jobs were done for us by a free-lance 'props' man from one of the London theatres. He used the oddest materials and finishes at times, and he wasn't much good at building structures like shelves, of which we had a whole drooping multi-tier terrace opposite the showcase.

Showroom 1932

Round the back, just outside the sink cupboard, there was an area devoted to the half-hearted display and demonstration of stage lighting spots and floods, gelatine colours and the like. Another of these purpose built wooden structures carried as best it could some of this equipment - the remainder used the floor, with or without the benefit of stands! There were three outdoor floods made of copper and one interior flood (500W Pattern 37) of the same metal. It did not give much light however because it had a stainless-steel reflector, whereas the others used silvered glass. Chromium plating was not used yet, and as for super-pure anodised aluminium, that was not even a shape of a thing to come. The two spotlights were plano-convex focus lamps (Patt. 43 1000W and Patt. 44 500W). The Patt. 43 had just replaced, except in hire, the original Strand Patt. 23, which was a 6-inch focus lamp supplied with either a 15 Amp carbon arc or an "aluminium sliding tray with adjustable Goliath lampholder to take 400-1000 Watt filament gas-filled lamps."* Adjustable it certainly was - in all directions, provided one did not get the wrist across the live pillar terminals. The arc version had an asbestos curtain instead of a lid at the back. Even the "planished steel" lid was lined, like the rest of the lantern, with asbestos millboard. Both this and the curtain used to ooze fibrous dust at the slightest provocation.

Looking back now, everything was wrong and had to have something done to it - even though one did not realise for decades after that inhaling asbestos dust was not a good thing. Memory says that the optically-ground lenses used then gave somewhat better images than the crude systems would suggest in our own moulded-lens times. But the 'spotting attachment' shoved on the front to give a clear-cut profile could reduce output to one tenth. And the other attachment, the Mangin mirror to increase the light by re-directing some of that from the rear of the filament, was an awful nuisance. It could do wonders for the light, but had to be readjusted every time one moved the lamp tray to give a different size of beam. Optical effects still used arcs, and so did follow spots with but one pioneer exception. This, the Stelmar, will come up later. What defies analysis at this distance in time is how the place was kept clean. There is a vague image of Mrs Ventem feather-dusting the tables and pushing an old O'Cedar mop around the lino but there were not only table or stand legs to avoid but the many prop fire grates lying around. As to the fitted carpet in the theatre, the only vacuum cleaners that come to mind were those used along with sewing machines as car noises. There were also rain and surf boxes with two kinds of wind machine - manual and motor. Overall there was the floor above, exposed boards without a ceiling, whence droppeth a gentle but dusty rain!

If the 'new' showroom was a peculiar place, the demonstration theatre was even stranger. It could be said that it contained nearly everything the young Bentham disapproved of. This must not be taken to mean that I was not happy there or that the use of the space could have been bettered. Entering, there was a stage one foot high with a pros. opening of 13ft across the right hand end and to the left there was a partition well clear of the ceiling complete with a door and three projection ports. Insofar as the ancient floor could be so described, it was a flat-floored house. As to seating, except for a grand opening where a buffet and C.B. Cochran would be the attraction, it had not been visualised that more than a handful of customers at a time would be there to see the demonstrations on the stage. Curiously, the same mistake

* Strand Electric *Modern Stage Lighting Apparatus* catalogue, 1924 edition

was to be made post-war when our bombed King Street theatre was rebuilt to seat a dozen or so, much against my will. More of that in another chapter. For the present there was an odd array of chairs of which no two were alike in type or design. The same could be said of the drapes on the stage - curtains, legs and borders. This singular anomaly arose from the sharing of the theatre with Hall and Dixon Ltd. Their office was at 19 Garrick Street just down the road. They were one of the firms which used to 'do' cinema decoration, curtains, seating and other furnishings. They also did things like the new house tabs (1933) in His Majesty's when they got the chance, but it was the cinema boom which provided the real market.

Mr. Dixon is only memorable as a quiet small grey man who did practical things on his occasional visits but Geo. S. Hall (as he actually liked to describe himself) was a pushy little man very formally dressed. He looked a typical draper; one could imagine the tape measure round his neck. This is not to belittle him: he knew his stuff - but in those days it was much easier to judge what people did from their appearance. Probably this was because most of them had actually done it, beginning as apprentices. There was, as far as I know, none of this being an 'executive' transferring with ease from the world of potato crisps, to that of office furniture and thence to stage lighting. Thus although Geo. and a bank manager might wear the same suit, the way they stood up in it would be different. Today, none of those persons the customer actually deals with in either type of place, seems at all likely to become a director or a top executive.

Looking around, rather like Flora Poste in *Cold Comfort Farm*, I had to bring order somehow or other. Nothing I gazed upon or used in this, the *Seecol Theatre*, was right. It was like people who clear up a serious accident - where do they start? In my own case the 'mess' was no accident. What was there had either evolved that way or was there by design. If you are selling chairs for cinemas you have one of each on display. From cafe to balcony, where ere you sat Hall and Dixon could prop up the posterior. There were Lloyd Loom creaking cane, chromium- plated tubular (the latest thing), arts and crafts wood, a super tip-up and one not so super tip-up. However, there was a good large table but finding seating to put customers around it to discuss their plans presented a nice exercise each time. What really floored me, though, were the walls - particularly the fourth wall, the proscenium, which everyone had to look at. This was the age of tortured plaster - Marblecote and other such textures. No surface was left alone. They were raked and combed into thirties chevrons, triangles and semicircles which were then rubbed in by picking out in bilious greens or oranges and inevitably some gold or silver paint - a New Discovery not long tinned. Not for us the French greys and the eau-de-nil of architects. Even the name *Seecol* for the theatre and the catalogue was a torture. It was the Strand trade mark and stood for Strand Electric and Engineering Co. Ltd. but suggested an ointment for bunions and piles, whatever they were! There was something called Zambuk around at the time which claimed to soothe most such things; Seecol was an obvious competitor.

Eventually, there was a 30-way Seecol Grand Master switchboard out in the auditorium and we were ready to fix a date for C.B. Cochran. Everyone - bar one - was very proud of this giant switchboard with its shafts and cross- gearing all chromium plated. And in those days such plating was really something. You didn't have to apply things to protect it; there was sufficient chromium to protect itself whether on car or Grand Master. Incidentally, the finish was special to this job and the Stratford-upon-Avon board which had preceded it. This Grand Master had my sole design contribution in that field: sixty chromium round-headed screws. There was a pair to each of the turned wood 'beer-engine' handles and they gave visual and tactile indication of whether one had turned the handle to lock onto the master shaft or not. Without the modification one had to rely on memory.

The theatre opened officially in March 1933 using chairs hired, along with the buffet, from J. Lyons: not the tea shop or Swiss roll departments but the one which used to do the Royal Garden Party and the like, so there was nothing to complain of there. Nor was there in the show. After the formalities, L.G. Applebee talked about lighting including Samoiloff and UV effects with appropriate demonstrations. Geo. S Hall did his bit about the curtains and such. As a finale I forsook my role of accompanist for soloist and "fully illustrated the theory of colour lighting by which

Seecol Theatre

the tones are dictated by the mood of the music" which revealed me as "no less an artist than a technician." To quote the *Kine Weekly*. The first of my three items was on a pair of white festoon muslin curtains. The colour lighting effects (back and front) were so distractingly beautiful that the audience did not notice that the left one was a different quality from the right! The second number was on a pair of black casement curtains. These were a real pair. They were my only identical twins, so to speak. I had insisted that we must have a set of blacks to hang behind the muslins so that they could be lit from the rear as well as the usual from top and bottom front and sides. Used solo, the folds of the blacks took colour from the sides and imparted to them a superb richness. The music was MacDowell's *AD 1620*, a 10-inch Columbia record of G.D. Cunningham at the organ. This solemnly surged 'Atlanticwise' towards crescendo and quiet reprise; ideal for lighting accompaniment. It was destined for an important role in the life of my Light Console. Back on the Seecol Grand master the finale was a dawn on the cyclorama to music of the same name by Ketelbey of *In a Monastery Garden* fame. Here, although there were five twinkling stars drilled in the cyclorama to begin (the Shakespeare Memorial Theatre had thirty) the scenic masking at the bottom jarred. Quite literally; for the ground row there, was painted as a low wall and had two profile classic vases stuck equidistantly on top - that props man of ours, at it again. Fortunately, these profile pots could be unscrewed. The masking of the bottom of a cyclorama is very important as neither the floor or any hint of the equipment must be seen. The limitless sky must end somewhere but where? The real solution which I hit on within the year was the inclined plane. A piece of framed ply (no hardboard then) painted matt white lay at an angle of rather less than 45° to the stage to catch the spill from overhead light aimed at the cyc. The whole thing, although strictly neutral, suggested a sea and sky with a horizon which could be defined or not by bringing in the bottom lighting from behind the plane itself. The device, now commonplace in television studios, served as an ideal base for the music which quickly ousted Ketelbey from my repertoire. Why him anyway? He came like the MacDowell and the Tchaikovsky 4th. (which was destined to go into my repertoire, virtually for ever!) as part of a random selection of records loaned free by Marconiphone along with their new twin-turntable sound system.

A digression on sound will not be inappropriate at this point. Reproduction of gramophone records using thermionic valve amplifiers became popular in the late twenties. Domestically the thing became known as a radio-gram but in the theatre it (minus the radio bit) was known as a Panatrope. This was the firm of Brunswick's trade name for it. In the cinema the term Non-Sync was applied to differentiate between it and the sound-film (talkie) equipment - the Vitaphone version of which used special long-play records. A particular feature of sound reproduction was bass boom which people mistook for quality. In the home it was probably a reaction from the enforced lack of bass with the acoustic gramophones. In cinemas, it may have been a product of the sound system. In theatres the record of the National Anthem was so bad as to make it impossible to judge the quality of the system. However, within our small theatre the Marconiphone sounded, to our ears then, rather good.

Until my Light Console went into action, the purchase of gramophone records at 3 shillings for a 10 inch or 4/6d for a 12 inch was not to be thought of. Eventually visits to Remington Van Wych's basement opposite the London Hippodrome - Moss Empire's Cranbourn Mansions office door to be precise - did see Strand cash purchases made. It was not the only thing those visits saw, for soon they had a Marconi high-definition television on display: a great floor-standing affair with a large mirror in the lid. Apart from the need for some choice of our own, purchase of records was necessary as our Marconiphone not only called our tune and played it but scraped it off in record time! It was not just the 'great' horseshoe magnet, between the poles of which the pickup armature had to oscillate, but the weight of the cueing arm itself. This was a large casting formed with a quadrant to carry a calibrated scale which when the release was gingerly operated (no dampers or dashpots then) certainly gave you the exact groove but how the designer expected the shellac disc to survive the weight is a cause for wonder. It looked good and was theatre-proof: a Grand Master board man would be quite at home with it. A world away from the flimsy affairs to which we have become accustomed. Not only did we try all types of steel needles, religiously changing them after playing each side, and the semi-permanents but also Van Wyck's special thorns to prevent record wear but they proved unable to preserve themselves for even one transit of our heavy pickups.

The solution was duplicate records or sets (maximum playing time was 4 minutes): thus Lohengrin Prelude Act I, for example, occupied two sides but of different records. The rehearsal sides became rough indeed. For most rehearsing I had to operate the gramophone myself and where, as so often, the new side began on something very active, this meant a mad dive back to the console bench; even, in the case of the King Street theatre, through a trio of doors and down a flight of stairs. No wonder I still feel 'the breaks' even after decades of long-play. That Tchaikovsky 4th had four sides to the first movement alone!

As I write there are probably only three other people to whom that old showroom and theatre in Floral Street conjures up vivid memories. They are Lew Burroughs, Len Jordan and Paul Weston. Len came over from Hire department as my first assistant. His job was to look after the showroom, once the theatre and R&D (Research and Development) became my main preoccupation. He stayed faithfully in that post until the building was, almost literally, pulled down around him. Say, four and a half decades of showroom. Another man of long service is Paul Weston, again of four and a half decades; but not in exactly the same work. And yet in a curious way for so much of his long service in Strand/ Rank Strand he has been playing the same role but growing with it at the pace of technological change. Paul's first job with me was theatre boy, a role originally played, once the Seecol theatre was complete and ready for action, by Lew Burroughs. There was much to do. Even the simplest of regular demonstrations had scene changes and music from records. Quite how this was done I do not remember, since the latter was out front in a small office and scene changes involved work backstage, of course. Not that there was any off-stage space whatever. We never had any; even less then if possible, than we had in the later King Street theatre. A parsimonious feature was that the stage floor did not extend right up to the walls. Instead there was a ragged gutter roughly 9-inches wide by one foot deep either side inhabited by tripe* and rats. Both Lew and Paul were (and are) thin - it must have been the most important qualification for that job. Somehow or other, whoever it was had to disappear between changes, but like a conjurers cabinet there was, seemingly, nowhere at all to hide. There was no overhead space or height either. The projection screen and the ultra-violet act drop were tumbled - just! All gauzes, muslins, blacks and scenery had to go off to the wings which weren't there, and were already populated with side lighting. Remember too, those were the days when all sources had to be hidden behind masking.

Looking back it is the scenery that is the biggest puzzle: there was, as memory and my archive shows, quite a repertoire of music items each with its own set or sets and there *was* nowhere to store them. The small space behind our flat plaster cyclorama was destined to house the Light Console dimmer bank; but at this time was occupied by Eddie Biddle's optical effects workshop. Well in character was the absence of any door or fill-in for the emergency exit gap left at one end, except an inadequate sheet of corrugated iron which had to be lugged in and out of position. Since the Biddle space had an open fireplace and grate, sometimes used for heating and at others to burn up waste, one had the piquant situation of *an open fire within our stage fire risk*. It goes without saying that none of the drapes or scenery was fireproofed. The real hazard, not infrequently encountered was the need to damp the fire down hastily when a customer wanted to see the twinkling stars or anything far from flamboyant demonstrated on the cyclorama alongside.

When I went to Strand, I went there with a Light Console under my bonnet, so to speak, but there was not the slightest thought of getting them to make it or of becoming involved in lantern design. The aim was to learn how stage lighting was done backstage in the *real* theatre and then bunk off and *do* lighting. The trigger to do something about R&D was the discovery that Strand Electric from inside had nothing better to show than what we hired from them as amateurs outside the firm. My work with my model theatre had accustomed me to powerful (relatively

* Stage term for flexible cables

speaking) narrow fixed beams from overhead and the sides; a more or less permanent layout with everything under individual dimmer control from a compact panel 'out-front'. The reality was that with one exception (the Stelmar spot) nothing that could be dimmed had any punch, and anyway the 1000-Watt Stelmar was three feet long and so expensive that the new Shakespeare Memorial Theatre of 1932 could only afford four, and the 1934 installation at the Covent Garden Opera had only nine. This ace spot was also in the hire stock, as were some 2kW focus lanterns. Hassard Short liked to specify them for his shows such as *Wild Violets* and *Stop Press;* but as 'ours' had only a 6-inch PC lens, this and the large lamp bulb and filament made the things rather a sham. It may have sounded good to specify a 2kW but it was little use.

Something had to be done but there was absolutely nothing available with which I could experiment. All that one could do was to take a lamp tray out of an existing spot, put it on Hall and Dixon's table (if Geo. was out of the way), and prop up the odd reflector using a telephone directory (and there was only one to the whole of London then). What one was trying to do was to adapt the principal of the Mirror Arc which had become popular for cinema projectors while I was with Basil Davis. Before too long I was given some money to buy a few retort stands, but we didn't get a proper optical bench until after the war. The firm did not even possess a voltmeter which would read anything above a hundred volts D.C. A whole shelf in one of those showcases was a jumble of such instruments: all were completely useless and had been bought only for use as props. They would be collectors' items now. The only thing that actually worked was a small Weston instrument in a musty leather case. Our premises, like most of the theatres at that time, were on a D.C. supply. To get A.C. power, one had to use a rotary converter - which did have a voltmeter on its control panel - but the whole lot was in the old machine shop next door, now ruled over by the formidable Frank Weston of optical effects fame.

A very long cable kept in a heap by the machine had to be unrolled, laid across the shop floor, down the entire length of the showroom and thence into the theatre. Although it was 'heavy tripe' the voltage drop was deep indeed; and load dependent. Output could be boosted at the machine but I had to have a voltmeter. Mansell agreed with me, and decided to buy two so that the new works at Gunnersbury could have one also. Recollection suggests that there was a short period in which we attempted to share the same one! These were Record instruments in a nice polished wood case with a leather handle, brass engine-turned knobs and terminals. It also had a very ingenious way of changing the actual scale behind the pointer to correspond with whatever shunt one was using to measure amps.

The Strand called itself "Electric and Engineering Company" but, as we see, it did not have the most elementary tools of the trade. There was a Megger somewhere in the Contracts department and there must have been another in the factory but everything was run on a shoestring. The Jim Jordan, originally Mossy's foreman at Mansell and Ogan and later to become Strand's Works Manager and afterwards a director, had many tales involving the principles of monetarism. Complaints, for example, over an expense claim for 4d. were supported by the fact that had he got on the tram two stops later and got off one earlier it would have been 3d. Rate of pay was in scale with this attitude too. People continued to work for the firm partly from sheer habit, I think, and partly because they liked those they worked with or for. There was what can only be described as an 'esprit de Strand'. This survived all hazards; even for a while after the take-over in 1969 by the Rank Organisation, with the incessant shuffles and rearrangements which were to follow. Joe Davis relates in "Tin Mug"* when he joined Strand in 1925 it was for "the princely sum of 3½d per hour".

It is of course a great mistake to think that Strand Electric was unique. It must have been typical of a large number of small specialist firms. But there was also the glamour of working if not on, then for, the stage. In fact there can have been few men at Strand who never went backstage. We were part of theatreland and located in the heart of it. Maybe the job was only to install something or to mend it; but a considerable proportion did work after hours as 'showmen'. This moonlighting could cause problems if suddenly his department within the firm had to work overtime. The bush telegraph would go into action and a deputy for the Duke's, the St. Martin's or wherever, was despatched to the stage door on time.

Tight financing of little things - meanness, perhaps - was to persist right up to the Rank take-over. It was identified, not always justly, with Henry Myers, who had joined Strand from C.B. Cochran's office as company secretary in 1925; the post he continued to hold until his retirement at the end of 1964. Better known in Cockney rhyming slang as 'Screwdriver and Pliers', or just Screwdriver, many were the tales (apocryphal or otherwise) about him. This one I vouch for as fact. In my second year as a director a decade or so later on, I remarked on the poor turnout our AGM attracted. It was held in our theatre where I was accustomed to good houses whereas, in this case, only two shareholders and two press came.

Some sherry next time would, I suggested, make the occasion less like the interment of an aged workhouse inmate: after all our annual figures used to be very good. With the support of Stanley Earnshaw this was voted a good idea and twelve months later Henry turned up with a bottle and some glasses, whose content bore the relationship of a dingy to a schooner. No question of finishing the bottle arose: Henry spirited it away upstairs somewhere. When, many years later, Jack Sheridan

* *TABS* Vol.21 No.3, December 1963

retired, there were found in the depths of a cupboard in his office (our boardroom) some six or seven bottles still bearing the remains of our annual orgies.

What on earth was the key I used to prise open the cash box so carefully guarded by the three director-owners of the firm it is impossible for me to determine fifty years later. It is an onlooker - an historian - who writes now! That me of so long ago was a very shy person; it may have been obvious that when he really did push an idea, it must have had such an inspired origin that it could not be bottled up. The brash self-assurance of a whizz-kid might not have cut much ice with those three 'old' wise men.

Before long a photometer* was very necessary. Applebee had an ancient grease-spot instrument in which you had to match the incident light to one of a series of thirty-three grubby minute spots of diminishing brightness. It was a hopeless task, but the photocell types of photometer had just been introduced. How L.G.A. ever came to possess the photometer is a mystery. Foot-candles and photometry never meant anything to him, nor did it need to in his work.

A primitive turntable of two large discs of wood with calibrated edges riding one upon the other, with a dose of wax polish between, was devised to fit in the tripod stand of the Stelmar and we were all prepared for some crude photometry. But not quite. Lew Burroughs, having run out the tripe cable would be dispatched to start the converter while I lurked apprehensively in the comparative security of the Seecol theatre. All was well, he would re-appear and we would begin our readings when the volts would go off. Lew would rush and re-start the machine; only to have it knocked off again shortly afterwards. Frank Weston could be very, very awkward and his attitude to me and this kind of technical mumbo-jumbo was not helped by his assumption that as a man many years (in fact, decades) my senior in age and theatre experience, he was in charge of me. It was characteristic of Arthur Earnshaw not to define the frontier between the young upstart and the cantankerous veteran. He had to do something about it before long; and the result was a door; sprung-closed with a loud bang by a heavy weight and tracker-wire. Geographically, the power converter, like the WCs, were in Frank's territory, with equal right of access: the wash basin remained in mine. Ian P. Neatly† would have found much to criticise, as must have the female members of our Seecol theatre audiences, as the arrangements were so dire that we could not bring ourselves to put up any public admission that we had any such thing for them at all!

Eventually a mock-up 1000-Watt Mirror spot (to become Patt. 73) in a crude metal box - made for me by the tinsmith next door, probably while Frank was away -

* Instrument for measuring intensity of light

† "There is a Tide in the Affairs of Men' *Sightline* Vol.15 No. 2 pp78-79

was ready to be demonstrated to the big three. They used to hold a board meeting more or less every Thursday afternoon and they would readily come over to see whatever I had to show them. It was all beautifully direct: it made me intolerant for ever of organisational machinations, even at the G.E.C. Basil Davis as a resident consulting engineer had been sufficient unto himself. Phillip Sheridan, who had just returned from New York, had sent over something for me to connect up so he could show it off to the two others. It was the latest thing - a Kliegl ellipsoidal spot with rhodium-plated reflector, G.E. cap-up pre-focus lamp and 6 x 9-in. moulded step-lens with black risers. I am not sure of the wattage - it was probably 500 or just maybe 650.

When all had admired the neat American production model and how its bright light could be shaped, it was my turn. The scene can be imagined, especially if the fact that P.S. (as we called him) was an excitable Dubliner is kept in mind. My spotlight looked, and was, a monstrosity but it was something which could be shaped-up for manufacture within measurable time in our own works, without importing anything. We did copy that moulded step lens, using the Kliegl one as a pattern, but all the rest was homespun with an 8-inch diameter silvered-glass reflector and G.E.S. A1 or B1 1000-watt lamps. Not for us the delights of pre-focusing - we had to wait until after the war - and cap-up burning didn't arrive until 1962. There was not much drawing involved; I was allocated a first class man, Harry Coe, and bit by bit it was devised and made on his bench. It is this one that appears with the Kliegl lens (and minus any colour runner because I thought it spoilt the outline), in my catalogue dated 1936. There is a funny contradiction here. Historically, it was published Autumn 1935, but the late date was used to extend its commercial validity. This is something for the thesis writer to be canny about.

Due to the major changes incorporated in the Kliegl spotlight and the custom which grew in the United States of referring to the type as "ellipsoidals" a certain amount of haze surrounds what we were all trying to do in the early thirties. The key word is *Profile*. None of us ever used that word then as far as I know; but it was a means of shaping the beam of light at will that we wanted. Not only without the great loss of light inherent in the use of a 'spotting attachment' but also with a great increase of light when compared to the standard lens spot or focus lamp. The Stelmar, whose patent applications are dated Sept. 1925 and 1929, was based on an adjustable gate with an elaborate ellipsoidal reflector system between it and the 1000-Watt tubular lamp. The gate, usually an iris diaphragm, was focused by a 6 x 12 inch optically-worked PC lens. The whole thing was geared to longish throws. The system was a precision affair with two concentric reflectors and a tiny step-lens in the centre plus, of course, a spherical reflector behind the lamp. It was almost telescope-grade work.

Casting around for a clue which would lead to something more compact and hopefully somewhat less expensive, I first wasted some time (and money!) over a

Schwabe lantern which I called the Double-Focus spot. This was among the odds and ends from the G.E.C. showroom when they closed down their stage lighting department at the end of 1932. It used a series of separate lenses in a narrow double-deck housing. For the wider angles, the beam went straight along the top, but for the narrow ones it was diverted back and forth by two mirrors and emerged from the lower deck. We made six or so but two things were off-putting: our lenses and mirrors were poor quality compared to the German ones and I tried using a Mogul (Large) pre-focus holder for the lamp. The holders could be purchased from Major but dimensions were still subject to international discussion. Furthermore, soft-solder was used by the lamp maker to join base to cap. This was incredible! The lamphouse itself was based on the German cylindrical one with a good current of air; in at the bottom, up past the sides of the lamp bulb and out at the top. The Germans had not used a pre-focus lamp but I was both anxious to give such a good idea a trial and also to avoid the fiddly filament line-up process which our theatre people were unlikely to bother with. The much cruder mirror spot in which I had nothing better than my own ideas and what came more or less to hand was more suited to our theatre as it was then. It couldn't have a pre-focus lamp so there was lining up to do with a new lamp - which incidentally could be a B1 if you wanted the longer life and the tilt. Paul Weston was to prove the best adjuster for any that had to go on show.

My best lantern was the Patt. 56 1000 Watt "Acting Area". It was foolproof with a long life GS lamp. With its 26° beam angle and good, not too sharp, cut-off, one simply had to hang up a row of them overhead to get a punchy light which, so long as the stage cloth was also light, could correct its verticality to some extent. The reflector was of a silvered cathedral glass designed for me by George Lovell of Robinson, King Ltd. He was the patentee of the Sunray silvered glass reflectors used by Strand Electric from the early twenties for their compartment (Samoiloff) battens, and most of their other floodlighting equipment: thus one heard "17-inch Sunray" and the "12-inch Sunray" as common lighting terms backstage. The principle involved a broken surface resembling a large number of tiny lenses. The result lost all filament striation and was ideal for flooding, but the Patt. 56 was to produce a narrow beam with minimal scatter, hence the cathedral glass in this case. George Lovell was ideal to work with; never making a fuss, but intrigued with a new problem he would come back with test samples in next to no time.

I still have his drawing of this reflector - in pencil on a sheet of detail paper - with conical spill rings added by me, also in pencil. The only ink around is a very, very large blot of India ink, which suggests that I was about to trace the thing but knocked the pot over and was not allowed the finance to buy another! This lantern had no trouble in replacing the wasteful wide-angle Arena flood with a deep hood, or the Strand copy of a German acting-area which had been used in the new installation of 1934 at Covent Garden. My lantern gave ten times more light for the same wattage. It did not look so neat and streamlined, but it was efficient. I never saw the original German unit which someone had copied, but it cannot have been quite as poor in output, so it must have lost something in inept copying.

It was Robert Nesbitt who made the Patt. 56 fashionable. Using row upon row overhead, and booms of Pageants in the wings, a style of installation was created, peculiar to this country, which became 'the way' to do any kind of stage spectacle. In a sense it was an anticipation of Svoboda's massed use of Nedervolt lamps in the 1960s or fixed beam PAR lamps of recent years (1980s, say). The Patt. 56 is inseparable from the Patt. 50 Pageant. This was the first 'parallel-beam' lantern over here - what the Americans referred to as a beamlight; a much better term, but there was no connection between the two - it was another case of ingenuity doing its own thing. Outsiders imagine that inventors go around copying each other; there must have been a first somewhere. Archaeologists have wasted a lot of time on how-did-it-spread investigation and have come to the conclusion that the answer can be: it didn't. The true answer being simultaneous invention. Even in our time it is possible to be so busy following up one's own ideas as to have, literally, no time to read about anyone else's.

Before the thing was named the Pageant it was referred to as the "Double-B" lantern. The other 'B' was not the well-known B. Bear (he had not joined us yet) but Jack Bennett. He was one of the two outside sales representatives who looked after special non-theatre work. The other rep was Jim Murray and they could not have been more unlike: Bennett was dapper and smart and Jim was not! The pageant to be staged in the empty moat of the Tower of London, as part of George V's Jubilee, needed a line of narrow beam lanterns mounted high up along the roof of the temporary stand. Shows of this kind were always in charge of someone of high rank in the Services, so Bennett must have been told to make some small searchlights. In due course the sample, of exactly that, appeared in the Seecol theatre

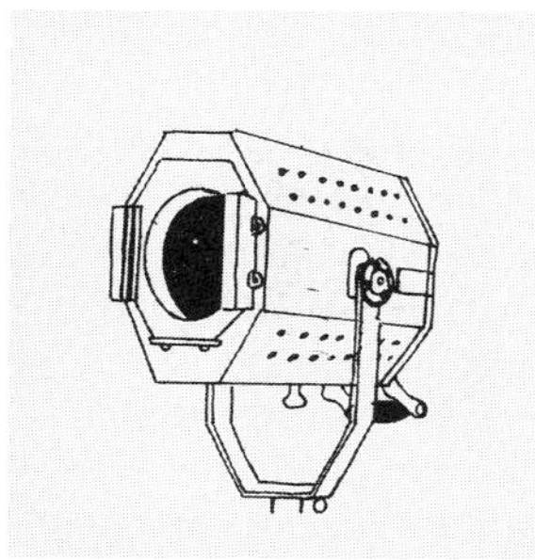

Patt. 43 Focus Lamp

Patt. 73 Mirror Spot

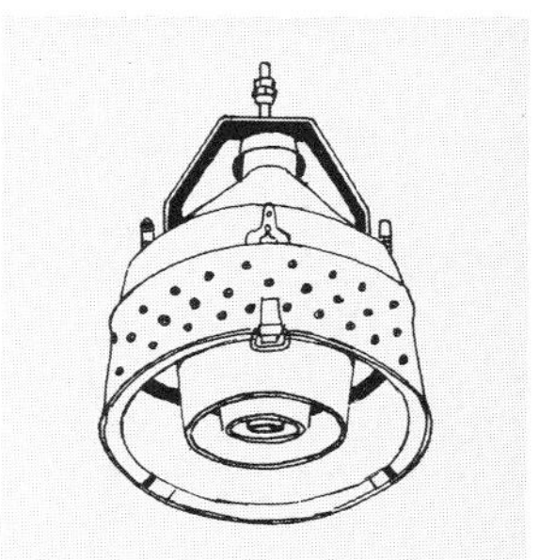

Patt. 56 Acting Area

(where else?) for test. It gave a nice punchy, if streaky, beam with a lot of side scatter. My interest was aroused, but not for a special for the Pageant itself - though I did go to the show - but as something to punch sunlight through windows of the many box sets of those pre-scenography days. Design of spill-rings did not present much difficulty nor, in those days of cheap labour, did their manufacture.

The first show to try out the new lantern was at His Majesty's and featured the film star Ramon Navarro in a constant change of costume and a Ruritanian romance which survived a run of just one week; and it opened on a Tuesday! On the Monday evening the two Earnshaws took me out for a pre-show sandwich (in Leicester Square and it was the first time I heard of liver-sausage!) and then via the stage door to the roped-off front row of the stalls. It was a public dress-rehearsal and the house was full. Our big moment did not come until the romance 'peaked' towards the end of the last act. The curtain rose and there it was - the best moonlight yet seen on any London stage. Two Pageants (just two!) way up on the fly rail (out of sight of course) shone brightly down into some sort of courtyard. As far as I recall they had the stage to themselves at the opening: perhaps Navarro had not managed his quick-change!

Two versions of the Pageant were made, an indoor and an outdoor, and it came as a surprise to me to find that both were ready in time for the Silver Jubilee of 1935. But the Strand Electric press book states that ninety were used at the Tower, and sixteen were certainly used on the spire of Salisbury cathedral as part of the same celebrations. The indoor version (Patt. 50a) was slower to take off, being restricted to sun and moon work for a while. Theatre people did not like the filament striation and a diffuser of cathedral glass had to be added as standard. Before too long people became less sensitive and it is an interesting quirk that when twenty-five years later I deleted the Pageant to ensure good sales for our new mass-produced Fresnel, the Patt. 243, there was much lamentation. Yet the latter gave exactly the soft-edge at one time considered essential - and with an adjustable beam angle as well!

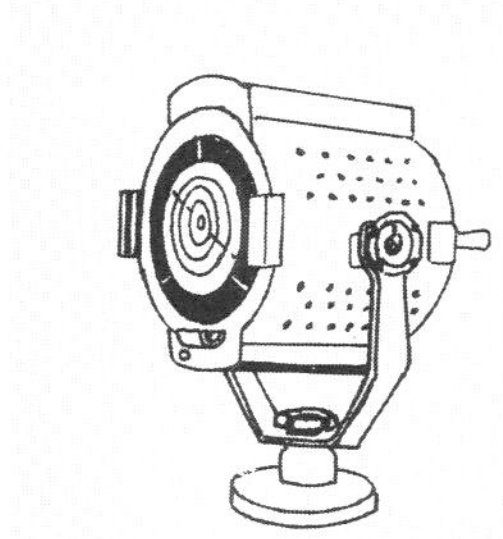

Patt. 50 Pageant

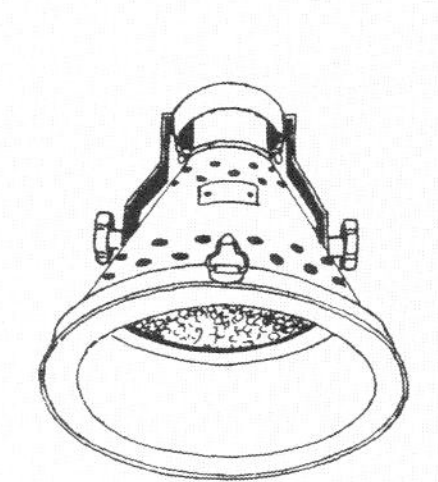

Patt. 35 Arena

Patt. 60 Flood

Until my catalogue of 1936 was published, theatre people never knew of beam angles and cut-off angles, to say nothing of polar or other beam distribution curves. I had come to consider such things as essential due to their presence in the GEC floodlighting catalogues. Everything in the Strand range, whether old or new, had to be dragooned to conform to this discipline. The dear old 17 inch and 12 inch Sunrays which had squirted out a happy flood, found themselves rejuvenated, so to speak, as medium or wide angle versions of 1000 and 500 watts respectively: eventually becoming Patt. 49 A or B in the one case and Patt. 30 or 60 in the other, for some unknown reason. I had no drawing board, except a small one to use on the kitchen table at home, so I had to resort to squared paper when necessary to do such work at Floral Street. On the whole the amount of drawing required was minimal - it was more a matter of stimulating the imagination of the man who was to make the prototype. In our British way we set about design by taking what was to hand, adding a bit of this or that and then making a simple sketch to get the idea over. The American luxury of special lamps and components was not for us.

As an example, one cannot do better than to take the Arena flood. This old Strand flood got its name from Bertram Mills Circus for which it was made in the twenties. Though intended to hang high above the ring, its Sunray reflector gave a very wide angle beam. So wide and smooth in fact, that I was able to use the selfsame reflector for both the Patt. 60, just referred to, and for an entirely new 500W flood (Patt. 55) for lighting cycloramas at close range - particularly with three-colour mixing. The circus used to hang a valance around in an attempt to keep the light out of people's eyes and in stagework the grossly inefficient hood already mentioned was sometimes used.

I would love to know how the various items of the Strand range, which I was 'correcting' without being asked, came into being. Only George Lovell knew about optics and reflectors but as he was not in theatre lighting someone had to give him an idea of the distribution of light required. Very often all I had to do was to get a reflector position altered slightly in relation to the lamp filament and maybe have the inside of the lamphouse painted black. It was absurd to make a wing flood by putting a big lamp in a ventilated metal box and shove a silvered glass Sunray reflector behind to *brighten* the light; then supply it with equal fervour to light a backing close behind a window or to gild cinema drapes 40ft or more wide from the side. I hate having to write about this clever Dick, or rather Fred, who came in and within a few months had put everyone and everything to rights. Especially as I had, and still have, such respect for my three bosses of those early thirties. They were such men of the theatre - they really knew the work and the people. I have to repeat - they belonged. Perhaps that was why the technical side was such a botch. Botching or vamping to get the show on is, or at any rate was, the essence of theatre production - short cuts abounded. A man of resource, compliant to the needs of the moment, tends to be intolerant of technological discipline. Besides which, in the days we are considering, there was no technical training in theatre whatever; good or bad practices were picked up simply by being there.

After a while an extra fillip to technical discipline and classification was given by Arthur Earnshaw's idea that we ought to have a new catalogue. He was certainly right. Early in the thirties Major Equipment published a superb catalogue properly bound as a hardback in a golden cover with an Art Deco design embossed upon it. Strand's was still a dire loose-leaf affair almost indistinguishable from that of the, by then defunct, firm of Digby on which it had been based. Stanley was told to get on with it, he consulted me and before long it was mine.

The Major catalogue looked good both inside and out but the range of equipment - aimed mainly at the super cinema market - was nothing like as complete as ours was shaping up to be. With the GEC's illuminating engineering catalogue formats in mind it was not difficult to think up a framework in which to work. For the same man to be designing both catalogue and the range of equipment which it was to enshrine was ideal. One lantern, the Patt. 61 Optical Effects Projector, never got any further than a mock-up which could be photographed; so it is no good archaeologists trying to seek traces of this. Yet the Patt. 61 had a full page to itself with specification and a dimensioned line drawing. It was introduced as "primarily intended for use on the stage" but it could be "used with considerable success on front of house throws up to 100ft". Of course, if someone had ordered the thing one would have had to bustle about and make it from scratch but nobody ever wanted it and meantime it looked good in my catalogue - completing the Effects Projector range; Patt. 51 1000W (one of my new ones), Patt. 33 20-40 amps (Strand traditional) and Patt. 61 50 amps. Another unique item (quite literally!) was the Patt. 74 Baby Mirror Spot. The Patt. 73 Mirror (profile) spot made its debut in this catalogue and in the same way that there had long been a 'Baby' version of the Patt. 43 lens spot (focus lamp). In this case the Patt. 74 illustrated had been made and lit up. No others were made and the item was deleted from the second edition of the catalogue. A similar fate befell the Patt. 80 Baby Pageant Lantern 12 Volt 100 Watt with an "Effective throw" of 150ft. Where did the idea of identification by pattern (Patt.) numbers come from? The answer has to be Strand's predecessor, Digby's catalogue (they too had a Patt. 23 but it was only an arc).

Here we come slap up against either a commercial barrier or a technological one. And of the two I think the first was the one that niggled. The ELMA was a wall around the big lamp suppliers which could not be breached by the likes of us (Jules Thorn had only just started on his path to take them on). A baby spot simply had to have a 500 Watt lamp, but this filament was obstinately enclosed in the same sized bulb as the 1000 Watt class B lamp. There was a smaller tubular A1 size, but it was frail and could not be tilted. And one thing was certain: anything calling itself Baby Spot would have to be used in positions of acute tilt. The 100 Watt Pageant idea also had to vanish but resort was made to 36 Watt car headlamp bulbs and two low-voltage lanterns appeared in the next edition; one a reflector cum spill-ring unit with built-in transformer (Patt. 81) and the other a tiny lens spot 3 by 5" (Patt. 87), which was to prove useful for the ceramics at the Paris Expo of 1937.

The Patt. 81 was something rushed out for a frantic Phillip Sheridan. George Black had fallen for the idea of having hundreds of these things massed as battens and booms at the London Palladium. The ones he installed were neither made nor thought up by us but we *had* to have something to cover this craze. But it never caught on as a style of lighting, unlike the Patt. 56/50 combination was to do. I was sent off to see the show from the front stalls but came back unconvinced that they were a success, which suggests that there was nothing dramatic in the way they were deployed. Nevertheless this was Nedervolt lighting in 1934, and it is a pity that neither the man who sold the idea to Black and Charlie Henry nor the firm (not one of the theatre regulars) can be named here. I can't even remember whether Flanagan and Allen were in the show!

If having catalogue editor and R&D Führer as one man pushed new items forward, there was one item which unfairly found itself relegated to the back pages down among Strand Shop Window Lighting as three lines without an illustration. This lantern was the 150 Watt Baby Flood - in effect a single compartment of a batten. The reason for relegation was that as a one beam angle lantern it did not conform to the facing spread format of the other floods - medium angle to the left, wide to the right. Looking at those pages, back nearly sixty years, the solution stares me in the face but there is no going back now and doing the right thing by it. Anyway it proved quite capable of looking after itself for it was to survive, in one version or another, to be listed by Rank Strand until 1979 at least!

We went to a first class printer for the catalogue - Hazell, Watson and Viney of Aylesbury, who then also had an office nearby in Long Acre. There was no difficulty over the choice of typeface: Gill Sans (sans serif, of course). It came off the press towards the end of 1935 though it bore the date 1936. That Christmas Eve the house phone buzzed to summon me over to P.S's office where he and Arthur Earnshaw were waiting to declare how pleased they were with the new catalogue and present me with the gold watch which I wear even as I type these words. It came from Davies the jewellers in St Martin's Lane next door to the London Coliseum; and they are still there, with a new shop-front but otherwise unmoved. The watch, any kind of reward, was quite unexpected but was just the right touch to show person to person that they appreciated what I had done for their firm as summed up and displayed in this catalogue. Did I but know it, that catalogue was to be the end of an era, and within two months I was to have a new board of directors, one of whom envied me and what I did. However, before we come to that upheaval it is necessary to return to 1932 and examine lighting control over those three years. Unlike lanterns and the rest, control of lighting was nearest my heart. I loved lighting but not as something detached, to be done and move on to the next job. Lighting was something to be savoured and enjoyed, which could only be done by working the switchboard oneself. The devising of such controls for lighting and the technical side of making the ideas work held equal attraction.

IV: MORE FLORAL STREET
Grand Master v. Light Console 1932-36

When I joined Strand Electric the 'Age of the Grand Master' had just begun (as far as the firm was concerned) and my self-appointed task was to undermine this confidence, somehow or other. At that time there were two switchboards considered as supreme achievements, to be regarded with something like awe: in the Halifax Little Theatre and in the Shakespeare Memorial Theatre. The latter had just gone into action on St. George's day 1932 as part of the installation for the new Elizabeth Scott building at Stratford-upon-Avon which had been despised by some at the time as looking like a factory but nowadays it is a familiar and cherished feature. So much so that even the RSC, who have torn down so much inside, have not interfered with the spirit of the outside. The other theatre was built by the Halifax Building Society and was an anticipation of something we have grown accustomed to in recent years; a commercial development which included a theatre as well as an extension to their own premises and some shops. The theatre was known as the Alexandra Hall and seated 600, of which 200 were in the balcony. The proscenium opening was 26ft with the familiar orchestra-cum-forestage conversion in front. It all seems to have been mainly for the benefit of an amateur company - the Halifax Thespians.

The consultants for both theatres were Ridge and Aldred but Halifax's real claim to fame here was its 42 way Grand Master - the first such control to be made by Strand. It is important to make quite clear that it was a real one. The term is often glibly used for some ancient outsize switchboard with levers and shafting on the front and resistance dimmers directly behind. To be a true Grand Master the thing has to have a master wheel to which the various 'colour' shafts can be locked and unlocked to move their dimmers up or down. Two things result from this: firstly, the design of the cross-gearing to join the shafts together at will and, secondly, a self-release or trip to avoid too much friction when 'early' dimmers arrived at either end of travel. The cross-gearing on these first models took the form of great toothed-bevels; a very crude device whose teeth could involve wheedling the shaft to and fro to get engagement. On later models the bevels were permanently meshed with a spline-clutch inside to effect engagement. The self-release dimmer lever was a dodgy device needing much careful setting, preferably by a fitter of the name of Syd Medlicott. To work, there had to be some residual friction to continue to operate the arm which lifted the locking shoe. Other firms tended to use a spring trigger which tripped the lever for good. This was the method adopted by Mickelwright of Alperton, a firm which acted as a sub-contractor to most of Strand's competitors. American practice for a long time was to use a slot which gathered dimmers en route, thereby reducing lighting to an overall nonentity before the final fadeout. At least our methods over here kept the dominants dominant to the end. But Germany did all this much better, if much more expensively.

The Halifax board had what was decidedly unusual at the time - Mansell and Ogan's Cecil plate dimmers. The common dimmer Strand used around then was the Hasemayer which was imported from Holland. These Dutch dimmers were of ingenious construction and must have been cheaper than Mansell's. Eventually he took the elements out of his plate and mounted them on an open frame. This, the Sunset dimmer, became our standard for most loads; only really large ones went onto open-coil resistances. The elements did facilitate accurate steps to suit a proper relationship of travel to light. Cost was critical and sixty contact dimmers were not unknown. Somehow Major Equipment managed to get some jobs in competition and use the Cecil plate when Strand had quoted Dutch. Cecil was obviously not named after Moss Mansell and I had a vague notion that the invisible Ogan might be a Cecil. The answer proved to be simple, the firm moved around a lot and at the time of that dimmer conception were lodged in Cecil Court off St Martin's Lane!

By the time of *the* catalogue, dimmer contacts were listed as eighty or a hundred, though some special 120-contact versions were used on the demonstration theatre ground-row circuits when my Light Console took over in 1935. The close range and the slow speed drive showed flicker otherwise. These special dimmer frames had to be resurrected in 1950 for the same reason in the case of the cold-cathode ceiling coves at the Royal Festival Hall.

The Grand Master was to endure for a very long time. Not only were the things so substantially constructed that once installed there was nothing to wear out, but it was not until well into the fifties that I was able to get a Board edict that no more were to be made or sold. In 1981 there was a affectionate account in *TABS** of working the Grand Master just removed from the Bristol Hippodrome in favour of a Duet memory system. That particular board was installed in 1948 and with 96-ways, I would not be alone even then in regarding it as an anachronism. The Theatre Royal Bristol had a small Light Console put in two years earlier but the ice was hardly broken as yet. The truth was that the people who sold such things on our behalf remained to be convinced.

Bristol was the scene of a notable close encounter between myself and a Grand Master installation in August 1934. The theatre was the Prince's which was later to

* "Farewell Old Friend" by Gail Hardman, *TABS* Vol.38 No.2

be destroyed during the Blitz. Although I was nothing to do with Applebee's Theatre Lighting department (TLD) and was the sworn opponent of his type of installation - based as it was on battens, footlights and Grand Master philosophy - he did ask me if I would go and do some colour lighting for the odd cinema opening up and down the country. This did land me at places like Stockton on Tees (my first experience of a sleeping car, 3rd class of course), Llandudno and Sale. I have always been reluctant to set off on any journey though I have always enjoyed the being there and especially the having got back. At the Pyramid, Sale I did not even get a welcome to put me at my ease. The electrician resented my being sent there. He had got everything arranged. For the first half he would be in the projection room and do the curtain lighting and any changes in the auditorium. There were two switchboards and during the interval he would switch over and go down to the one on the stage to do the variety acts; all of which had either rehearsed, or told him what they wanted, before I was around. Incidentally, as the name implies, this cinema was Egyptian in style and the second of the two Christie organ consoles, the one for use on the stage, looked as if it has belonged to Tutankhamen. I stuck to the electrician with no hope of anything to do. There would not be even a chance that either of the switchboards would go wrong: that kind, simply doesn't.

Come the interval and we adjourned to the stage. Suddenly, like a fairy story or a backstage romance, the unemployed young understudy got his chance. The electrician had dissolved into a jelly before my very eyes. The first act was about to go on, and everything changed in the twinkling of an eye. The electrician had left his lighting plot behind somewhere in the projection room, he thought! I enjoyed vamping that second half: taking hasty instruction as each act went on, or guessing or ad-libbing. It was a perfect justification of the cinema practice of putting the board in the prompt corner at stage level. Afterwards, there was a celebration in our Manchester Hotel with Drury the architect, Applebee and Geo. S. Hall who had motored up for the occasion. My tipple would have been ginger beer and Geo. was, if memory serves, a tea drinker.

At the Prince's in Bristol all was planned and not left to chance. The new installation would be inaugurated with a colour music solo 'played' on the Grand Master as a curtain raiser to the play *Ten Minute Alibi*. Originally intended for the first two nights only (two houses a night), it was extended (by public demand) to cover all performances from August 6th to 11th. The item was announced in the programme as "an elaborate demonstration of the beautiful new Stage Lighting Effects. This demonstration has been devised and carried out by Messrs L.G. Applebee and F.P. Bentham." It was, however, no duet. L.G.A's role was his usual one of selling the theatre the Grand Master, floats, battens and the rest.

According to the *Bristol Evening World,* "It was effective enough to fascinate a large audience by its constantly changing colours for at least ten minutes. ...

And there was unrestrained applause at the beauty of the colourings which was altered by the operation of dimmers." And so on for $6^{1}/_{4}$ column inches no less! Mind you, there was not much to create all this "beauty" either on or with. A pair of decidedly second-hand greys were dropped-in between the standing box set for the play and the house tabs. This limited things to the colours in no.1 batten and the floats plus some modest side lighting to pick out the folds. The board was on the prompt side perch giving me as operator an acute side view. What I did see very well was the band in the pit. About half a dozen musicians played Amy Woodward Finden's *Four Indian Love Lyrics* with as much of the fervour for "Less than the Dust" and passion in "Kashmiri Song" as they could muster. It had been a matter of checking with the leader that morning to see what they had at all suitable in their repertoire. My curtain raiser stint done, I recall stealing across the coconut matting upstage past a young girl ASM who sat on top of a pair of steps: perhaps, it was because the stage door was on the O.P. side or maybe just to get another look at her. Anyway she had a very important part in that thriller - she performed the many resets of the hands of the clock upstage centre.

There is no record of the Prince's Grand Master but it was probably like that at the Regal Edmonton, of which board there is a good photograph to prompt my memory. And memory is quirky. I can still see myself at the Regal in 'white tie and tails' of immense length as Mossy turned to me and asked for the loan of a sixpence (never repaid!) in the cloakroom so that he could reclaim his coat. Unlike the Curzon opening I was overdressed on this occasion and felt rather awkward, especially when I went backstage for the stage show officially, but quite unnecessarily, to stand by the board. The electrician (Charlie Passmore, destined decades later to do Thorn's Son et Lumiere jobs) looked me up and down and I felt a show-off; a black tie would have been just right, and after all I did possess a dinner jacket - one had to! All this reads very strangely now. But for the happy chance which was to provide regular visits to Glyndebourne in the more recent past, rare indeed would have been the opportunity to air my mohair 'tuxedo' - and it was mohair , adapted off the peg instead of "barathea, of course sir" from one's tailor. Although barathea was a fine woollen cloth that suit would be very heavy today - a reminder of the unheated decades of my younger days.

The Regal Edmonton, like the luxurious Regal Marble Arch before it, was built for A.E. Abrahams and the architect was the same - Clifford Aish. Unlike Marble Arch, with its overhead vines and bunches of internally illuminated grapes and so forth, the interior was relatively plain and straightforward with the usual art-deco wall scrapings. The great feature was the triple proscenium arch of three 3-colour lighting coves, one inside the other. In this case the lighting of these was from Strand equipment with the compartments side by side (instead of alternating) and thus the light from each colour was even, at point blank range. I am hazy as to whether I had anything to do with this; I suppose by that time I must have had; but the real, if unwilling, originator was R. Gillespie Williams, then of Holophane, whose speciality was auditorium colour lighting. The cove surfaces had a white lacework pattern and the colour mixing was not controlled from the Strand Grand Master but from a Major remote control panel in the projection room. This had been invented by Percy Newton while we had been together under Basil Davis. Newton had tried to interest Mansell in the idea but Mossy had simply shown him his own clutch and that was that. I remember Percy's poor opinion of that primitive clutch, his own being something more sophisticated. However the real interest in that Major panel lies in the fact that it could preset 1/4, 1/2 and 3/4 intermediate positions. Although Major had made a very neat up or down reversing 4-preset panel for the reversible motors at the Trocadero Elephant and Castle, at Edmonton they let Percy Newton down with an unnecessarily vast affair and no more were ever made.

However, that board is quite remarkable for one thing - it had to have 2-way switches to determine whether each dimmer was to move up or down from level of the preset it was at. The circuit did not automatically instruct it as to which way it should move. Although Newton must have shown and discussed his circuit with me I did not spot how it could be done until the need arose in my early years at Strand Electric.

The stage of the Regal Edmonton was really something special: a depth of 46ft with a plaster cyclorama right across the back and a proscenium opening 56ft wide and 32ft high. The grid was 54ft high and the stage had a 39ft revolve with four lifts in it, each rising 5ft and sinking 12ft. The cyclorama had curved ends and a trough with a double-row ground row. The top was lit by a double batten of 500W G/S lamps in 12-inch square compartments. There were four 4-colour ones and between their 6ft sections five pre-Patt. 56 acting areas - the inept copy by Strand (not me!) of a German model. There were only 8 dimmers for these twenty AAs. There were three 1kW triple floods in the wings each side and an illuminated walkway round the orchestra pit which had separate lifts for the band and the Christie organ console. By now the reader will begin to wonder where the spots were? As with so many cinema stage installations, however elaborate, the spots were conspicuous by their absence.

Leaving follow-spots on one side for the moment, there were only twelve spots mounted slap in the centre of the balcony front. And it really was 'inside' - no hanging in full view. The twelve had solenoid colour change (4 colours and white) but the Patt.73 was not yet available, so they were 1kW focus lamps with 6" x 10" PC lenses (Patt.43A for the archivist). The optics may have been run of the mill but I had been called in by my ex-boss Basil Davis and by L.G. Applebee, whose job it was as manager of Strand's Theatre Lighting Department to doctor them. The problem arose from the shallow throw: how to confine the light to just above the footlight but just clear of the cyc? The lamps were Osram A1s and like all other ELMA makers, with but one exception, the filament in those days was much taller than it was wide. As a result of my R&D activities I knew that Philips had a much less frail, more compact filament which was virtually square. There was little else for it, as Basil Davis agreed, but to smuggle in twelve of these lamps without a word to anybody; nothing must spoil the G.E.C. claim of supplying 'Everything Electrical' - their reward for loaning his services as consultant.

Needless to say, as in the music hall, arcs were relied on to pick out any acts or a band leader or his crooner or whatever. I think there were two 80-Amp followspots in the 'dome' and two in the projection room along with a couple of Brenographs, all of which would have been supplied by J. Frank Brockliss. The Brenograph symbolised the well-equipped projection room of the day, though it was seldom called on to perform more than a few of the many optical tricks claimed for it. It consisted of an open framework carrying what were virtually two optical benches one above the other. Each had an arc lamphouse and a series of optical mounts, all of which could slide to and fro. Slides, gobos, chromatropes, moving clouds and other effects were projected and blended on the screen or house tabs during organ interludes and the like. But at Edmonton the triple proscenium and footlights (floats) were more likely to be used for this.

The Strand Grand Master board was along the pros. wall Prompt side at stage floor level, a favourite position in a house of this type. It had 72-ways arranged as three tiers with the master wheels in the middle. The layout of the handles was very confusing, nothing came logically to the hand. This was due in part to the fact that most of the lighting was in four colours and three into four does not go; and partly the effect of phase separation regulations on the location of the dimmers. Thus the colour shafts were the top two to left and right of the masters. Each ran from the left: Dips Centre, Dips OP, Dips PS, Batt 4, Batt 2, Batt 3, Cyc Left, Cyc Right, Cyc Centre, Cyc Pit, Batt 1 and Float. Imagine what it was like trying to mix the red, green and two blues of the cyc with any finesse. The bottom shaft either side had all the odds and ends like the circle spots as three circuits and the acting-areas and so forth. The solenoid colour change switches were right down on the floor below the grand master wheel. It might be thought that operation of the lighting was not all that important but it was. The visual side of the show depended on almost continual lighting changes with little rehearsal and a scanty plot.

Applebee and I visited the place several times during the progress of the job and were there at the rehearsal on the day of the opening. I cannot remember what the films were but I do remember setting the flame effects, on tall stands in the wings, to appear above the ground rows of Moscow in front of the cyc. There were clouds also. As this went on, Napoleon seated on his horse "supplied by Chapmans Tottenham Court Road" according to the programme, came up on one of the revolve lifts. Unfortunately the animal showed every sign of wanting to lead the retreat from Moscow at rehearsal and during the performance Napoleon had to appear as a foot slogger. All of which should make it superfluous to name the composition the orchestra with Sydney Torch at the organ were bashing out! On the last entry of the Marseillaise the triple pros. was dimmed-in as red, white and blue and brought the house down. What had impressed me backstage earlier on were the words, "Don't forget the piano cable." The voice came over our local speakers and was that of Dave Abrahams (the son of boss A.E. Abrahams) seated at the sound control and rehearsal station out among the first night audience, four rows above the cross gangway in the circle. From there every show was monitored and talked through - and this in 1934! The piano was a grand one on which Sydney Torch had just played a duet with himself from the organ console in the pit. The electro-pneumatic remote action relied on a multi-core cable and I was just wondering, as I stood in the wings, had they slackened it off enough to strike the piano when over came the warning. Dave was a real professional because the tabs had been dropped-in and he could not see what was happening. It was cinemas such as this which went in for advanced technology, not the theatre, and it was there that I felt certain my first Light Console installation would go.

For example, long, long before it was permissible to suck your microphone in public, a cinema stage like the Gaumont State Kilburn had a large installation of counterweighted mikes controlled from the wings to pop-up through traps in the floor wherever you walked. In fact, The State was a failure from my point of view since it had another even bigger Grand Master, although I tried to sell H & G Cinemas (Hyams and Gale) a portable panel version of my console with Compton luminous heads to use in this kind of circle position. Mick Hyams (another of those sons) remarked with half humorous admiration that it was so small that it could easily be stolen! This little remembered (even by me) alternative to the organ form was even made up as one colour to function in the Seecol theatre using the Light Console relay. Photo-montage of this was used to illustrate the idea in certain publicity but archivists beware - a full installation was never made. Indeed at the time of the Regal Edmonton neither had the Light Console itself, though a provisional patent application had been filed on December 20th 1933, and a specification for manufacture exists which is dated 25th October the same year. But before we trace that adventure it is back to the Seecol theatre more or less complete but not officially open as it was Grand-Masterless.

I was sitting in the showroom during the slack season, a lone soul amid a sea of ancient fittings, when a stoutish gentlemen entered and said he was building an opera house and wanted to see our optical effects. I was young and a nobody, whereas he obviously wasn't either. We went into the theatre and using a temporary

12-way teak slider board sitting on the floor and a 6-way affair with various types of dimmer and handle they used to cart around at exhibitions, I did a passable demonstration on our cyc. He never had a good word to say about anything I showed him. Even our star turn, the optical wave which used to make our customers goggle and marvel, was no good because the waves merely surged and would not break and roll up the beach.

He dropped in several times of an afternoon at irregular intervals: his sole purpose, seemingly, to tell me how unsuitable Strand equipment was for this 'opera house' of his. Even when our super chromium-plated 30-way Grand Master stood there in glory, he did not think much of it - but that made two of us! According to him, the only people who had the right kind of control and the rest of the stage lighting equipment were the Germans. I knew he might well be right about the latter as I had fallen for the German type of lighting layout while still at school but I knew that he was wrong about the control: there was only one man who had the right idea about that - myself! By now I knew that his name was Christie (an ex-school-master from Eton) and that he had something to do with the organ builders Hill, Norman & Beard, and lived at a place called Glyndebourne. Years later I was to learn that he was their chairman and driving force behind the firm from 1923, but his interest in organs was on the wane as mine was on the 'wax' at the time of our brief encounters.

There had always been an oddity about Christie cinema organs. Wurlitzers were made by Wurlitzer, and Compton by Compton. Christie, although bearing the name in great letters across the music desk at a time when the others had a modest plate, were made by Hill, Norman & Beard; a name familiar in church work.

Although for engineering reasons (dealt with later in this chapter) I wanted Compton to make my Light Console, the order had not been placed at this time - it was not to happen until the end of 1933 - so it is interesting to speculate on what might have happened if I had told John Christie of my ideas then. Would there have been a Christie/Bentham light console in Glyndebourne, colour music recitals, or even a colour music version of some of the Ring? How fortunate for music in Britain that I kept that quiet. All this might have happened because I now realise looking back at him lecturing me in the Seecol theatre, that instead of one crackpot there were two! Both of us were equally ignorant of the problems of staging Wagner with whose works we were quite besotted. John Christie was at that time around fifty, and Fred Bentham was twenty-one or so. Christie had position, authority and wealth, travelled widely, knew German opera houses, including Bayreuth, well. Bentham was limited to what he had read of these plus Henry Wood's Monday Wagner nights at the Queen's Hall Proms, together with a few broadcasts on the wireless and some 12-inch gramophone records.

It is easy for me in writing of those times to think of that Fred in the third person: both marvelling at and critical of what he did. Anyone who has attained over-mature years will know the feeling. Some things remain vivid or bits of paper turn up which promote or set one musing; but there remain gaps as to what that chap, who was oneself, thought and did and why. I do know that young Bentham was obsessed with the idea of replacing the plump casts and the crude scenery and effects he had learned about, by Appia-inspired settings and lighting. The latter to change in colour, form, intensity and tempo to express the mood of the music. Music Drama would become Colour Music.

Christie too, by all accounts, had the strangest ideas as to what he could do in his tiny opera house. The great opera orchestra problem, still difficult today, could be solved by using a small band with the organ to fill in, as for a special features film. It seems to have been the technical side, especially the lighting, which fascinated him; but, unlike me, not as an inventor. All the requisite lighting equipment existed. Not here in England, the stuff made here was hopeless: it was the German Schwabe system complete with the great cyclorama and pros. bridge-perch array which held the key to everything. Backed up, of course, by the standard compact regulator with levers at 1¾ inch centres to operate dimmers remotely by long stretches of tracker-wire over pulleys. The dimmers could be tall-frame resistances tapped to a vertical linear commutator, or, much better, large transformers with multi-slider commutation all around, generally referred to as 'Bordoni transformers', reputedly after the Italian inventor. What is certain is that all that equipment was much more expensive than anything Strand Electric then could dare to make for the UK market.

Expense did not deter John Christie. The German system went into Glyndebourne with a 60-way Bordoni transformer as the dimmers. For some reason the regulator lever unit was not German but appeared to me to have been made by Mickelwright of Alperton. The mechanical facilities were very limited compared to the genuine German article. The reader must bear in mind that when the Glyndebourne opera house was completed and opened for its first season at the end of May 1934 it was much smaller both backstage and out-front than what we have come to know over the years: and one cannot think of it even as it is today before the proposed re-build, with a proscenium opening of under 30ft as anything but on the small side for opera. How Christie could ever have conceived that Wagner was a practical proposition for 1934 can only be explained in terms of absolute faith in powers of German stage lighting. Get that right and all things were possible*!

A photograph of the Glyndebourne backstage in *The Times Weekly Edition* taken shortly before the place opened† shows everything German with the exception of the compartment battens which look like Strand B-type. L.G. Applebee, as manager of

* In reality it was two men, Fritz Busch from Dresden and Carl Ebert from Berlin, who had chosen to leave Nazi Germany who were to make the 1934 season and thereafter such a success.

† See *CUE* No. 30 July/August 1984

the Theatre Lighting Dept. for so long, must have had a go at selling Christie something - it would be quite unlike him not to. In any case, the famous Schwabe double-tier cloud machine ex-Plaza cinema Regent Street turned up in 'my' showroom for overhaul by our effects expert Frank Weston. I was not told, but someone must have arranged it. All of a sudden, it was hauled up on the outside crane to hang among the large crystal chandeliers for some weeks while Frank tinkered with it or got his assistant Eddie Biddle to do things to it. None of John Christie's visits coincided with its stay there - perhaps a notion of a Teutonic breakdown was distasteful.

There were diverter mirrors to the ten lenses in the bottom tier driven via axles and bevel gearing from one motor and eight in the top tier driven from another motor in the same manner. A third motor rotated the whole machine. Each lens was a high quality objective and with its individual cloud slide and condenser it constituted a projector, only the 3kW lamp being common to all. It was an elaborate and very expensive machine, proper in the context of the great German stages but absurd in the cramped confines of the Plaza cinema. Who on earth managed to persuade them that this, complete with horizon lanterns etc, was appropriate to a cinema stage 21ft deep is not known. GEC were the Schwabe agents in the twenties, so perhaps it was H. Lester Groom, that Heidelberg-scarred manager of their stage lighting department.

The object of the tier motors was to ride the clouds over each other for greater effect but this stuff had been badly damaged and was stripped off. It is important to put the Glyndebourne lighting in its proper context. Listening to John Christie at the time and long afterwards, one might imagine that the rest of the UK merely slopped light all over the place using just battens and floats. It is true that theatres had only the basics and that almost everything important had to be hired for a show, but it could be and it was. Not even the Schwabe installation was unique; Basil Dean had been using such equipment at the St. Martin's in 1923 and in 1924 for his superbly lit *A Midsummer Night's Dream* at Drury Lane which I can still conjure up in my mind's eye. There was Terence Gray's Cambridge Festival theatre of the twenties and *White Horse Inn* at the London Coliseum in 1931 had a complete cyc and its Schwabe lighting. All C.B. Cochran's shows were properly lit and staged. Even the tiny Westminster Theatre (1931) had a permanent cyc with an appropriate Strand installation which Molly McArthur was able to use with remarkable effect in its opening years.

Exactly one month before Glyndebourne opened for the first time, the Royal Opera House under Sir Thomas Beecham inaugurated its entirely new stage lighting installation with brand new productions of Beethoven's *Fidelio* and Wagner's *Ring*.

It is curious that even I, who was up there on the cyc end of the control and brought face to face with the practical side of staging opera for the first time, had forgotten, until this point in this chapter, the historic relationship of the two installations. There at Covent Garden was for the first time the great Hasait* cloth cyc from grid to floor encompassing the main stage with the associated pros. bridge and perch structure. As to the lighting, the stage connected load was 700kW A.C. and 150kW D.C. There was seven weeks to do it yet, no part of it came from Germany; it and its unique (literally) remote control was by Strand Electric.

No credit for any part of that installation can be claimed by myself but whereas in time I was to 'do' Covent Garden, those other gardens down at Glyndebourne have kept themselves clear of Benthamism. Even when in 1964 they had at last to pension off the Bordoni (unlike Covent Garden who - coincidentally - did the same with their 1934 control that year), they resisted any control of mine. Instead of a system C/AE desk they insisted that Strand make a control desk to the design of their Lighting Manager there - Francis Reid!†

At Covent Garden in 1934 there were to be 175 dimmers controlled as 130 ways on the remote panel up on the PS bottom perch. The previous control of 1903 had been under the stage without a view of anything so it was just possible that there might have been several Grand Masters down under. We must remember that these were the days of the Beecham international season of opera in May and June only. Even with rehearsals and the De Basil Ballets Russe de Monte Carlo which always followed, the stage lighting was used for less than one third of the year. Until 1934 Covent Garden opera productions had used traditional painted scenery and someone, and I can only think it was Beecham, decided that they must go modern with a great encompassing cyclorama and all that entailed. The Germans were well used to such techniques but over here any cycs used in theatre had been tiny and usually confined to the upstage area. For the new Covent Garden stage lighting the cyclorama would not just form part of the installation but a major part - 184 kW no less. This alone was half as much again as the total stage lighting load at the Stratford Memorial Theatre; Britain's, and Strand's, largest permanent stage lighting installation in a theatre till then.

It must be realised that neither Strand or anyone else in this country had a suitable system; it had to be designed there and then. I should like at this point to repeat that I played no part, nor was asked to, in this control. My "I was there"

* Max Hasait was technical director at the Dresden Opera, who devised a method of keeping very large cloth cycloramas taut when unrolled around a stage.

† Francis has described his control, and the ones which preceded it and succeeded it in *TABS* Vol.35 No. 2

Royal Opera House, Covent Garden 1934

experiences had to do with working the board, which I found myself doing at the rehearsals as the 'great expert' on mixing the three primary colours, red, blue and green. The whole of the great Hasait cloth cyc was lit on this principle with double wattage blue. The new *Ring* had sets by Gabriel Volkoff and was directed by Dr. Earhardt who brought Max Hasait (with charming daughter as interpreter) along as technical adviser. All had been brought up on the Schwabe 7-colour system - dark, mid, light and steel blues, green, yellow and red. The cyc controls were at the on-stage end of perch panel and one sat on a tall stool hovering right inside it. (This view was mucked-up post war by hanging red traverses for curtain calls.) There would be a call from the stalls for yellow cyc (no mikes then) and to a murmur of satisfaction I would bring up the reds and the greens gently to the required level.

Suddenly there would be a German curse from below and a cry, "Kein Grün". Hasait had wandered on the stage and chanced to look up aloft. With fury at my non reaction he consulted his daughter and shrieked "Not Green". There was nothing for it, out the greens had to go. Whereupon Earhardt out front would make a bigger noise - he was a big man - "Kein Rot". Frenzy would take over until they returned to the stalls to find themselves beholding soothing yellow once more. We never did get this sorted out but the three colours stayed and tales of subsequent battles fought on the perch during public performances lost nothing in their retailing to me, once I returned to the safety of the Seecol theatre at the other end of Floral Street.

Fortunately Charlie Storer, the chief operator, was one of those who simply got on with it no matter how the storm might rage, a wonderful man who had been there for years on the old board. I was overawed also by the way that Jack Croxford, Syd Cheney and most of the large temporary staff knew the operas. In spite of the brand new set of three-dimensional rocks no one had to tell them where Wotan might need a spot, Brunnhilde a patch to snooze in or Flosshilde a drop of Strand ripple. This a reminder of happier days, when the Rhine's only pollution came from gold and maidens.

It was for this 1934 season that the great bridge and triple perch structure, which is such a feature of the Covent Gardens pros. as seen backstage, was built. This, the new counterweight system, cyc track and winding gear was by The Lift and Engineering Company while Strand Electric did the electrical installation. Just upstage hung the main cyc bank - five rows of 1kW 17-inch floods with silvered glass reflectors. A second smaller bank of these hung further upstage. Even the groundrow trucks were made up of 500W 12-inch floods; seventy-two in all. There were five compartment battens, all with silvered glass Sunray reflectors and between the 6ft lengths of each there were five of the feeble pre-Patt. 56 acting-areas. All these had to be made on top of other work in the days when lanterns were manufactured in batches of a couple of dozen at a time. There would be nowhere to store anything at our new but small works at Gunnersbury. Vans did not take much of a load either, so transport from there would be quite a feat in itself.

What that installation was short of was spots, and the few there did not, with one exception, give much light. This was the age of the plano-convex lens focus lamp. Back-up from arcs was essential at times and all the many optical effects in *The Ring* always used arcs. The exception was the Stelmar spot. There were six of 1kW, one to each perch and three out-front in the dome with 30 Volt 30 Amp lamps and remote colour change. Somehow or other, Stelmar has got associated with the later Brockliss arc follow spots of 1935, but Strand were making these 1000-Watt projector lamp models at the end of the twenties. It may well be that the Stelmar* design represents the first theatre use of ellipsoidal profile spots in the world. They were 3ft long however, dimmed from the board, and were manned on the perches so as to be redirected rather than used to follow. The Stelmars, and this particular usage, were to remain a feature of Covent Garden lighting for many years. The Patt. 50 Pageants, Patt. 73 Mirror Spots and the Patt. 56 acting areas were not,

* The inventors were Steele and Martin, hence Stelmar.

of course, to appear for a year yet: and neither was my Light Console. And there lay the snag from my point of view. The original wiring diagrams and console layout are dated 17/3/33 but this 70-way prototype had not been ordered until late autumn. Such techniques were out of the question for a rush job on the great scale and of the importance of the opera house. Something more basic had to be provided.

The key man was Moss Mansell, as inventor of the magnetic clutch which Strand and I were going to use in one form and another for three decades. At that time the largest successful installation was still the nineteen ways in the Regal cinema Uxbridge of late 1931. In a personal letter to me of April 30th 1957 Mossy, as we knew him, says of his clutch, "I do not think it would have been used at Covent Garden had not Basil Davis seen its advantages over the 'Grand Master'. The then directors of Strand Electric (excluding the Junior) did not think much of it or in fact any of the ideas of said Junior." The "said Junior" was Mansell, of course, the other two were the joint managing directors Arthur Earnshaw and Phillip Sheridan. This remark confirms the distrust of novel technical solutions to problems in UK theatre at the time. Imagine, a 130-way Grand Master with 175 direct-operated dimmers behind it! Impossible, it would have to have been split as two boards below stage somewhere. But Basil Davis was a real theatre consulting engineer and could see what nonsense that would be. I wonder how he came to be appointed as consultant in 1934 to the Opera House?

When the separate small works moved out of the Covent Garden area in 1932 to the new factory in Power Road Gunnersbury*, Mansell became works director and his own team, under Jim Jordan, became the shop for 'advanced' work while the Strand engineering shop under Dusty Miller did the Grand Masters and the traditional stuff. The machines, which they shared, stood with the overhead shafting drive as a kind of 'steelhenge' between them. There was a further shop, of Strand origin, to do sheet metal work including floats, battens and the various lanterns.

Mansell and his foreman Jordan (later to become in his turn works manager and then director) played safe with the Opera House *switchboard*. All circuit switching, blackouts and the rest was off-loaded, so to speak. A direct-operated switchboard, made by Miller's 'traditional' shop of course, was mounted on the same perch but further off-stage. It included all the live (phase) side, with the dimmers downstairs in the basement being in the neutral return. This was a pre-war practice derived from the old DC days when switching was in the positive and dimming in the negative. My book of 1950† declared firmly that "The regular practice in the past of putting them in the neutral is inexcusable." That old practice had been taken for granted by

* The building still survives in 1992, in spite of the minimal expenditure on its construction and what is more the occupier is Honda (UK) Ltd.

† *Stage Lighting* (Pitman 1950) p.326

Ridge and Aldred, very responsible consultants, in their book of 1935.*

The difficult problem of a remote motor drive with a large variable speed range was overcome by not having one! The clutch drive shafting was extended right up to the perch to terminate in two pairs of capstan wheels just under the control panel. The vertical capstans were for slow motion and the horizontals for 'fast'. Freewheel gear was fitted to prevent reversal of the shafts which did facilitate the extra slow inching, much in demand in opera, but meant a lot of work if a chorus of lights had to reverse. Each dimmer way had a flush-mounted 2-way and off switch. Up to raise, down to dim and centre to stop. These would be set appropriately, followed by a slight stoop to the capstans to move them. The tempo was essentially *lento*. Fast work resetting lots of switches and lugging round the two capstans locked as one was out of the question. Some masters were fitted, to inert groups quickly when a small change had to follow a large; and the, all too likely very slow, cyclorama sky changes came off different shafting from the rest.

Indication of dimmer position was from a rear-illuminated dial above each switch (these were re-calibrated Rolls Royce petrol gauges!). Two operators were used at the time and the second man's role, except when there were a large number of switch change-overs, was really that of an 'electric' motor thereby allowing the chief to concentrate on hitting the required levels. To those who today are brought up on memory systems, or even preset boards, this will appear crude indeed for our famous opera house. But if the equipment had to be made in Britain this was beyond question the best solution in the time, and at the time. To keep the record straight, the Americans did have the General Electric multi-preset thyratron reactor by now; but the remote panel would have had to go under the stage, due to its size, as in the 'old' Met. in New York and both cost and delivery would have put it right out of court.

The 12-volt DC Mansell magnetic clutch was to survive unchanged until 1954. The re-design then reduced dimmer centres from eight inches to five and at last a spring was incorporated to clear the pole-piece from the wheel and remove the gentle scraping and jarring sound characteristics of a "Strand" clutch job with its motor idling at the ready. The clutch was a very simple device but it worked - any problems were solved very early on, except one. This was the limit switch at each end of travel. The clutch had no inertia; the moment the current was cut it stopped dead. We had to make our own limit switches for years and all sorts of things were tried: gravity mercury, mercury with trigger spring, with silver contacts, and without and so on. The trouble was that it had to operate both at speed and at the slowest of slow crawls. The mechanically-minded reader can imagine the problem; it was as tough in its way as that other perennial problem - spotlight shutters which can move freely but stay put! Even when the Burgess micro-switch turned up post-war to solve

* *Stage Lighting Principles & Practice* (Pitman 1935 & 1940) p.46

the problem for us, we encountered trouble with a few on the 216-way Light Console banks at the London Coliseum. With immense patience this was traced by Burgess to female assembly of the contacts on 'certain days of the month', believe it or not.

That London Coliseum console was number 13 which went in for *Call Me Madam* in March 1952; but what of the very first one? The nearest I can get to a key date would be one evening in March 1935 at the Seecol theatre. The Compton console and relay had been delivered to us at the end of August the previous year and I had been in a state of frustration ever since, as the empty frame of the dimmer bank haunted the Gunnersbury works. At last on November 19th Mossy wrote to me that he "was hopeful that they would be back on this job in a matter of a day or so," and they would concentrate on getting it "to Floral Street in its simple form, and worry out the other gadgets later." This suited me because the basic dimmers and contactors were all I needed for the colour music which would dull all other critical faculties in any audiences. Needless to say, being our own job it was dropped in favour of urgent real work that paid money. Anyway, that March evening came at last.

The dimmer bank had been assembled behind the cyclorama in what had been Eddie Biddle's workshop, and Percy Pillar, the fitter, and his mate had gone off promising to begin the action wiring next morning at 8 o'clock. The rats took up their position to picket the premises and dispatch me homewards with the minimum delay. They could not know that my anxious heartbeats were not rodent but relay inspired. That night was to be the 'night of the nuclear test'. Would the slender silver wire contacts of the Compton relay work (without protest) the coils of a Mansell magnetic clutch? They were fine for the tiny primary valve magnets of an organ; but for the 12-volt 0.4-amps of those great coils?

It may appear strange that this all-important test of the nucleus around which everything revolved should have had to await delivery of a complete 2-manual 70-stop console and cross-relay plus a 35-way electro-mechanical dimmer bank.* The orders had, after all, been placed a year or so earlier; surely it would not have been impossible to take a clutch coil to Compton's factory in Chase Road, North Acton - within walking distance of my home, then at Crownhill Road, Harlesden - connect up and test? Here we come to the nub of the matter; the Light Console, according to its inventor's philosophy, *had* to work! The possible behaviour of the Compton contacts had been discussed with their Mr Pollard and it was thought that they would be alright, so long as condensers were fitted to encourage a snappy spark. The inventor reckoned that having come thus far the three directors would in

* As only 35 dimmers were needed, their controls were duplicated on both keyboards to give a 70 -way console effect.

an emergency not balk at paying for the thirty-five pairs of up and down relays (or 70 pairs if the contactors were troublesome) whereas this extra on a cost which had already been a problem at the outset might have made the whole thing a non-starter. Some idea of what I was up against is given by a letter to me from Mansell dated June 16th 1933 which I still have:

> *I am sending herewith schedule of material duly priced, and shall be glad to have your views. It seems that with the cost of the console the total would be little less than £1,000, and I think it hardly likely the directors will go to this expense. Certainly I would not be prepared to recommend it. You must bear in mind that if we sold equipment of this sort at a profit of 20% on cost, we should have to sell 5 before we recovered our experimental charges.*

That it went on as costed is a tribute to Arthur Earnshaw and Phillip Sheridan who managed to win over the third man. Mind you, that youthful inventor pulled every string he could; including one revealed in *LIGHTS!** for the first time ever.

Back to that March evening: there were some drums of twin cotton-covered bell-wire ready to hand and taking some of this I ran lines across from the up and down clutches and full-on and blackout contactors for one channel to the appropriate staples on the Compton testboard. The battery and motor-generator set to provide the 15-volts DC had been working for some weeks while we had tested the Compton side and there was no need to run the shaft motors or to have lights: all that had to be done was to get the coils to click on and off and watch the spark at the relay - especially with the kind of rapid action required for jazz. I was all alone in a way that I was never to experience in my work at any other time - the only inhabitant in the tiny island of my own arcane technology.

I understand somehow, though I don't remember, that I simply said to Mother on my return home that night "It works". The following morning a start was made on the action wiring of the dimmer rack using exactly the same techniques as they had used one year earlier up the road at the Opera House. This involved running out bell-wires along the bank frame from every coil terminal, taking them across as a taped-up bunch to the Compton relay, ringing out to identify each, whereupon their man Roy Skinner would solder each wire to the testboard. Roy stood around watching the Laocoon-like struggles of the Gunnersbury folk for nigh on an hour when he signalled me out of the dimmer room into the theatre and suggested he should show them how to make-up the whole thing in a single organ cable fashion. He had no

* Vol.3 No.1 February 1992

difficulty in selling the idea to me as I seen it done in the Compton factory and had been completely won over as with everything they did. However I do not remember any difficulty with Percy Pillar* at all, and imagine that he was as intrigued with the idea as I was. So we sent his mate out for a bag of 1$^1/_2$" oval nails. They had to be ovals as they have minimal heads making it easy to slip the tied-up cable off.

Our one-foot high stage had a shallow forestage in front of the footlight painted 'Geo. black', and this was an ideal bench as we were all young and unlikely to suffer from backache. Taking the necessary measurements, Roy nailed out the forestage

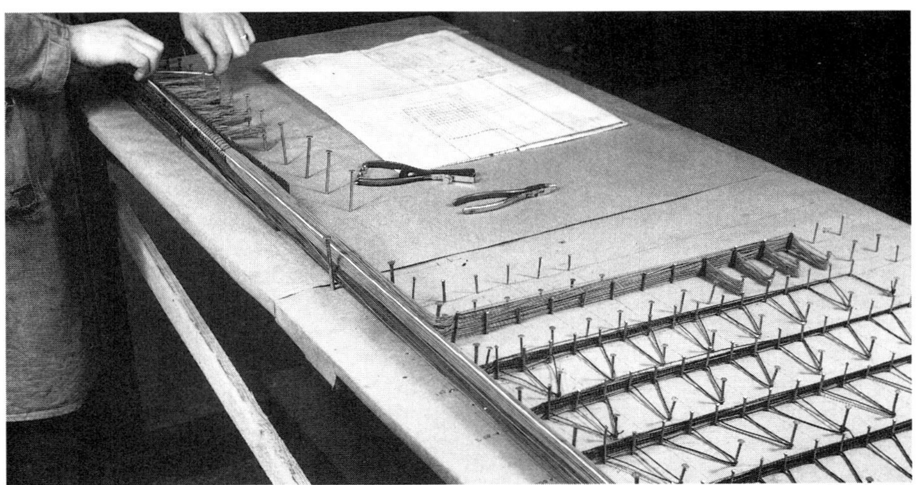

"Tying out one continuous wire"

accordingly but did use a separate piece of wood for the close $^1/_4$" setout of the testboard end. And later that day we had the first ever jig-made cable used on a piece of Strand equipment. Tied-out with macramé twine it only had to have the ends cut to be lifted off and laid along the horizontals of the dimmer bank. This technique of tying-out one continuous wire so that identification was just a matter of getting number-one in the right place and the rest would automatically fall in line was used by organ builders for everything including the main cable from console in orchestra pit to wherever the organ chamber with the pipework might be. We were to have some very long cables in places like the London Coliseum or Her Majesty's and it was just a matter of finding the correct distance, preferably in a straight line,

* About 50 years later I learned that his real name was Fred!

between the ends and walking to and fro or devising a Heath Robinson overhead shuttle to get the wire from end to end. Our works were to become very expert at this work and some real craftsmen were to be found at Gunnersbury who were to rival Comptons.

Although with the arrival of plastic covered wires post-war, colours came to be used in the tied-out cables, they were not strictly necessary and must not be confused with the elaborate colour coding essential with telephone multi-cores. I only ever used one single wire in colour before that time and that was on the Lisbon job and it had dire consequences when I tried to connect-up at the bank testboard the large and complex loop cable which came over from the Compton relay. One row, try as I would, simply would not come right. Having threaded-in all 108 wires there was still an empty staple! What I had forgotten over the intervening months was that we had put in an extra wire at the last moment and instead of tying it in I had simply used some red ink to colour (and identify!) the dangling end.

The cable between the relay in the dimmer room and the console was of course part of the Compton contract, and within its flexible Greenfield metal hose allowed the console to be anywhere in the auditorium. It was on a rostrum with castors which enabled one man to push it around. Indeed on the occasion of the visit of a certain Major Bell, having given a show-off demonstration with all stops out, I concluded by dramatically pushing it with one hand right across the theatre with the words "and it is movable". This was a challenge and the reason for it was that he was a cinema consultant to the new Paramount cinemas then being built and always recommended our rivals, Major Equipment. The cable had a Compton multi-way plug at the console end; a sort of tie-press studded with rows of contacts of which the sprung side were standard BC lampholder plungers. Seen in terms of today's multi-way plugs and sockets it would be another Heath Robinson device; but it was neatly and nicely made of wood, and it worked.

The first Light Console was important, not only for the ergonomic techniques it represented then and the developments which followed post war, but also for the introduction to Strand Electric of organ type electro-mechanical action, wire contact relays and all that went with it. In this the choice of the John Compton Organ Company was of fundamental importance. Left to themselves the natural firm for Strand to join up with, in the extremely unlikely event of their ever wanting to, was Christie Organs. For years they had shared a stand, along with Hall and Dixon, at the annual C.E.A. exhibitions up and down the country. My choice of Comptons arose from the fact that they did not use pneumatics on the console or at the relay; Wurlitzer, Christie and the others did. It was quite natural: as you have to have a blower to make the pipes speak, why not keep electric work to just opening small primary valves? I had never met anyone from Comptons or seen any of their equipment until my mind made up, I went off to meet their Mr Taylor at their new

First Light Console and Grand Master contrast

factory in Chase Road, out at North Acton, not far from that Savoy cinema of chapter II.

Two books were very important in this context, namely *The Electric Organ* (1930) and *The Cinema Organ* (1932) both by Reginald Whitworth which indicated Comptons as the firm. Although both were published by *The Musical Opinion* they were not musical books as such. They were not books on organ building either and they certainly weren't aimed at cinema organ fans. What they dealt with in considerable detail was "organ action" i.e. the means employed by the principal firms to connect pipes via an electric cable to the keys and stops at a remote console. Accessories such as couplers, piston action, swell pedal control were all there and description was aided by special line drawings by the author. It would be fascinating to know how many copies he sold, for it was an esoteric subject indeed.

Anyone, including myself, looking back from the 1990's to the 1930's must wonder at our complete rejection of the automatic (auto-selector or Strowger) relay systems. In my own case, my addiction to colour-music and the playing of lighting is sufficient explanation, but what of others? The arrival of the dial-phone to replace the old manual exchanges attracted a lot of limelight. The desirability of preset lighting controls was around in 1930 while I was at the G.E.C. and I am haunted by the notion that the idea did surface of a dial preset to call up by number. I wish I could find some real evidence to this effect. Did it merely arise as airy talk between we two Basil Davis assistants in our tiny office across the corridor from his scarcely larger one in Central House? After all, Percy Newton was devising the preset control at that very time which did, as described earlier, get installed in the Regal Edmonton projection room.

Speaking for myself, another influence would have been the need to use versatile yet standard mass-produced equipment made by others. The Compton organ relays assembled in wooden boxes to suit each particular job, spelt a freedom that telephone relay racks did not. Anyway, the Compton electrics were more compact and much less expensive and I soon found myself incorporating them in circuitry other than the Light Console. It is important to stress that the market for sophisticated control was small indeed. The majority of those who sought my advice day by day were amateurs with virtually nothing to spend. Having been such an amateur myself, it was not difficult to change gear and look at any problems in their terms. The biggest one was the dimmer. How on earth to fade lights in and out cheaply? Not that there were many circuits in most cases.

On that cue enter the Questors, Ealing or more exactly, Alfred Emmet. I never did join them as a member; but thanks to him I certainly got much involved in their first theatre. This was to be a conversion of a Roman Catholic mission chapel, by then a Boy Scouts' hall, which has become known as the 'Tin Hut'. The conversion took place between June and October 1933 when I had just started my second year with Strand Electric.

I recall being picked up one evening at Ealing Common station and driven by Alfred to the hut in his small car, which after a while he gave up, never seemingly to drive again. He always was careful to live within an easy walk of the railway station and of The Questors theatre. On arrival at the Tin Hut, I found it a small version of the Memorial Hall Acton Lane Harlesden, the hall I had been used to. It would seat just about half the number and had many of the same faults except *that* stage extension. To compensate there was one other, *no toilets* - neither male nor female. I had been called in to advise on a lighting installation but have never been able to stick to just that. There had to be a cyclorama, and as masking I adopted the permanent ceiling of the Festival Theatre Cambridge, as described by Harold Ridge, instead of borders - even for open-air scenes. Along the top of the up-stage edge of this were three circuits of 'home-made' cyc floods with gelatine colour filters, while in the cyc pit there were three circuits of china-sprayed lamps, an important component in those cinema cornice colour lighting days. Initially the primary colours were used. On October 14th 1933 the theatre opened with speeches and at this point I cannot do better than to quote from something I wrote for the July 1987 issue of *Questopics*: "It was a matter of pleasure and pride that I was the first to stage any kind of 'show' before an audience... What did 'my' show consist of? I told an audience clad in their dinner-jackets about the wonders of the new stage lighting installation; two old German Schwabe spots out-front, two baby-spots and four baby-floods behind the pros. and six cyclorama circuits. But this was not just talk; the three top cyc. circuits actually worked!" The control was in the 'wings' actors right and it was just as well that the primaries red, blue and green were used because I was able to tell the audience what I was going to mix, go and do it and stride back on stage. The first real production was a new experimental play *Dragon's Teeth* on the 6th December.

On July 14th 1934 I actually did some colour music there, but what my solo pieces were I cannot be sure. One item the programme 'identifies' as "Le Coucher du Soleil" but what was its real title? It was obviously a sunset since it was sandwiched between "Soleil" Debussy's Arabesque in G and "Clair de Lune". My title was invented by the dancer Gwendolen Foreman's husband Cyril Thomas. She and I did a mixture of duets and solos, so to speak. Possibly it was really Elgar's "Evening Song" which was in my solo cyc repertoire at the time, but the English was thought to jar! There were six liquid dimmers at that time and these could be plugged-in as appropriate using the switchboard they built to the circuit, which I was to use again after the war for Strand's Junior HA boards. A good idea of that pioneer theatre can be gained from its use as an example in my *Stage Lighting* book of 1950. As to The Questors themselves, the story of their sixty years was published in 1989 under the title *A Few Drops of Water**. Looking right back, the great amateur division was between those who hired their scenery from Capes of Chiswick and that ilk, and those after my own heart who made their own.

Amplified sound rated low in the list of amateur priorities then and I had to bring my own HMV table-gram and extension speaker and stand them on the front edge of

* by Gwenan Evans and others: pub. The Questors Ltd 1989

the stage either side of the pros. opening. Both Gwen and I had to limit our pieces to the 3 or $4^1/_2$ minutes discipline of the old 78s. Extreme economy even extended to a lecture I gave there on the history of theatre planning a bit later. Slides were out, so I made large drawings on sheets of paper pinned along the top of a blackboard and turned each over as necessary. Odd social evenings as an excuse for get-togethers were a feature of the early Questors seasons; I remember one at which someone gave a very good imitation of A.J. Alan telling one of his radio adventure stories. My contribution was colour music of a most peculiar kind using slides and an unaccompanied violin record. This was all a bluff based on a recital B. Bear and I had seen advertised and had attended to find ourselves the sole members of the audience in a largish hall. A continental genius with a heavy accent played his own compositions for unaccompanied violin, while his wife projected slides of one kind or another including some nude statues on the screen. We simply had to unload this on someone and 'B' took the role of the foreign genius with no English. I fear some of our audience never did learn the truth. But the oddest Questors event for me was the result of an SOS from Alfred in December 1936. Tonight's show was *Everyman* and his switchboard operator had been taken ill and as he was playing Everyman himself, would I takeover the board? Alfred would work it for the curtain raiser (The *Shepherd's Play* from the Wakefield Cycle) in order to give me time to get there. There was no chance of writing my own plot and he literally gave me my cues by catching my eye as he played the role. For my part, seeing that the year had begun with the playing of my Light Console to the HRH Prince George, the Duke of Kent, and to George Bernard Shaw, to end it on six pots was to come down to earth, or rather earthenware, with a splash!

Shaw prompts a quote from Basil Dean's 1888-1927 autobiography *Seven Ages* * in which he tells of his encounter after his Schwabe-Hasait demonstration for the G.E.C at the St. Martin's theatre in 1923:

> *...greeting me in the lobby at the end of the demonstration, he saw no cause for congratulation. Instead, it was; 'I'll take good care ye'll not use any of those contraptions in my plays, young man. The audience would be so busy staring at your clouds they wouldn't listen to my words.' Of course, he was right.*

At which point the curtain rises on my next chapter and another young man's Shavian encounter.

* pub. Hutchinson & Co., 1970

V: KING STREET
Lighting for Entertainment 1936-39

Hitherto the Gods had been kind, almost indulgent, but 1936 was going to alter all that. Sitting in the Piccadilly Line tube on the way from Sudbury Hill to Covent Garden I opened up my *Daily Telegraph* (a strange choice even then for the more-or-less socialist I have always been!) and there was the prospectus for Strand Electric Holdings a public company "incorporated in England on 3rd February 1936". It was the morning of February 13th, eight weeks after my three 'old' directors had presented me with the gold watch. The new chairman was an absolute stranger - F.L. Blow JP and the secretary was a man called R.L. Tillett ACA; obvious denizens of the City. Blow, later to become familiar to us in Strand as 'old fly-blow' of course, had two directors to keep him company - one was our own Phillip Sheridan and the other Hugh Cotterill.

Cotterill's appointment was difficult for us to take, for he was a member of the opposition - Major Equipment Ltd. He was a well-known name at Major, but quite what he did there was uncertain. I had read the odd article by him in the cinema press and had met him at an occasional meeting to try and get a standard for the Mogul prefocus lamp cap. He was a languid Oxbridge type*, a rare bird indeed in cinema and theatre of those times. Fortunately, 'B' Bear (a *Times* man faithful to the end!) had joined Strand the previous Autumn as assistant manager of the showroom and Seecol theatre; although things were never clearly defined. This meant that there *was* someone to ponder aloud with. In a couple of weeks our two departed directors gave a large farewell dinner for everyone who was someone, or nearly someone, in the firm, at the Comedy restaurant in Leicester Square (the scene of my own 21st birthday dinner in October 1932). There were lots of speeches among which Phillip Sheridan invited all back there to another in two weeks time to meet Blow, Cotterill and Tillett - a gesture typical of this excitable Dubliner.

A mystery remained as to why only he survived of the original three. Arthur Earnshaw was not yet sixty-four and Moss Mansell was just fifty. Mossy was in fact to get himself back in our very much larger works at Talbot Road in order to act as personnel manager (including the canteen) during the war. Why did only two sell out? After the war when Arthur Earnshaw's son Stanley and I became great friends

* Westminster and Cambridge if I recall

and by which time I also had joined the board, his explanation - repeated more than once - was that his father and Mossy assumed all three were going; but the signing was done in alphabetical order, and after they had, Sheridan did not. This may be the purest fiction for all I know, but it was an idea Stanley certainly carried around with a sense of injustice; and he was not the kind of man to harbour a grudge. As to questions of health being behind the two premature retirements, the fact is that it was Phillip who had suffered a serious illness about the time I joined the firm, and who died in the December of our first year as a public company. The two sons, Mr. Stanley and Mr. Jack as they were known to us, and R.L. Tillett joined Blow and Cotterill as directors on the Strand Electric Holdings board one month later in January 1937 (the first two had become directors of the original Strand Electric and Engineering Company in May 1935). Some sort of City scandal caused Tillett to be replaced by Henry Myers in November 1942, Blow departed three years later and Jack Sheridan became chairman as well as managing director; a role which he had taken on with the death of his father. Stanley became joint managing director and L.G. Applebee filled the empty seat. Five directors were to be the rule until September 1963 when the number was increased to six, so that Jack's son Phillip could join the board.

All this is to anticipate: my two Comedy dinners over, what I had to digest was that for the first time in Strand Electric I had a rival for my esoteric jobs. Hugh Cotterill was perhaps three years older than I, but he had money and was a director of all companies within the Holdings group. It soon became obvious that he saw himself as my director boss in the matter of the catalogue and publicity which I had been doing; but above all he saw himself as running a research and development department. What I could continue to keep to myself was the showroom and the Seecol theatre. At this point the reader may wonder why I didn't pack up and go. After all, my original intent had been to stay but three years.

What tied me to Strand Electric more firmly than any contract was my Light Console and the opportunity it gave to pursue my mania - Colour Music! Until we sold one to some theatre or cinema that I would want to go and 'work' in, there in the Seecol theatre I must remain. And in this I had, most opportunely, the best assistant I could ever have had - 'B' Bear. Like me he had been drawn to stage lighting through his work as an amateur. The artist in him responded to the Light Console and how it could be used. It was his idea that we should set up a "Light Console Society" so we would develop a repertoire for *the same audience*. He proceeded to do this. Appropriately there are exactly one hundred and one cards in the membership envelope which survives to this day. There are the obvious names, like Alfred Emmet and Leonard Walker, but others, such as Donald Wolfit (then at Stratford), seem improbable. However, H.H. Prince Yurka Galitzine whoever he was, did accept for October 7th.

The recitals went on at intervals during 1936 and 1937 and we had appreciative audiences with good discussion afterwards. They then had to come to an end as the lease ran out on the warehouse in Floral Street in which the Seecol theatre was housed. I can still recall the dismay expressed by some of our members who had become addicted to these experiments in lighting and music. They, and we, were consoled by the thought that a new and better demonstration theatre - a veritable temple to colour music was to be constructed in King Street across the road. But, alas, that did not open until February 22nd 1939 and one way and another the times were hardly propitious!

Thanks to something which called itself the Faculty of Arts we were able to try in addition to our seven Light Console Society recitals, experiments with some dance students under Lydia Sokolova. She was a link with a distinguished past as she had been one of the names in Diaghilev's company. A link with a distinguished future was the young Robert Eddison who read among other things some "Extracts from the Psalms". His fine voice took 'B' and I by surprise. There were three of these "Dance-Light Recitals" in a matter of six weeks. Stage management was by Lew Burroughs and the programme states that there was "At the piano ... Alix Falls", though I have no recollection of how we got it in and, in our limited space, where we put it when it was in! A year earlier in 1936 we had, I suppose, registered our two most distinguished visitors: H.R.H. the King's brother and George Bernard Shaw - the one and only. As events were to turn out, the latter was the one to have the enduring effect on my life - unbeknown to him. What he saw and discussed was Colour Music but what he, a teetotaller, led me to (I being also T.T.) was the creation and the running of a regular sherry bar - as I have done for some years now.

It happened like this. The visit of H.R.H. will come up later in this history (chapter IX) but this is an appropriate place for the Shaw visit as it was directly connected with the second blow I received in the first half of 1936; a quite unexpected tragedy out of the blue. Father was keen that the Art Workers Guild (of which he had become a member in 1922, at the same time as Oliver Bernard) should visit the Seecol theatre and see my colour music. The Guild did have occasional visits as part of their regular Friday evening programme. Father stressed that they would expect free scotch as well as the usual refreshments (this requirement vanished with the outbreak of war although they did continue to hold some nineteen meetings each year - albeit in the afternoons).

So Father was there that April 28th in 1936 when the Guild paid their first visit to us. The meetings began late at 8pm and were restricted to members "and one *male* guest each" (this rule remained for a further three decades). The house was already full and seated. I was ready to be introduced by the master for that year, Harry Morley, appropriately a painter, before I began my lecture on "Stage Lighting as an

Art" when Bernard Shaw arrived to murmurs of "It's Shaw..... it's Shaw". Stephen Stanton, an architect and one of the two honorary secretaries (the other was Cecil Thomas, a sculptor) gave up his seat in the front row and there was G.B.S in all his white-whiskered prime waiting to hear *me* lecture!

Somehow or other, on that occasion at least, I never put a foot wrong. The assemblage sat through the whole programme and received all the colour music items with particular enthusiasm. At the end Shaw got up and in that wonderful soft Irish voice of his spoke about stage lighting; concluding, not unnaturally, with an admonition that lighting such as mine would be a distraction to his plays. My own diffident but firm riposte, was that his plays would be a distraction to my lighting. The youthful thesis being that there was, in the emotions evoked by changes of colour, intensity and direction of light, something too important to be forever shackled to mere illumination of actors and scenery. It is a view I still hold. At the very least, pursuit of this art form by lighting designers would act as a safety valve and remove much of the temptation to complicate lighting and lighting plots when actors are on the stage. Thanks to war, and serious ill-health, that crusade was destined to become a lost cause - relegated to a stimulating and refreshing personal hobby. It was to be the life of an illuminating engineer, inventor and writer for me perforce.

The meeting adjourned for refreshments and scotch, or rather scotch and refreshments, and in due course Father and I found ourselves alone at the bottom of the stairs to Floral Street. Much to my surprise, before we emerged he paused and turned to me, seized both my hands and declared he was proud of me. He wasn't demonstrative in this sense. It was an age when it simply wasn't done for men to show emotion; but this was his Guild and the evening had been all that he could have possibly wished from his elder son in front of his friends and fellow artists.

Eight weeks later this healthy and active man was dead. Septicaemia had killed him in a matter of days; not one of the medical weapons to be available so soon after was around then. Thus it was at the age of twenty-four I was swept into the Guild on a wave of emotion in which Brother Percy Bentham's sudden death, a colourful novel art form and a rare visit from G.B.S (who was an honorary member) were inextricably mixed. My election to the Guild was by committee under a long since obsolete rule XI. Such election was very rare in those days; it being usual to submit the candidates and their work to the verdict of the brethren. In this case I hadn't ever thought of myself as worthy of the Guild or been asked whether I wanted to join. The letter informing me that I had been elected came as a complete surprise; as did the craft which Guild ingenuity had created for me - Decorative Colour Worker - what could be better?

It was my insistence over many years that the Guild should return to something like the civilised whisky tradition that led to my being told that there could be a sherry-bar, provided I arranged for the running of it. Something I have, much to my surprise, enjoyed; I am sure that 'B' would have approved though he never lived to see it.

It is sad that I never asked 'B' Bear to put on paper the tale of how he came to join Strand Electric. He went to the same school (St. Dunstan's) as Stanley Earnshaw and Jack Sheridan but would have been their junior. He was on terms with the Sheridan family, particularly Phillip, and must have been a frequent visitor to their home. His first job was in an insurance office. It was Stanley who first introduced us in the stalls bar at the Palace and left us with a 'pair of briefs', a scotch and a ginger beer respectively. During Act 1 of *Anything Goes* with Sydney Howard, 'B' fell asleep which I attributed wrongly to the scotch. Nor was it the show, for as I was to find out he was a Sydney Howard enthusiast like Stanley. Decades were to pass before I learned that he (and I indirectly) suffered from something, called narcolepsy.

When 'B' first joined Strand he scandalised everyone with the free way he spoke about Phillip and Arthur, Jack and Stanley. Though the first named was "P.S" to most of us it was "Mr. Earnshaw", "Mr. Jack" and "Mr. Stanley". Speaking personally, it was not until I had been there some thirty years and been a director some time that I even thought of them as Jack and Stanley. But then I have never been good at Christian names. In my Father's day, use of a surname without prefix was the sign of a closer relationship at last. At public school neither boys nor masters ever used anything but surnames. I never went to B's home in Orpington and I got the impression that he didn't often go there either. Certainly we were rung at home by his mother one Sunday who asked if we had seen Bernard; which flummoxed us for a moment since we had no idea that his name was Bernard. The 'B' was followed by an 'E' but what that stood for I have no idea. And here we come to the point that our very long friendship and great periods of working together were based solely on this common objective - stage lighting.

Until sometime in the 1950s when he acquired his small flat on the fourth flour of Russell Court, we never knew where 'B' went to get his night's rest. But once there, the entertaining he managed to do was legendary. The kitchen was little more than a cupboard and he would serve his guests as first and second sittings all in the same small room - drinks, of course, kept the others occupied meanwhile. Although nearly a pauper, 'B' nevertheless lived his life in the grand manner. He always used taxis and when we went out to eat it was somewhere extravagant (to me, anyway - a teashop and café man pre-war), like Stone's Chop House in Panton Street. A show would follow either because he had been given a couple of pit passes by some electrician, to be exchanged at the early door for the metal tokens* or because we

* Tickets were not issued for the unreserved Pit and Gallery seats. The heavy metal tokens had to be surrendered on entry.

wanted to see how well some new Strand lantern was used. I saw my first *Candida* (the revival of February 1937 at the Globe) because they were using two pageants (Patt. 50s) to get the sun streaming through the window instead of just lighting the backing with floods. My friend Phyllis from Watford joined us on that occasion and we stood waiting for her on the pavement outside during the first interval. Her problem was to get from Watford High Street station to Euston after office hours. Fortunately most shows were late starts - to allow stalls and dress circle to dine, and still some would push through late. Discovery of an express, steam of course, which did the bit from Watford to London non-stop solved our problem. Even so, I could occasionally find myself waiting to the last possible minute in Euston if fog meant the train was late. We had an understanding that zero hour having passed it would become a first interval rendezvous. Cinemas with their 'continuous performances', even in the West End, were easy - especially as they all had some sort of café restaurant. Our next step-up was one of the four Lyons' Corner Houses; but they could take up precious time as tables could not be reserved. Of course the girl never, never paid or contributed towards the cost of the outing - or was expected to!

Good Friday Music

When after a while 'B' gravitated to outside rep work (via the 'Lamb & Flag' or the 'Bird in Hand' or further afield, the 'Salisbury' pubs) he still faithfully played his part in Colour Music activity. My own private rehearsals would go on in the evenings after six but Saturday afternoons - the firm was open until 1 o'clock anyway - would be when he and I would get together to work out ideas and make any scenery bits and pieces. The ancient 2kW electric fire was used to toast something or other and was then put on its back with a cheap kettle on top to make tea. This is the way the sets for the *Good Friday Music* or the *Dawn* and *Siegfried's Journey to the Rhine* were created. They were mainly long muslin drapes but with cut-outs behind, backed by blacks or with a vista through to the cyc. We had five 3-dimensional columns for use with the cyc and of course the inclined plane groundrow. Optical effects and special silhouette pieces were used in front of the cyc for the overtures to the *Flying Dutchman* or the *Hebrides* - the latter a nice evocation of Fingal's Cave which neither of us had seen.

Usually it was a matter of a scene change for particular items in a recital or a demonstration. The change being covered by talk or a Hot Rhythm number on the house tabs and pros. cove; but three more ambitious works required changes within the progress of the music. They were Stravinsky's *Firebird* suite, the Mussorgsky/Ravel *Pictures at an Exhibition* and the Vaughan Williams *London Symphony*, complete. We usually did only the first movements of symphonies; for example, Schubert's *Unfinished* and Tchaikovsky's numbers 4, 5 and 6. Inspired by the Toscanini record, 'B' even had a go at the second movement of Beethoven's Seventh. He considered a ticket to see the Maestro a must when Toscanini gave his first series of concerts at the Queens Hall with Adrian Bolt's new BBC orchestra in June 1937. Off he went to queue for the entire morning until well after lunch, and thanks to him I was able to attend several of those historic concerts. In return, I managed to get him to come along to the Queen's Hall to learn that our own Sir Thomas Beecham also had something special to offer. In some respects 'B's outlook could be very narrow!

The *London* was the nearest we ever came to naturalistic sets. The Mussorgsky *Pictures* was more or less sprung on us as the finale to the first Faculty of Arts Dance-Light recital by Sokolova's choreographer, a man called George Aries. Sokolova was so ecstatic at my interpretation of the *Great Gate of Kiev* finale that she declared that it made her want to tear her clothes off and stand there on the stage in front of our five columns - fortunately, she did not as the destruction of the scale of our small stage would have jeopardised that Great Gate! As I write this I can only look back in wonder over nearly sixty years at the prowess displayed by Lew Burroughs, and his successor Paul Weston, in doing those scene changes in such a cramped space.

There were no dancers used in the *Pictures*. The idea was that George Aries would outline his plot for each scene. The 'his' has to be stressed because it differed entirely from the composer's version. And what the audience saw was mine, which resembled neither. My version was abstract - I simply based it on the emotions stirred by Ravel's wonderful orchestration. I am sure I could not have got off the ground with the original piano suite, fond though I have become of it. We were to do *Pictures* several times but never again with commentary or programme notes! The sets were adaptations of what had been devised for the *Firebird*. From the moment I first saw, or rather heard the introduction of Stravinsky's *Firebird*, sitting on my own in the circle of Covent Garden, I knew it was a must for Colour Music treatment. So too was Massine's *Les Presages*; it was the De Basil Ballet season. I eventually did both - solo in the Seecol theatre when the Light Console was installed at last. In that Tchaikovsky 5th, the music used to cry out at times for the lighting, to soar away where the dancers could not follow; yet at others the dancers were so right; doing what the lighting could never do. Massine's symphonic ballets demanded the aid of lighting in a way that simply did not matter with his other compositions. But the season was short, and chance (on which I had come to rely), never brought Leonid Massine to the Seecol theatre.

Usually my outside jobs involved some problem with an intriguing slant. Before dealing with any such customer demands it is necessary to get one of our own out of the way, something which haunted us in 1937. It was what to do when the lease on our premises on the north side of Floral Street expired. I got deeply involved in this since the need for a demonstration theatre, and a good one, was taken for granted by the Strand board of directors. No argument on my part was necessary - even the City types could see that what we had was a success. At some time or other buildings running between Monmouth Street and Shorts Gardens had been acquired with the idea that the whole Floral Street operation would move there, virtually on the doorstep of the new Cambridge Theatre at Seven Dials. I had planned a theatre and showroom conversion on the top floor, when it became apparent that the latest Charing Cross bridge project, with its long flyover approach, would be a threat to our proposed location. No such bridge scheme ever went ahead and London still has only a rail and footbridge across the Thames at Charing Cross. We were not to know that; so there was nothing for it but to find somewhere else. One of the empty semi-derelict properties inspected, found suitable but rejected by our board of directors later became the Ballet Studio half-way down Floral Street. Eventually No 29 King Street running right through to Floral Street and adjoining our No 24 was decided on.

Provision of a theatre was a teasing problem. The basement was much too low and the ground floor not high enough. Above that, the building was set back about

4-ft making the upper two floors much too narrow. No. 29 King Street was immediately alongside what was then the Westminster Fire Office, a building of considerable architectural merit; it and all this side of King Street has been subject to a conservation order for many years. Thus although what I write about now was completely demolished and rebuilt as yet another great office development, it has been done more decently than one might have expected and the actual King Street facade remains complete with 'my' fibreglass caps from Pinewood on No. 30 (they must wait their turn in chapter IX when we were to become Rank). What we were dealing with at 29 was once an early 18th century house where the garden had been built over to form workshops or warehouses, occupied at one time by Deans Rag Books if I recall aright. There was an architect, a Mr. Scott, an assistant attached to our estate agent and he would look after the technical side of any alterations to the buildings - all I had to do was to think something up in terms of what Strand's directors would be likely to pay for. The work that had to be done looked pretty daunting.

King Street 'Temple' and shadow set 1939

The basement and ground floors had to become one, somehow. Part of the ground floor might remain as a balcony but the rest had to be cleared. But what about the lines of cast-iron columns? There were two lines one immediately above the other and they supported the outside wall of the first and second floors overhead via a series of short beams. The solution was to pick up these with pairs of RSJs running across the theatre to be and fix them in the party wall between us and the Westminster Fire Office. The offending columns could then be taken away. This structural discipline was the inspiration behind my decor for the colour music temple I intended the new auditorium to be. The fact that the place was extraordinarily high for its width was good at the stage end, especially as we still did not have any wing space; but it was also stimulating in the auditorium. I was able to apply Gordon Craig's "Never be afraid of verticals" advice.

The wall to the audience right was dictated by what remained of the multi-column days plus the new diversionary structure: the wall to the left duplicated this in fibrous plaster as near as possible. The whole was in two tones of grey and all colour and any decoration came from the lighting and therefore could be changed from the Light Console. In all there were 36-ways of dimmers in the auditorium and 39-ways on stage. Fading out the auditorium automatically changed the thirty-six over to the stage as the tabs opened.* This patching was an economy measure but even so I can only wonder now at such expenditure as this theatre and its equipment represented. All this was going on with war clouds gathering everywhere - 1938 was the year of Munich. Furthermore, I was not there to goad it on for a large part of that time.

The new theatre opened officially on the 22nd of February 1939 by Leslie Henson, the famous comedy actor. The programme was almost wholly colour music: Elgar, Verdi, Wagner and Tchaikovsky (1st movement of the 6th). Also Petis, Mills and Schobell, three people to write one short piece; but what a piece *Bugle Call Rag* was, as played on the organ of the Regal Edmonton by Sydney Torch (a 10-inch record) and on the auditorium of the new Strand Electric theatre by Fred Bentham! Everything worked out just right there to get the new art really on its way; furthermore in just under two months time there would be a 70ft high tower feature in the centre of the Ideal Home Exhibition dedicated to a month of free public colour music recitals. But health and a war were to close that chapter prematurely: but not this one!

It is curious how we humans manage to bear such things as ill health: mind you I had been lucky, looked at one way, to make the opening of that theatre at all. The brunt of the supervision had fallen on 'B' as the intermediary between bedside and

* see *CUE* 17, June 1982 for full article with photographs

building site. All this had its beginnings one year earlier when the chilly winter wastes of Bellevue Park Glasgow saw the completion and testing of our various equipment for the last of all the British Empire exhibitions, to open that Spring. There were four major Strand jobs: three indoors and one outside on the hillside. I was mixed up with three, one of which was on that hillside. The Victoria Falls in the Rhodesia pavilion was solely the province of L. Stokes-Roberts who though he had joined me as an assistant for a while after 'B' had moved on, simply got on with it. My own inside job was H.M. Government pavilion - the cyclorama behind the great globe which flashed-up the progress of the British Empire in red light as, by one means or another, we acquired this chunk of land or that. Some such display was always a prominent feature at international exhibitions. Our pavilions have become much more fun since we have had no Empire to take seriously and there has been James Gardner to design our displays. At Glasgow it was Stephen Thomas who asked me to advise and quote for the job. As to the hillside, that was for the GEC Illuminating Engineering department - Strand were only sub-contractors for the control equipment. But for my kind of mind it might have been a relatively simple job albeit involving large loads. The north cascade consisted of three flights of seven illuminated stairs running down the hillside with a stairway for the public either side. There was a pool and fountain between each flight and big jet-changing fountain at the bottom opposite the Paisley Road entrance to the exhibition. The architects were Sir John Burnett Tait and Lorne and I assumed that, as had been the case with the fountains at the Paris Exposition the year before, there would be a restaurant and other vantage points from which the whole display could be viewed. I was not to know that no such provision would be made and the sightlines were such that the only place to see the lot was from the top deck of a tramcar outside the Paisley Road entrance! A cycle for the display was devised to last for about half-an-hour (though it may have been longer), and approved by R.O. Ackerley who ran the Illuminating Engineering department of GEC at that time.

The fountain had a clutch-operated dimmer bank whose cycles were triggered from cams on the jet-changing hydraulic action. All went well except for the Compton couplers which were not too happy in their wooden boxes in the damp room under the fountain. It was the cascade flasher that embodied real trouble. Like an ass I assumed that 'sign people' knew all about flashers. After all, London at night was full of signs chasing and spelling-out names in the rooftops. That is what people assembled in Piccadilly Circus to see. So I merely made a chart of the cycle I wanted and gave it to our signs department (Strand & Interchangeable Signs Ltd.) to get on with. In overdue course it was sent to join the dimmer bank and other stuff at our works, then at Talbot Road West Ealing. Odd's cams and switches - it was terribly primitive and threatened trouble. Instead of one cycle drum and some nifty switching to put the three flights of stairs in phase and out of phase for matching and contrasts, there was an enormous drum, vast in length and circumference, in which every circuit on the entire cascade was represented by a mercury switch to be lifted by a peg to be screwed into the drum for every change everywhere*. Time was against me, there was nothing for it: the Heath Robinson contraption had to be preset and made to work somehow. This meant rigging a line of pilot lamps and overnight after overnight sessions for me at the works. I sat in Dusty Miller's tiny machine shop foreman's office along with a strange smell as each row of switches was set. It was months later before the source of that smell was revealed. Being with Dusty as he took his morning break one day, I noticed that he stuck his cheese sandwich into the guard of the small bowl fire which had been my sole source of heat. Some cheese oozed out onto the bowl, there to remain until scorched off or baked in!

The length of the flasher contraption meant that the partition between the lighting control section and the pumps proper had to be omitted, hence the threat of damp to the Compton couplers. Apart from the fact that the drum never did accurately control each change up the hillside with any precision (there was always a circuit or two which was late and worse) the whole device was a humiliation for me in the eyes of the engineers from the G.E.C. Here had been a chance to out-do that Ipswich Supply Company job I had devised for Basil Davis in 1931. As the sightlines up the hillside were so bad it did not show as much as it should have. The Paisley Road sophisticated automatic dimmer did its job, matching the appropriate set of underwater lamps to each particular arrangement of water jets whilst illuminating them with a changing colour cycle.

If there was a really sophisticated solution to a series of problems then it was the G.P.O† pavilion. This was a job which 'B' had got and which we did together. There too trouble lurked. He had been in contact with some G.P.O. engineers in much the same manner as was to happen with television in the fifties. He thought it might lead to something. These engineers no longer had anything directly to do with telephones (if they ever had) but formed part of a display team. The G.P.O was very publicity conscious at that time and, for example, had a gauge 1 Bassett-Lowke model railway with which they demonstrated the pick-up and dropping of mail from trains in motion. The G.P.O. Film Unit was very active with John Grierson and Alberto Cavalcanti associated with it. This was early use of documentary film for commercial propaganda, albeit by a State enterprise. Cavalcanti had designed a pavilion in plan with a mock radio mast in the centre going from floor to ceiling and

* Unknown to me then but I was to learn in 1981, this switch changing of lights resembles somewhat change ringing with bells. That art has been going on for centuries in church towers in this country; but not in Europe.

† General Post Office

out through the roof. At intervals around the walls were large cut-outs painted red representing maps of those parts of the world on the Empire flying boat routes. Canada must have been omitted because memory says that the only regular passenger flight across the Atlantic was Pan Am's Lisbon to Bermuda flying boat. However, the Empire routes did get as far as Australia and that was enough of a teaser for 'B' and I!

What we had to do was to dim the lights in the pavilion every ten minutes and project the image of a flying boat which would start on the map of the British Isles, fly round the hall, pass over the intervening map cut-outs and end up in Australia. *Light and Lighting* of June 28th 1938 has a semi-technical article by an anonymous contributor (myself!) which gives accurate details quite beyond me now. But our troubles are recalled with ease. Suffice it to say that because of the central mast we had to have two projectors instead of one and these had to be concealed and rotate in circular pedestals only 3ft in diameter. Between these and the walls were eight columns standing out roughly 5ft from them and, due to the elliptical plan, they were in effect irregularly spaced. All this plus the notion that it would be nice not to betray the source of the projection (nowadays fashion would dictate the opposite!). This led us to dream up ultra-violet projection onto a fluorescent wall track. Since the throw was over 30ft and the only light source available was a 125-watt UV (black) lamp, that should have been quite enough problem to get on with. But 'B' and I went on to compound it by suggesting that the moving clouds in the ceiling high up overall should also avoid visible rays, by means of UV projection. The Strand anthracine fluorescent dope was so inflammable that it simply could not be sprayed in the hall, so it was sprayed onto ceiling paper by Eddie Biddle in the Sign department's spray booth. This was located on the floor above the Seecol theatre in dire working conditions; roll upon roll under UV lamps.

The Stelmar optical system was used for the clouds, and the German double focus diverter mirror system was included to keep the aeroplane projectors down to size. They were probably conversions of a couple of my Patt. 83* failures. The light had to be collected from the front of the lamp as passage through the black glass envelope three times would have left virtually nothing to pass through the slide and objective lens. We were determined to have decent clouds and got Kodak to make us some on glass - after all, the usual problem of heat did not exist with a 125W source. Nevertheless, this was a grave mistake. Testing a couple of slides before sending them up north, we found that the whites were not passing sufficient UV and there was nothing for it but to clear those areas down to the glass. Being Saturday there was nowhere to seek advice but Brasso metal polish seemed to work, so that became

* see chapter III

our occupation that weekend. The task completed, I made some joke to 'B' that it would be just our luck if we unpacked and found the slides had gone yellow during their journey to Scotland! Needless to say, that was exactly what we did find.

Hours were spent using splinters of wood and water to scrape patches of emulsion off the slides and yet retain the suggestion of clouds. We might just as well have got Frank Weston and Eddie Biddle to make the slides up in their usual manner using Photopak coating - a task they excelled at. It may be wondered what the Post Office engineers made of all this. The truth is that they knew us very well as we had all spent some days together in Paris the previous year visiting the 1937 International Exposition. After adventuring around Montmatre all night we ended up in the small hours in a cinema populated by lesbians, only because 'B' said we must see *Le Million*. 'B' promptly fell asleep. After that experience, the sight of us seated on the floor with the intention of spending the night scraping bits of glass would not rate as peculiar to those engineers. They knew, as did most of Strand Electric's customers, that the curtain would go up somehow.

My main wish to go to Paris arose from the fact that I had designed some tiny spotlights (focus-lamps) for Stephen Thomas to use on the ceramic display in our Government pavilion. This pavilion by Oliver Hill was a real step forward in exhibition design for Britain. At last that Empire map feature had been ditched and 'modern' architecture and display used to good advantage. There were a couple of oddities: a giant cut-out of Neville Chamberlain, our Prime Minister, fishing; and the fact that alone of all those privileged with a prime position on the Seine, only the U.K. turned its back on the river and presented blank walls and a dreary unfrequented terrace on that side. Others put their national restaurants overlooking, or floating on the river, but our 'pub' was as far away from it as could be.

Germany and Russia confronted each other across the grand avenue down from the Trocadero, where the now familiar fountain display was brand new, down to the Eiffel tower. Colossal sculptures of pure Aryan mother-with-childrenhood and Ardent-aspiring workers warned of things to come within their respective pavilions - or rather temples. Even so, I was still taken aback on entry to the German one; the regimented lines of great framed showcases on either side of the 'processional' gangway struck the keynote. Germany had put the clock back - the Bauhaus sunk without trace. For something exciting to accord with my beliefs at that time, one had to turn to the Polish and the Swiss pavilions. Our little party of three 'GPOs' and two 'Bs' was conducted around backstage and underneath the Trocadero fountains by guides whose real preoccupation was amplified sound. Wherever we went, there was sound to be demonstrated. It was "Voici les amplificateurs," here, and "Voila les amplificateurs" there, and to get them off the subject was an impossible task. The highlight of the tour was the central control for all the external loudspeakers. The martial music was killed mid-bar, and something soft substituted nearby, while something clashing and loud was put on in the area beyond. Phoney announcements were made to demonstrate speech quality, but the peak came when all the loudspeakers were killed to show the power of those on the Eiffel tower. These were turned up full blast and must have shattered the ears of those people nearby. They certainly could cover the entire exhibition from the tower - aural chaos was all about and around that night!

Back in Glasgow, after our all nights of hard work, the projected clouds looked quite well. With a feeling that we literally had 'scraped through' we made for the nearest exit as the trumpets sounded in the distance to welcome His Majesty King George VI to declare the Empire Exhibition open. Our thoughts turned to our beds in 'The George' in far off Buchanan Street. This had been our second refuge. Our original lodgings had been a boarding house further up in one of those strange Glasgow tenements where the ground floor and basement are quite separate from the top floors, into which there seems no way of getting! Thus we went down into the basement to bed. It had sufficed until high tea on the Sunday. A scandal developed when one of the female lodgers asked another lady to read the tea-leaves in her cup - on the Sabbath! Coming at the end of a day in which we had been itching to tackle our many problems, but work was not permitted, 'B' found 'The George'.

Curiously, in Paris it had worked the other way round. Somehow or other our reservation at the Hotel Strasbourg must have been a bridal suite; it can't have been anything else. Mirrors everywhere and a great canopied bed like that by Oliver Messel for *Helen* but of an older period. Next day we sought out our G.P.O friends and joined them in a cheap pension in one of the back streets near the Rue de Rivoli. There it was I drank Pernod for the first and last time - and saw three doorways for the first time. It was on that occasion that I came to appreciate the merits of black coffee, for that dinner was but an overture to the outing which landed us up in that *Le Million* cinema. Cafe Cognac was what I stuck to thereafter until I became tee-total once more on return to England. Even that return sticks in the memory. We arrived in London at about three in the morning, so we walked from Charing Cross station to Floral Street and let ourselves into the Seecol theatre, took down a pair of Geo. S Hall's best quality tabs and with each of us amply cocooned, we went to sleep.

I honestly believe it was the only time I ever found a use for that particular pair of drapes. Glasgow left an enduring legacy - a dull ache just under my lowest left rib; a grumble which persisted but which was not sufficient to complain of or go and see our doctor about. I took it with me, along with my brother and my cousin Donald, for a week's holiday in Lucerne and Lugano. The visit to the island of Triebschen should have been the peak of the peaks around for this Wagner enthusiast, but it is still largely memorable for the tightly stretched khaki short shorts of a girl tourist as she bent over the showcase in front of me to study the detail of a Wagner score more closely. We have become accustomed to posteriors under pressure these days, but all three of us found that German one an irreverent big blot in that hallowed house. Of course we would not then have been aware of where Wagner's own interests lay.

We were certainly aware that trouble was brewing over the border and Donald and I were very pessimistic about the situation. We saw our only hope as a pact with the U.S.S.R. which was said to be under negotiation; but we did not believe, rightly as it was to turn out, that it would ever be signed by Chamberlain's government. What there was no doubt about on the night train home was that I was in pain. If it had been on my right side I would have diagnosed appendicitis, which I had (but did not have the operation at the time) as a child. Fortunately our compartment, unlike our journey out, was empty but for us. So Phil and Donald occupied one seat while I stretched out on the other. Back home at Pebworth Road I was sent straight to bed and within two days I was in private room number 2 in Wembley Hospital with a pleural effusion.

Three things stick in my memory: two unpleasant, and one pleasant. It was my first time as an 'inmate', and the unhappy wailing cry which echoed down the corridor as they wheeled a little boy off to the operating theatre, "Not want my tonsils out - I want my tonsils!" is still vivid. So too is the drainage of the liquid from my pleural cavity performed by my own doctor, Doyle, in my room the same morning. This involved a couple of 'locals', as at the dentist, then pushing a hollow needle into my back somewhere. This should have been simple enough, as I was to find when I had it done to me at home during the war by Doctor Gompertz, who was by then my GP. But Doctor Doyle was a man who had obviously shone on the rugger field during his training, had one eye on Chamberlain (then in Germany), and the other eye on Ireland where he intended to retreat - and eventually did. The Sister, who to those eyes of mine was elderly, fussed around. "Are you sure you wouldn't prefer me to do it? That what-ever-it-was is a bit tricky; let me give you a hand." Other confidence inspiring commentary went on behind my back, geographically, not metaphorically. Doyle refused to surrender the needle in the scrum and eventually a piddling sort of sound proclaimed that they had struck if not oil then some sort of liquid. By which time the young nurse out-front noticed that a drop of cossetting was needed.

I got on very well with these young nurses because my room was so convenient for them and I was obviously trustworthy. The first time it was put to the test, I was taken by surprise. I suppose I had been tucked-up for the night about 9 o'clock. Laying there in the moonlight there was a tapping on my partially-opened window; I was on the ground floor. To my call, "Who's there?" I got a shush, and, "Please ring for Night Nurse, but if Sister comes don't say anything - I'm locked out!" Fortunately the Night Nurse came and opened the window for me to enjoy the process of climbing over the window ledge. Thereafter I had something to look forward to at night! In recent years TV series such as *Upstairs, Downstairs* have made us aware of the servile role 'enjoyed' below stairs and the strict code of morals enjoined on them by master and mistress alike. This went on into the twenties, but we need reminding that such a code was rigorously applied to nurses in hospitals between the wars and in the case of the big name hospitals, like The London, they also applied during the war. Nurses, however well educated, were treated by Matron and the Sisters as if they were schoolgirls, servants, or privates in an army. Locked out after ten o'clock was the rule at Wembley.

Chamberlain came home from Munich waving his scrap of paper at the end of September and shortly after I came home from Wembley to a convalescence of 'take-it-easy' seasoned with something Dr. Doyle believed in called Quarcol, plus immense desert-spoonfuls of a sticky sugary stuff, in a large jar, called Radio Malt. The jar was so large that when I let go of the spoon accidentally it was sucked under and had to stay there to the end; it would have been hopeless to dredge for it. This stuff was for vitamins and the other was to keep my temperature down and tone me up, I think. It was all very primitive. Before long Doyle came to see me with Dr. Gompertz, who was taking over the practice, and this was the best thing that could have happened to me. He was a stern but human GP who made the best of the resources then available to him. He did not believe that a doctor who didn't prescribe medication every time was not doing his job properly.

Faced with some weeks stuck at home I bought myself a Murphy television set. Those were days when Gordon Russell had to do with what later became known as the 'styling' and in consequence the floor-standing affair with radio and a decent loudspeaker was decidedly out of the rut. The screen was 9 or 10 inch, small in today's terms but not then when 12 inch was the largest and 6 inch ones were common. The picture was extraordinarily good, because it had a black level clamp circuit. In dark night scenes and blackouts the screen went a real black not a nondescript grey. This refinement was dropped later probably for the same reason that one cannot obtain unwatered bacon!

By the time I bought my set the Baird system had been shut down and in consequence the set's electronics only had to be suitable for the 405 line EMI system; but the second studio at Alexandra Palace did not reopen till the end of 1938. What the BBC managed to do with one small studio was remarkable. What would be obvious on the television at home to us now would be the lack of depth of focus in the Emitron cameras. People sitting on a diagonally-placed bench or around a table could only be hard-focused one at a time. In a discussion or a love scene one was very conscious of the lens being tracked to and fro although the camera remained on the same shot. The fact that the background was out of focus except in establishing shots did not matter. In fact I got so used to it that when at last I did go to the cinema again I found the detail, the wood grain on the door behind an actor, positively distracting. This was in much the same way that in the early talkies we, who had been brought up on the 'silents', did not always find the sound track a help. I could go on and add that sound effects on the radio or backstage are often far from welcome.

To my mind there is no doubt that part of the reason why Rudolf Cartier's earlier 1950s production of Orwell's *1984* made an indelible impression was the nightmare quality of the out-of-focus of the derelict areas of the White City site and buildings. One's imagination was able to go into play and viewers were not shackled to the exact picture on the screen. The later version of his, using the much improved equipment in the studio, showed a more lavish production in clearer detail which at the time I found something of an anti-climax. This latter version is the one which was recorded by filming the cathode-ray tube, and extracts turn up in BBC TV anniversary celebrations from time to time - at least I think so. Anyway this early type of 'video' of necessity provides the out-of-focus component whose absence I regretted in that second version of this bad dream. But was it a bad dream? With Churchill's "iron curtain" of 1946 ascending across the Continent nearly a half-century later; we find, as so many of us suspected, *1984* had been all too real.

Since fate ordained, one way and another, that my role in pre-war television was only that of a viewer; this is no place for its technology. However, Fred did concern himself with its future. For example, in April 1937 he made a contribution to the discussion of Jesty and Winch's paper "Television Images".* The last of six paragraphs confirms his mania as follows:

> *Even the short period during which high definition television had been a public service was sufficient to show the difficulty of obtaining enough programme-hours of material in the future. There was no equivalent of music for television, seeing that a view of the orchestra had no attraction. In radio last year music accounted for over 50% of the total hours. Therefore he would conclude with a prophecy that in the future when screens were larger and colour an accomplished fact, light in the guise of 'colour-music' would have a very large part to play. Perhaps television would provide the*

* IES Transactions Vol.II No.8 1937

> *necessary impetus to the development of this art which had been so long deferred.*

How wrong can you be....?

By the time I had my set, BBC television had become really professional in much of what we actually saw on our little screen. Visitors who came to gawp at our wonder toy were captured and held by the show itself. Seeing that there was usually only one hour each afternoon and $1^1/_2$ to 2-hours from 9pm, it was amazing what was covered. We had plays, ballet, even opera and of course variety acts. A memorable regular was *Picture Page* with Joan Miller. BBC TV did not have its own newsreels then, but alternated between "Movietone" and "Gaumont British News". However, it did put out topical specials of which the *News Map* series was the most outstanding. It featured experts in the studio, for instance Peter Fleming talking in depth on China. Such talks were illustrated with maps drawn by J.F. Horrabin who was present to modify or accent, on camera, parts of them as necessary. What Horrabin, a craftsman of imagination, did was the kind of thing which was to become commonplace in the computer-graphic age, and he did it with only the traditional artist's materials to hand. Some television outside broadcasts were now possible and leaving aside bits of paper waved in the air, the "boat race" and the like, the most important has to be the first theatrical performance from St. Martin's Theatre on November 16th 1938. It was J.B. Priestley's *When We Are Married*, which had us glued to our armchairs out at Harrow. Unlike the BBC radio then, BBC TV had the sense to see the role for female announcers and they literally outnumbered the male by two to one. The slim brunette, Elizabeth Cowell, still evokes a sigh in me.

Occasionally our television picture would become afflicted with a pulse which began slowly, became faster and faster until it slowed down and vanished. It did not annoy so much as intrigue. I discussed the symptoms with the man who supplied our set. He also had been intrigued; but had failed to get a satisfactory explanation - there was something to be hushed-up here. Of course there was; what we suffered from was the basis of that key pre-war invention - Radar. The Ally Pally (Alexandra Palace) mast signals made their way to our aerial alright (we could actually see the transmitter mast on the far horizon on a clear day); but they could become confused by their own reflections from any passing aeroplane. Hence the varying speed of pulse depending on its distance. It was certainly not something to air publicly with the Hitler menace hovering over us. There were many less technical reminders in the news as to where we were heading. The Penguin Special paperbacks of 1937 *Germany Puts the Clock Back* by Edgar Mowrer and of March 1938 *Blackmail or War* by Genevieve Tabouis confirmed one's worst fears. The H.G. Wells film of his

The Shape of Things to Come seemed all too likely to present a true picture of our future, if we had any. Looking back from my present conservationist stance, it is a matter of wonder how that Fred derived some comfort from the scenes of post-war reconstruction in that film. Perhaps it was the Bauhaus/Corbusier/Rationalist spirit then still alive in him; or possibly it was the effect of that last part of the Arthur Bliss score!

The IES "Television Images" paper above also concerned itself with a "translucent surround" for the cathode ray tube screen. This was a frame with its own illuminated border. The idea had also been discussed and experiments made in the cinema. Eye strain and contrast were all mixed up in debate. A sort of inner pros. frame with low 3-colour illumination regulated and mixed automatically by photo-cell operated thyratron-reactor dimmers was advocated and tried, in the Alhambra-Odeon Leicester Square I think. It was all very complicated and expensive. My notion was to adapt my cyc ground-row inclined plane idea. Flats would be sloped inwards either side with the inclined planes joining them along the top and bottom of form a complete frame. Painted matt-white, no lighting would be needed as it would pick up an appropriate level and colour of light from the screen scatter. I took out a provisional patent; but of course the impending war put a stop to such finicky concerns and after the war bigger screens soon became common. But for my own TV back in 1938-39, I made a frame on this principle out of cardboard with a couple of wood-lath legs: it weighed nothing and was simply leaned against the set - and it worked a treat. A real invention and another 'who-knows if?' in my career!

Invention and the patent process was by no means a straight forward affair and things don't seem to have got any simpler since then. The trouble is that the LAW comes into the matter, and endless debate and delay inevitably follows. Possession of a patent guarantees nothing, in spite of the fact that an official search preceded the granting of the patent. In the 1950s some rival tried to stop our making the single dimmer automatic mixer of 3 or 4 circuits. They quoted their recent patent number. My reply to their lawyers was to refer them to the GEC patent of 1932 for *my* 'Monarch of Bermuda' drum, which in any case we had been using off and on for years. More recently I found myself playing the role of an expert witness in a case which concerned remote position control of spotlights. Here it was not a matter of citing my own invention; but invention or installation by others known to me over the decades of my work. Quoting from my own memories was not enough, items had to be backed up by contemporary documents. It was certainly a case of my own archive to the rescue. The great frustration was the way the lawyers would not leave the text I submitted alone. Some editing is fine, but the engineering truth can get lost among the legal jargon. In a way it was a pity the matter was ultimately settled out of court and I never got a chance to perform, so to speak.

My first encounter with the law (our advocate was Sir Stafford Cripps K.C. no less) also got settled out of court. The punishment for my crime was the public mutilation of my beloved "1936" catalogue. Pages 81, 82 and 83, which come immediately before the Light Console, had to be removed and others hurriedly devised and substituted. A close-up of the Covent Garden control panel with Charlie Storer and a photo of one of the two Alexandra Palace BBC TV Grand-Masters formed the new page 81. At the other end it was easy to give the Light Console an extra page, which left me with page 82 to fill. The result was a description and photo of a Strand Remote Control panel having pairs of dial switches with which "the intensity and the *time* taken by *each* circuit to arrive at the intensity can be preset". The method to achieve the latter would have been the clutch impulse timer from the original Light Console. I say, "would have been" because this panel was not constructed as such. So where did the actual photograph come from? The answer to this is that it was the bottom third of the censored picture of the 24-way remote control panel installed in Greens Playhouse Dundee previously featured on that page.

That panel was 3ft.5ins x 3ft.3ins and operated the three primary colours in the float and two battens plus five cove and dome locations in the auditorium. The system was known as the "Strand Chromolux" and was intended to render colour-mixing skill unnecessary in cinemas. Applebee had to quote for such a scheme and consulted me. At home that night I drew something on squared-paper and was staggered how easy it was to devise a basic position circuit for each dimmer without the need for Percy Newton's reversing switches. All that had to be done was to put the requisite number of limit switches in series between the up and down clutches and get the dimmer to open a pair (fore and aft) at the point of travel to which the clutch feed was selector-switched. Why on earth hadn't I thought of this in those 'distant' Davis days at Central House, I don't know. Full of myself, I set out for Gunnersbury works first thing next morning, to show off my circuit to Jim Jordan (by then the works manager). His reply was to lift up his blotting-pad and hand me a bit of paper. He had produced exactly the same circuit that very same night - simultaneous invention!

The circuit devised, the next step had to be the selector to switch all three dimmers to positions to produce the various colour-mixes. The simplest thing was to adapt the slider dimmer format by substituting stud contacts on a panel made of syndanyo instead of the slates wound with resistance wire. Truly we live in different times, as I write these words fifty-years later. Imagine the labour involved in drilling the sixty holes at close centres to cope with the 20 triple contact positions to each switch. Yet we took it for granted. The technology we had to call on to solve each task may have been wanting; but the cheap manual labour certainly was not. The positions used for the colour-mixtures gave roughly 3/4, 1/2 and 1/4 light intensity and were also available as separate individual colours from three rotary selector switches, one above the other under each colour-selector slider. They also gave simple up, down and stop and formed the part of the Greens Playhouse control I was allowed to retain in my catalogue. So what precisely was this censorship about?

The truth was that it had been Gillespie Williams of Holophane who had the idea of the "Auto-Selective system" of three dimmers for mixing the primaries from one control knob. It was aimed at remote control of colour lighting in cinemas, whether on stage or in the auditorium. He was obsessed with the notion; but as pretty effects rather than my psychological ideas tightly tied to the music. My kind of operator had to be something of an artist. To make the projectionist's job simpler in the intervals obviously had its sales appeal. But the cinema owners believed in hard bargaining. Hence Applebee was asked to tender for something we hadn't got; automatic motor-drive colour-mixing, yes; but preset mixing, no. Since Jim and Fred were only doing what they were asked to do, they were classed as "innocent infringers", it was the firm that was in the dock. Personally I enjoyed the legal visits to our Patent Agent, Patent Solicitor, Junior and Senior Counsel. As far as I can see now; the key was whether it was the mixing idea or the means that was the important feature of the Williams patent. Their circuit used reversing motors to each dimmer whereas we had the Mansell clutch and one motor only.

After some months the legal costs were seen by Phillip Sheridan and Jack to be out of all proportion to the Strand business likely to result. Unofficial contacts were made via the GEC as intermediary to arrive at a sensible solution to the litigation without the lawyers. Agreement was reached by the two managing directors on April 16th 1937. Strand Electric would only make the equipment and Holophane would, as we say now, market it. Therefore all trace of our Chromolux had to be removed from my catalogue.

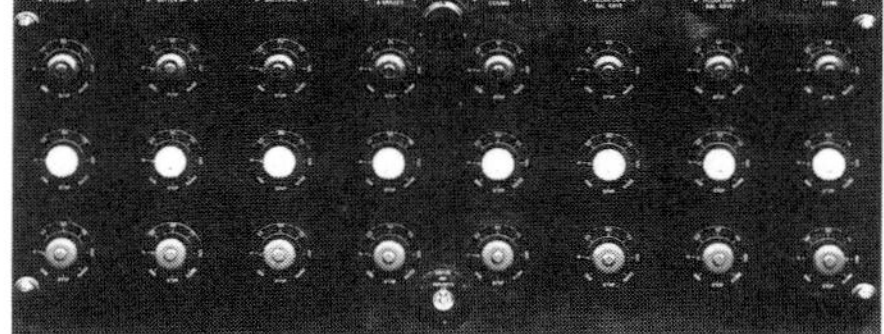

"Chromolux" before and after censorship

By that time colour lighting had gone out of fashion and installations were few indeed.

The war over, Holophane Limited did not take up stage lighting again, so Gillespie Williams moved to another of Strand Electric's competitors, Furse of Nottingham. There he launched a manual version of his auto-selector. Called the "Delicolor" its success seemed improbable. The cinema market was no longer what it has been and theatre was becoming more and more spotlight and other localised light based; so who would want primary colour battens? The answer was entertainer Jack Hulbert and we find his photograph posed with Williams at his side, on the front of the Furse Delicolor literature, while underneath in bold red lettering, "The American Theatre Expert, Mr David Murray, says, 'It is the greatest thing in the theatre world since Talking Pictures'. After a provincial tour the Hulbert show *Here come the Boys* (the other 'boy' was Bobby Howes) landed up in the Saville theatre. The system itself was a four-circuit dial unit with direct-operated resistance dimmers by means of cams. Each unit was 32" high by 24" wide by 44" deep. A couple of dial units might just be OK but by the time one mastered seven, as in the Rex Wilmslow installation later on, the friction which had to be overcome can be imagined. Delicolors did get put in here and there but they didn't worry me as the concept of theatre use was completely misguided whatever the claims and press praise. There were some within Strand who were concerned however, and the result was a detailed report of mine from Midhurst dated February 1946 which began: "When I was asked to explain why I don't believe in the Delicolor as a theatre control, I found it extremely difficult to know where to begin. To me the Delicolor as a theatre control is just crazy, and in consequence it was like being asked to prove black is not white. The report continues, "I think we have to admit first and foremost that we are faced by a fine piece of salesmanship. Here we have a piece of apparatus invented before April 1934 for cinema lighting; now put forward with no basic alteration as the 'last word' for the theatre"

Before too long "R. Gillespie" departed for the United States to become "Rollo G." and that was the end of the colour-mixing batten threat to theatre. Well not quite; but the Thorn Atlas adventure must await a later chapter. In a sense I should be grateful to Gillespie Williams; because it was the demonstration theatre he got Holophane to construct in their Vincent Square premises which put the idea into Arthur Earnshaw and Phillip Sheridan's heads that they too must have one - hence that appropriate vacancy for me in 1932.

VI: SAN CARLOS & KING EDWARD VII
Lisbon to Midhurst via Crail 1940-47

Shortly after Christmas 1946, three merry gentlemen could be seen one Sunday afternoon paying a kindly social call. Like the other wise men they bore gifts; in this case, they were in the shape of a brace of pheasants. Having arrived at their destination, one of them staggered down a corridor and asked a young girl, who was preoccupied at a sink, what he should do with the birds he bore. Whereupon she rounded on him furiously: "You ought not to be out of bed!" Indeed I ought not, having but a couple of days previously had some of my ribs removed.

It was my brother, of course, who startled the duty nurse at the King Edward VII sanatorium in Midhurst that afternoon and it was neither the first nor the last occasion of such confusion between us two brothers. Way back in my GEC Kingsway days he and I frequented the same restaurant - Whyteladies* in Bury Place near the British Museum. My brother was then a student at the Central School of Arts & Crafts nearby and came in early; he was a 'twelve o'clock' man whereas I was an 'after-two'. It was well 'after' once I went to Strand - for the lunch hour was our busy time, for amateurs. Miss Weedon, the proprietress of Whyteladies told me that her waitress thought for a long time we were one man who had two lunches. Memory suggests that three courses 'on the lunch' cost 1/4d. Mind you, that waitress could not have been very bright but a number of people continued to confuse us, especially when we became elderly. John English, in the bar of West Dean College, turned with a "Freddie!" only to find that it wasn't, it was Philip who taught there. The secret was to look for the moustache; I have never worn one.

We were not twins - I was his elder by a year and eight months - but 'socially' he was ahead of me. The fact that I was academically brighter (and that is not saying much) and did not go to work until nearly eighteen, whereas Phil went into Father's studio in Gunter Grove at fifteen and combined this with the Central School, gave him a more worldly-wise background - a kind of open university. I had to remain a schoolboy, and at a public school and therefore in a closed society. My model theatre hobby was no help either; his equivalent was the tennis club! Then Father's sudden death from septicaemia in May 1936 landed him at not quite twenty-three with the job of running the studio and the jobs in hand.

* Still there but now called Ristorante Italiano Fratelli

In contrast, my earlier years - indeed in a sense a large part of my forty-two years at Strand Electric - gave me rather a cloistered existence. Surrounded by 'buffers' I have ruled by ricochet, so to speak. The principal of these 'buffers' was 'B' Bear but another was certainly Stanley Earnshaw. 'B' used to say in the period of our greatest joint activity - the conquest of television from 1955 onwards - that he looked upon his role as that of a catalyst. This he certainly was in any discussion but he was also a front man. I had to have someone to do this, even when in reality I was quite on my own as in my first years at Strand Electric. Thus when 'old' Phillip Sheridan told me to put "Manager R&D" on my card, I suggested that it was better not to reveal the bald truth. Like Mr. Spenlow in Dickens' *David Copperfield* I needed a 'partner' to further my work. My 'Mr. Jorkins' was 'Frederick Bentham' who appeared as inventor on the Strand Light Console label, or in journals as author of articles on it and other innovations. I gave lectures and demonstrations to the drama schools and amateur groups; and afterwards they would gather round the console and ask questions. The girls - or perhaps it is only the young girls that were memorable - would ask about its inventor and I would describe some mythical personage. Looking back, I am sure that I had the feeling that the image of the true inventor with his youth and red nose would let his console down! I still possess, complete in cheap art deco frame, a cartoon clipped from the *Evening Standard* presented me by TLD* over on the other side of Floral Street. This would be shortly after the launch of the console and the cartoon had been adapted (and coloured!) from a series called "London Laughs". It showed a cinema organist up on his lift playing full-out. I have no idea what the original caption was, but the revised cartoon shows one lady in the audience turning excitedly to another to say: "Look at Charlie now, going all out with hands, feet AND NOSE!"

Charlie was the nickname I acquired from Harry S. Pepper of BBC Light Entertainment at the time of Radiolympia 1934. Watching me working the old Grand Master in the Seecol Theatre before the Light Console had appeared, he remarked to John Watt, "Charlie Rhubarb he play dat switchboard like one of dem dere Wurlitzers." The nickname stuck and in certain circles (which were to include the end of the Grand Circle at the London Palladium) I was always addressed as "Charlie" or "Charles".

This chapter is going to be unlike the others in that it will include a large amount of domestic background. It is essential material to explain why an intended sojourn of three or four years in Strand became forty-two and my presence in theatres on productions became so rare. Whether I was any good at that kind of work became irrelevant; quite simply, the long and irregular hours of real theatre work were not

* Theatre Lighting Department

good for me. The key is that terrible moment in my life when I lurked like a hunted criminal on the landing of my Mother's house in Harrow. Terror struck I had not the slightest idea what to do or say next. Here lies the explanation of the missing ribs when the tipsy three arrived at my bedside that Sunday two years or so later. And they were tipsy, having called at pubs known to 'B' en route for Midhurst. Sober or not they would not have been aware that this surgery had taken place, and I was not at that moment officially allowed visitors. My chance to have the first stage of surgical interference came while I was eating my breakfast. There was a sudden vacancy in the theatre; a slot to be filled. An understudy was needed for a chap who had developed a cold. Nobody else welcomed the role, they probably wanted time for prayer before such major surgery. Jumping the gun and getting my seven ribs out without anyone in the family being aware appealed to my sense of the dramatic. Soon I was taking my last bath unmutilated. One gazed at the semi-submerged torso with half a desire to show it off for the last time; a photograph taken perhaps? It must be so much worse for a woman. Men's clothes muffle or at any rate they did in those days. There was not much time for narcissism; for all the pre-operation prepping which would have been done the day before had to be crowded-in before I went down just after lunch. Not that there was any lunch for me; strictly I should not have had that breakfast.

The operation of thoracoplasty was a barbaric affair, performed only, believe you me, under local anaesthetics, just as if it were teeth not ribs to be extracted. Lots and lots of injections taking nigh on an hour went on in a room just off 'the theatre'. The de-ribbing itself took hours and three things stick vividly in the mind. First the noise: cutting through with the rib-shears made a hell of a row and to think that this is you being smashed up in slow motion. The second memory is rib number six. You can't have all seven ribs removed at one go - even though one would like to get it over at one bash. The body, as distinct from its occupant, would go into a state of shock. So the great wound (from neck curving round to waist) was sewn-up with fifty-six stitches, after four ribs out and three left to play after an interval break of a fortnight.

Now apart from the fact that it seems a dirty trick to play on the body to open old wounds, one said to oneself, "Well, it will be one less to come out this time". And one was wrong: because things are bigger and tougher. The weight of the surgeon bearing down on rib number six was impossible to cope with. Psychologically I was less prepared for it because the first stage, as it is called, had been less dire than I expected. Furthermore, though it was not a sharp pain, it felt as if he was going to break my back. And when lying down, if someone seems to be trying to break your back you give him a kick. Anyway that is what my body, as distinct from me, tried to do. Each time the surgeon weighed-in, up came my left leg.

There was nothing for it; my consent for a general anaesthetic had to be obtained. Easy? No it wasn't. This was where fear of cowardice in the face of the enemy intervened. Ex-public school and the general atmosphere which lingered just after the war made up an illogical hurdle to overcome. If Britain could take it - so could Bentham. But Bentham's body obviously couldn't and they eventually waved a trumpet-like affair in front of my face and I awoke to find that I was being sewn-up.

Officially twelve weeks *absolute* bed rest follows the last operation, thus making fourteen weeks in all. In my case it was a week or so less and one of the first things I did, when allowed to get up at last, was to visit the operating theatre on my own two feet, along with my next door neighbour, an Austrian who when well had done optical design for Pullins. The reason for this visit was not to return to the scene of the crime but to investigate the source of the third vivid memory - a remark by my surgeon that he could not see! By that time I had been promoted to floor representative, which involved collecting the mail from the bed prisoners. This should have been followed by graded walks up the sanatorium drive and after a few months return home to attempt a normal life. As it was, an involved X-ray, known as a tomogram, showed that five ribs had to be extracted on the other (the right hand) side. So back I went to absolute bed rest and two further sets of ribs came out*. A full fourteen weeks was to elapse before I set foot to floor again. A second Christmas was to follow within the walls of Midhurst and since I had spent one earlier on in Creaton sanatorium in Northamptonshire it is obvious that the process of cure was a long one.

It had all begun with that pleurisy and those five weeks in Wembley hospital in the Autumn of 1938. The seeds of this had been laid in bitter work on the fountains for the Empire Exhibition Bellevue Park Glasgow earlier that year. I recovered in time to open the new Strand Electric demonstration theatre in King Street which I had designed as a veritable temple to Colour Music. Thanks to 'B' I had been able to supervise the work from bed. Having got this open and done the odd show there, a visit to Earls Court to see progress on the Ideal Home Kaleidakon tower proved to be my undoing: I went down with pneumonia. While under treatment with the very new and vicious M&B693 chemotherapy, I had to be content with *Daily Mail* headlines like "HE SPENT SIX YEARS ON ONE IDEA - Too Ill to See It Yet" and the *Daily Mirror* "SUCCESS AS HE LIES ON SICK BED". Even *The Times* gave twenty-one lines to me and my troubles!

* To correct any image of a flabby Fred thereafter, I must point out that when removed in the proper manner the ribs grow again; albeit smaller, putting that part of the chest out of action. The power of our bodies to do their best to correct and heal themselves is, like the growth of plants after pruning, rather difficult for we engineers to believe.

I never made that fixture at the Ideal Home Exhibition, and it was left to 'B' and Paul Weston in turn to play duets with Quentin Maclean at the lakeside. Convalescence followed, concluding with three weeks in Switzerland. The night train back haunted the German frontier. With blacked-out stations and lots of troops about, all the signs pointed to war this time. No hope of another Munich reprieve for me and colour music; like I had experienced in Wembley hospital! Sure enough, before many days were out, Chamberlain was telling us that we were at war with Germany. I hastily returned to work only to receive, along with 90% of the Head Office staff, one week's notice. So that was what I had been trying to get well for.

It was sheer panic on the part of Jack Sheridan and the directors. Something they would no doubt like to be forgotten. No blame attaches to them for doing it to me. My health could still be regarded as very dodgy and if I had stayed quietly at home for some weeks then much of this chapter would not have needed to be written. But then I would never have been admitted to Midhurst. Where on being asked about my religion for the form, I said to the staff nurse, "Mind you write that down," and got the indignant reaction "And why shouldn't I write it down?" And I would never have one day married that staff nurse and had two sons.

I had got accustomed to the Irish nurses at my other ports of call behaving as if the writing down of the word "Agnostic" would produce an instant thunderbolt from on high. They would hesitate and say "Perhaps it had better be left blank" or "I'll put down C of E, in case!" Concern for my ultimate destination showed in extreme in the case of Rosie, a little nurse from Babies Castle at Doctor Barnado's. Strict chapel, she was very worried lest anything terminal should happen to me on one of my visits to the operating theatre. You see, she was aware that I worked in the Other Theatre. Apparently it was easier for this poor man to go through the eye of a needle than to enter the kingdom of heaven via all those stage doors.

An advantage of this kind of leisurely passage through sanatoria was that one really got to know one's nurses in all their infinite variety. Chats day after day over blanket baths and the like gave plenty of opportunity to find out about each other. Little Rosie wanted to become a missionary in Africa but I would not have dreamed of teasing her about it. My first school being a convent, I knew well what Hell Fire could be like and could appreciate her concern on my behalf. All this is to anticipate.

To return to September 1939: what the directors of Strand Electric should have realised, and the three founders certainly would have, was that you don't keep theatre under for long in a war. And certainly not in the "phoney war" period that followed the outbreak. After all, the infant Strand Electric had survived the 1914-18 war; so what had the firm of silver jubilee age got to fear? These remarks do not apply, however, to the next World War as anyone not as stupid as the politicians realises. Even theatre cannot cope with the nuclear contamination after the explosions.

"And why shouldn't I write it down?"

To sit around at home doing nothing after war had been declared, needed more courage than I possessed. So it was off to the Strand Electric works, which had recently moved to much larger premises at Talbot Road West Ealing. Jim Jordan, as the Works manager, found me a part-time job. It was back to £3 a week; and in the mornings I could be seen sitting on a high stool in the middle of nowhere shrouded in Union Jacks and gazing down a telescope, a phone in my hand. My role was not that of an over-patriotic plane spotter. My job was to check the cut-off angles of something called screen-pillars, or I think they were, destined for the Ark Royal and other aircraft carriers. I am much clearer about the Union Jacks. These were to keep out the draught. They were left-overs from over-optimistic stocking-up for the George VI Coronation. I was scared of taking another chill and these colourful layers over my overcoat showed that, whatever else was impaired, the inventive genius still functioned.

I did not keep this job for long. At the slightest pretext I would sneak back to Covent Garden. Also I was too strict, so there were far too many rejects during my turns of duty. The theatres soon re-opened. At first it was in the daytime only, but then as the bombers did not come, the hours were extended. Theatre people expected their props as usual. So although the windows on King Street remained close-boarded, I found myself taking the odd customer through the back door into something so gloomy that not even that old showroom of 1932 resembled it. One of these visitors was a girl so ravishingly pretty that had it not been that she had a stinking cold which made me keep my distance, who knows if I could have resisted temptation? Fear of infection can work two ways but the result is the same, contact must not be made.

If I had known it, I need not have worried about keeping a grip, however slight, on Strand; before long out of the blue was to come the touch of a magic wand. War or no war - someone wanted a Light Console! Applebee had quoted, in competition with the Germans, for a complete new stage lighting installation to go into the S'Carlos opera house in Lisbon. Those were the days, before Lend-Lease, when we were encouraged to export. This country had to get the money in somehow.

On behalf of the Minister dos Obras Publicas e Monumentos Edifos a letter arrived saying: "What about the piano?" The Strand quote had stuck to the usual Grand Master as the easy way but the Light Console featured prominently in the catalogue and its photographs intrigued the Portuguese. Certainly in this case it was the odd non-resemblance to any switchboard which sold it. But I anticipate. Applebee and I had to go out with our interpreter and clinch the matter in Lisbon. And what an interpreter we took with us! 'Old Martin' was an elderly French-Canadian who had worked as an engineer in Switzerland once upon a time and had worked in the theatre since. He was well known to some Strand people.

Lisbon seemed a long way away in those early months of the war. A full four days travelling of which there was a night in Paris and two nights on the Sud-Express. The journey started from Victoria early and inauspiciously. Old Martin had the temerity to complain about the coffee on the Southern railway train; not its quality - he had lived too long in England - but its temperature. There was no doubt about it, our coffee was nigh-on stone cold. The steward's retort to his complaint was, "It can't be." and that was that. It was only when we joined the boat at Newhaven and Martin retired to lie down below as a precaution against mal de mer that we got some peace.

It was a bleak grey day in the early part of 1940 and as the ship rolled and yawed a door banged shut loudly only to prime itself for the next big bang. Pursuing the hint, I decided that in the event of a torpedo it would be a waste of time for me to take to the boats and embark on the inevitable pleurisy and pneumonia cruise. However, once safely on terra franca all this vanished; for there it was, an excitingly novel train known as the "Michelin" in which we were to shoot off to Paris. It was a streamlined multiple-unit Diesel to Pullman standard and the Michelin bit came from the rubber-tyred wheels which ran on the rails.

Paris was by no means as blacked-out as London. Everything was very civilised except for the mutton. It was my first encounter with the raw deal French cuisine bestows on roast mutton. On the return journey we three saw the Casino de Paris show with Josephine Baker and Maurice Chevalier. We had seats in the front row stalls and I was much impressed with the torrent of saliva from the famous bottom lip. It could clearly be seen in the limes from where we sat. This prime location was due to Strand Electric of course. A certain M.Gabriel pulled off the trick. He had some connection with our firm, so did one M.Vernon at the Alhambra Paris. Indeed the whole 1930 installation in that Gaumont house was by Strand.

The Wagon-Lit Sud-Express left Gare St. Lazaire the following night and in due comfortable course we were deposited at Hendaye. There we had to change to another set of Wagon-Lits at Irun just across the frontier. This was in part due to the change of gauge. The Iberian peninsular used 5ft instead of 4ft 8½" but I rather think our short walk was due the fact that the Civil War had not long ended. As there were three hours or so before the train departure, we were able to look around the largely destroyed town and have a meal there. There were lots of troops swaggering about. Each man with an army blanket swung across his shoulders as if it were a cloak. It was all very Spanish. Dinner in the hotel featured "petits oiseaux" which turned out to be just that: a boney dish of starved sparrows.

Back on the train, the Wagons-Lits were the real thing this time. Built in Birmingham at the peak period for this type of mahogany-fitted carriage work. The French train had been more up to date - clad in steel and somewhat 'Bauhaused' inside. The Portuguese ones were well maintained working museum pieces from the real age of the train - way back before any British Rail marketing men were thought of. Round about midday the train crossed the frontier from Fuentes de Onoro to Vilar Formoso; exchanging a dirty squalid slum with the inevitable Spanish soldiers for a neat tiled station - complete with girl in her best National (or rather local) costume walking along the platform. This was the first indication that Lisbon might not be the dirty, greasy, Latin city my imagination had painted! The farewell to Spain had just involved each of us in solitary interrogation in an atmosphere heavy with garlic and a portrait of General Franco. Since it was conducted entirely in rapid Spanish, of which I knew not one word, it could not be said to serve any purpose whatever.

The reference to the tiled station may mislead. These were beautiful decorative tiles and we were to find that their use was common practice in Portugal. The train ran into Lisbon station through a tunnel. Yet when we went to catch a taxi we found we were on the top of a hill with the city spread out below. It was another of those cities on seven hills and a very lovely place it turned out to be. It was rather like the reverse of Waverley station where one suddenly ascends into Edinburgh and the city all around very much in view.

The interior of the S'Carlos opera house proved to be as beautiful architecturally as its city. This particular building opened in June 1793 having been built to replace the one by Bibiena which had been totally wrecked by the great earthquake of 1755. After 132 years of service it was closed in 1925 as being in need of extensive maintenance, and that is how we saw it fourteen years later. Although a great deal of restoration and redecoration had yet to take place to re-open it on December 1st, it was impossible not to be impressed. So much so that I was unable, when the committee adjourned for a 'natural' break, to join the others as each stood in his own private box, as if it were a palatial urinal, facing and admiring the auditorium at the same time. For my part I sought out a remote backstage store and braved the gaze of the ancient props with which it was crammed. Retrospectively, I find myself wondering whether there had been any provision for toilets in the original building or whether it was that the drains were by then in such a chronic state as to be unable to cope with even this piddling burden. All was well when the time came to install the job, and in fact our site office-cum-store was next door to, and in acoustic connection with, the backstage 'Senhoras' - so much so that I dubbed it 'Notre WC'. This caught on and it was always referred to as 'Votre WC' by those in the know. Another thing impossible to get used to, this time for all three of us, was the way our Portuguese chairman would start hawking noisily in the middle of business, go to the window, throw it open and dispatch a lethal projectile into outer space. Since we met each day in the grand salon immediately above the main entrance, we took good care to enter by the stage door. We found that spitting went on everywhere; it seemed to be a custom that nobody but us noticed. This was strange as everything was otherwise clean and tidy - certainly much more so than London is today as I write these memories. What Lisbon did have was beggars, something I never thought I would see here.

As usual, when Applebee was around we went to several shows. We had made the mistake of arriving a few days before Carnival so we had to hang around before the Portuguese would get down to business, however urgent. On the night itself we found ourselves in a variety house where the programme seemed to have been extended to infinity. The audience got more and more relaxed and we grew more and more restive, as lengthy turn followed lengthy turn at even lengthier intervals. It was like a very intimate family party and the fact that immensities of time passed without anything happening on the stage did not matter to them. Suddenly the woman in the row immediately in front of us turned right round and produced a large scent spray from her corsage. She shoved the nozzle at Applebee's chest and pumped the cheap contents all over his shirt - there was no escape. Another vivid memory is of a slender but shapely young black girl doing slow cartwheels centre stage at the Coliseu. Although well clad in today's terms, the effect of gravity was amply demonstrated. 'They' lagged until well past the vertical whereupon there was a sudden flop and bounce. I was just wondering if I was the only one with a mind like mine, when I caught the eye of a Portuguese nearby and language for once presented no barrier. Gradually members of the audience caught on and tittering broke out here and there, to increase with each unwitting wheel. The real lifelong impression to take away was the encounter on the first trip with the Portuguese fado. All three of us were quite unprepared for it and were completely captivated by a young fado singer in a largish theatre in a fairground of sorts just off the Grand Avenida running up to the Parc Eduardo VII (our Edward VII!). We talked of how Cochran ought to bring her over to capture London. What her name was and how she got on out there I have no means of knowing. What I do know is that on none of my subsequent visits did I encounter her equal.

On our return to England we had to set about making the equipment. Our large Talbot Road factory was full of work for the Admiralty (those patriotic pillars and landing lights and the like!) but Export still had a high priority. It was 'the piano' which might have stymied us because Comptons had gone completely over to the wood fuselages for Hurricanes. However J.I. Taylor, that superb improviser upon the organ and the firm's technical director, said that now we had an order for a Light Console they must make it somehow. So there it was a loner among an entire factory swept by Hurricanes. A photograph exists in which the three-manual console is standing there with a fairing for one of these aircraft, uncensored inadvertently in the background.

The "Battle of Britain" was by now in full swing but I had a private one which included dubious health prospects and a conviction that this was the last chance ever for me and my Light Console. When it and the dimmer bank came together at Talbot Road I had to have someone at the other end while we made the main cable - our first ever! Comptons could not spare anyone and Paul Weston was the only other one in Strand who had seen the technique, so there he had to be - and he was. The job was labelled in Portuguese throughout, so the works chap (Jim Haden) would trot up with the 26-gauge DCC enamelled wire and say "Tom Urd Pal R." and as I passed the wire over the nail would retort "Pl Vert Fr" or some such, and away Jim would go back to Paul. Every now and then we would have to drop the job and adjourn to the air raid shelter, there to watch with a great deal of non-comprehension interminable games of Solo. It seemed improbable that this job of mine would ever be completed, let alone installed.

This doubt changed to certainty when having at last tested and packed-up the dimmer banks and all the rest and dispatched them to the London docks, Hitler opted to concentrate bombing on that area. For three successive nights I could look across London from the house at Harrow and see the great red glare in the sky which signalled the end to all my ambitions. But in fact it didn't! The Lisbon equipment was in the basement of its blitzed warehouse and survived to be shifted up to Liverpool, thence to be embarked on a two month voyage. Two months to Lisbon must seem like a printing error. Lord knows where and by what routes the boat went but it certainly crossed the Atlantic to get there.

Eventually we were warned to be ready to receive and install the stuff. Theoretically, the three of us were to return plus Applebee's favourite foreman, Bill Pepworth, to go and put the job in. But France having fallen it was necessary to travel by air or not at all. And the Air Ministry decided that it was to be not at all. This was hardly surprising since there was only one Civil flight a week - a survival of the Empire flying boat era. There were only six places and this was the link with the entire Empire and the Pan-Am clipper to USA via Bermuda, as well! The party was reduced to Bill Pepworth and I but there was still no room. We lobbied A.P. Herbert, then an MP and the one who would know how important first nights and opening dates really were. The best he could suggest was that we should get our agent, Arriaga de Tavares to tackle his government. After all, it was they who were going to celebrate 'oitos seculos' of this and 'trois seculos' of that with a State re-opening of the Lisbon S'Carlos opera house. The idea worked. Armed with a Portuguese visa with "At the extraordinary request of his Excellency the Ambassador" written in red ink across it we were allocated a date and a couple of places.

The intervening days conspired with German aid to suggest that we would be lucky if we both made those places in one piece. Eventually, however, we checked-in at the Royal Bath Hotel Bournemouth on the appointed evening. This improbable luxury rendezvous was part of the Imperial Airways package. A car called to collect us, plus four aloof pillars of the Empire, from the front steps of the Royal Bath very early the following morning - long before dawn - and take us to Poole harbour. Travel by flying boat was unlike any other flying and this was my first flight ever. It was a decidedly nautical affair involving a tender and a jetty at each end: the fact that the boat took to the air for the voyage itself was incidental. We couldn't see out of our windows anyway, as they had been covered over. We had to take the take-off on trust, so to speak. Opaque white Perspex (or whatever it was then) was attached to each small window by four suckers and we were, in effect, put on our honour not to pull them open and spy out. There was no one to ensure that we didn't, the crew having departed upstairs, but we did not: not even Bill Pepworth the only one of the party who had not obviously been to public school!

Take-off in this packing case consisted of a series of jerks aloft as if we were being lugged up by a human team at the end of a rope. One of the air crew appeared, put a plate of bacon and sausage (which somehow I did not fancy) in front of each of us and departed. While I was considering what to pick out and nibble, a white glaze of congealed fat formed overall. The 'pillar of Empire' immediately opposite had wolfed the lot and presented a clean plate to my eye. I felt humiliated. It showed how tough the school of Empire was: not just a matter of chota pegs and sundowners, but big bangers and bacon at sun up. However, the sun was not the only thing that came up at that time, for the 'pillar' vanished hurriedly and was seen no more that trip. The word 'trip' is used quite deliberately because after two miserable hours we learned that we were turning round to go back to Poole.

The next day we did not get any further than the pre-dawn parade on the hotel steps. The following morning after three nights of Royal Bathing at the airway's expense it was now six comrades, buddies or pals who climbed aboard in Poole Harbour. We were not served breakfast, nor did a single one of us voice a complaint! The journey was dire: bumping along the odd hundred feet above the waves to dodge the head wind. When at last the Perspex was taken away, there it was - the sea - all storm-tossed waves just under the window. Fourteen hours the poor old flying boat 'Claire' took. Post-war in one of the very early Viscounts I did the journey in four hours; now it is advertised as taking one and a half. Two thirds of the way there the sun came out of hiding, the plane made for the sky and we sought out the hampers in the empty cabin below. The plane was literally stripped for action in order to take aboard the vast amount of fuel necessary. In peacetime there were many overnight stops in interesting places on the Empire routes and it must have been a very gentlemanly way of travel. These craft became better known for their role as Sunderlands in the war. They were very big for the time. Hunting around above the clouds for Lisbon a mountain-top suddenly stuck up through the cloud and our four engines revved and we cleared it steeply. I asked Pepworth, who had been in the Flying Corps in the previous war, whether it was usual and he said "No!". In some such way both HRH the Duke of Kent (my Light Console inspector) and Leslie Howard (the stage and film actor) may have met their ends when they disappeared on the same route some weeks later. The Claire itself was wrecked while moored on the river Tagus during the hurricane we experienced out there. It was Nature's own air raid; sheets of glass whizzed down along the street like so much airborne paper and a chimney stack was blown down our hotel lift shaft.

We found the Tagus and moored there in the sunset. There was such a pretty effect on the wide waters of the river that I was often to go down there to enjoy it during my six month's stay. We were lodged just up the road from the S'Carlos at the Hotel Borges. Short though the walk was - a matter of five minutes at most - it was ambushed half-way by the York Bar. In a letter I sent to Jack Sheridan which was then typed out and circulated round the firm to keep them abreast of our adventures, I wrote, "Here it is that Pep could, his work done, be seen tapping the barrel, muttering "grande" whilst holding his hands about 3 foot apart. Now the man does not need to be told. Here it is I come for my nightly beer instead of my usual milk so greatly do things differ." That long letter contains much detail but it is only now after all these years that I realise that one sentence must have been deleted by our wartime censor. There is no other way of accounting for something which I know I wrote not being there; but that must await its turn later on in this chapter.

Mind you, I myself had censored something. Lisbon was full of refugees most of whom were hanging around hoping for a chance to get to the USA, and every now and again there was a great clearance in the Hotel Borges, which filled again immediately after. Pep and I were lucky therefore to share a double bed room with bath. But all seemed far from well - I suffered from continual night-sweats. Was illness going to intervene once again? I had to take care and decided to spend a couple of days in bed, in case! I must confess to sometimes envying those who suffer from a physical handicap. That is something tangible to fight against, but what do you do with something where the doctor's recipe is to rest and not overdo it? This has been stated as: never stand when you can sit; never sit when you can lie down. So I remained in bed while Pep went off to the theatre to do what he could before our equipment was unloaded at the docks.

Far from improving I got worse, ran a temperature and perspired all day. Pep discovered that one of the English refugees in the hotel, a rum crowd from the French Riveira with no intention of going to England, was a doctor. He came to my bedside and pointed out immediately that it was infernally hot and did I know that our room was directly above the kitchen. In a sense his subsequent examination was unnecessary but it did give him a chance to ask for a guinea fee! All the hotel could find was a tiny little room on the noisy street but there I moved leaving Pep the grandeur of the double-room with bath. A return to my contemporary account is the best way of dealing with the arrival of the Strand equipment:

The apparatus was unloaded very smartly into the scene dock including the piano, but no relay, this took them from about 1.30 to 4 pm, there seemed to be a hell of a lot of packing cases. Then about 5 pm, there arrived (up the hill) three small lorries with three large packing cases. These were to go straight into the Dimmer room. It was obvious that the packing cases would not go through the door, so they were unpacked in the street. Lamps were rigged and the traffic stopped; by this time we had quite an audience. I will not describe the nervous strain of what followed, both Pep and I thought the lorry would tip up as the case was manhandled over the tail-gate. Unfortunately, owing to the layout of the room Teclado 3 (Manual 3), the largest section, had to be got in first. When this finally reached the ground and amid loud hammerings the case was removed we could see that it was not going through the doorway. However, ONCE the Portuguese do move, they do and no mistake. The masons arrived and in about twenty minutes the concrete and stone steps were removed using pickaxes only. Then began a terrifying spectacle, with groans, crashes and mighty swayings the section arrived approximately in position. The other two followed, the job being complete just about 9 pm.
While this was going on, the Customs Broker would persist in carrying on a rapid conversation in French about "cette jolie piece" etc. and as my heart was in my mouth most of the time it would have been difficult to talk in English let alone in French. The men worked from lunch until after nine without a break for anything, drink or food and they worked with a real will and never a grumble. Pep and I took turn to return to the hotel to eat our dinner. They deserved the drinks we stood them afterwards.

My account also covers the events of the next few days and includes a "tribute to the system which gave the Customs a complete list of case contents and ourselves nothing useful at all." It continues:

There was a touching picture at one time of Engineer Martins (in charge for the Minister) and Arriaga (Strand's agent) peeping through the partly opened lid of the 'piano' packing case to satisfy their curiosity. The general opening of the parcels, cases etc., reminded me of opening Christmas presents, all excitement. The rain effect (rain-box), for instance, everybody played with it.

> *While the console case was opened all work seemed to stop... From that time on neither the console or the dimmer bank has been free of visitors. Parties are conducted round by various notabilities who give voluble explanations with assurance. I feel certain from experience in England that they have got it all wrong. They are, of course, quite safe from my protests since neither they nor I understand one another... You can have no idea what it is like trying to get things done here. The language difficulty does not help, and it is very hard to see that 'our' men do only our jobs. There was a time when every time Pep's back was turned the men would vanish from the stage and start once again polishing the dimmer bank. Above all we are hampered by "tomorrow"; everything can be answered by "tomorrow".*

All this was in spite of the fact that it was a matter of days before the date of the Gala performance which had to re-open S'Carlos. There was a battle to be fought over the location of the Light Console. On our previous visit this had been settled, as I wanted, in the orchestra pit. On our return they indicated that there had been a change of mind and it was going on the stage.

> *Apparently everyone was for it in the pit except the Maestro. I put my foot down many times and the Minister decided after visiting the theatre at nearly midnight that it must go in the orchestra. Meantime the Maestro, who is also the composer of the Gala opera and speaks a little English, congratulates me on the console and says he doesn't mind it in the orchestra at all. It is moved there and I put the cable on.*
>
> *Five days later I am told that the Minister had been to the theatre the night before and had decided that the orchestra would not have enough room and the console must go on the side of the stage. This has to be investigated as the Maestro was still willing. It is the architect that has complained that it did not match the auditorium! Everyone agrees it should go in the pit but the architect is afraid that its presence will draw attention from his restoration of the auditorium.*

The Minister's decision was reversed and in the orchestra it has remained ever since. Though not in the prominent position I secured and held for it while I was there. These battles will be familiar to most of those who have done export installations or indeed any complicated technical job in a theatre. Lisbon was more special than most, so to speak. It was the great chance to show off my own cherished invention. It could well be the last chance, being a race against the hazards of war and illness. It just had to be right: I was going to light the show and work it from the console, there was no one else to do it. Thus, when on returning after a couple of days off for a cold I found a deep glossy blue cyc staring at me instead of the matt white one I had left, there was nothing for it but to get it re-painted. No mean feat since it was a great affair made of wood which encompassed half the stage. The Minister had once again to be involved.

Far more serious, indeed in retrospect a hurdle impossible to surmount, though I did give the matter some thought the night before setting off to the docks to enquire, was the missing console relay. This poignant episode must have been censored from my contemporary account above. Because where I described going up to the tired and haggard captain of the battered old merchantman, feeling an absolute heel to bother him about the relay which was to do something so unimportant as to make stage lighting work. Obviously, it was not done in wartime to describe a *British* captain as “tired and haggard”. I found him leaning against the bulwarks supervising some job on what seemed a singularly empty and weather-beaten small ship. He immediately suggested we take a look and led me into a hold in which the same emptiness ruled overall. However before despair could take over, there it was - the missing Compton relay - looking very small partially hidden behind a bulkhead. It was this which enabled the relatively few wires of the main cable to multiply and activate all the contactor and clutch coils and the rest. Without it there was no alternative to manual operation by a gang of slaves at the end of a telephone line in the dimmer room. The ‘piano’ would have been a fraud.

We did not get any current to run or test the job until November 22nd though we were ready four days earlier. However, we did open on December 1st - the appointed day. There was only the one rehearsal, the dress, and this of a brand new opera of which I was not even given a summary or any idea of what the scenes were going to be. We knew that they were building half a boat because we could see it, in the scene dock at the back. They had been at this for days, carefully planking out both sides of the hull so that we could not decide whether the action was to take place aboard or alongside.

Eventually out of nowhere a painted set was hung. It was at this point that some real theatre people made their entrance. Essentially practical, they were used to putting on shows whatever the conditions. The little stage manager was particularly impressive - a type we would all recognise in any country. It went without saying that I would light the show, work the console and mend it if it broke down. He would see that the scenery and singers got on and off the stage at the proper times. From his rapid French which I could not follow, I gleaned that the first act

S'Carlos Lisbon, November 1940

was a room in a palace, with a sunset, a couple of candle cues and a vision or two. The second act was aboard ship, opening as night with a slow dawn for the entire act. The last act was a full-up, fine day in the Black Horse Square in Lisbon and that was what was hanging there at the moment.

Well, the first thing was to get rid of the sky borders which formed an integral part of the set in order to give the cyclorama a chance. This was done there and then; and what had been a series of cutcloths one behind the other became painted wing pieces lashed to the carriage and frame machinery with which this old stage was still equipped. How to light this and the other two scenes had to await the dress rehearsal that very night, by which time the safety curtain (which had remained obstinately down so the Maestro could rehearse) would be raised, presumably. We met our stage hands and gave them an idea how the Patt. 73 spots on the bridges and the five 1-kW Stelmars out in the dome functioned. Those five must have been the last ever made.

Returning from the Hotel Borges after dinner Pep and I got a shock. It was quite impossible: the wings on both sides were packed tight with people who obviously did not belong on-stage or off-stage.

Who were they and why were they there? They were the poor people of Lisbon who had been invited along to see the rehearsal. Why were they not out-front? You cannot have them sitting in the new clean seats which will be bottomed-out tomorrow night by the highest in the land. By then I had two interpreters in train, one for the lower orders and the other for society contact. The latter was no ordinary man, and he and I set out to see the Minister who, with a select few, occupied the very grand ex-Royal box out-front centre. The poor people of Lisbon will never know why, magically, their fortune changed that one night and they were ordered to occupy the stalls!

Lanterns had been set to cover likely areas of the stage and except for the odd special it was a matter of painting the stage and action from the console as the drama unfolded. We have become used to a view of the stage from the lighting control nowadays: but until then it had been all theory. But it worked! The vibrations at the base of my spine from my immediate neighbours, the basses and cellos, were peculiar and the Act I vision extreme stage right could not be seen from pit left, of course. But Pep was able to give me a commentary on the phone. For the final scene I got all the colours removed from the spots on both bridges (a total of 18 Patt.73s plus spots elsewhere - about thirty-six in all).

The fleecy clouds floated by to begin with - they had to be shown off - and after I had slowly taken them out I adjourned to one of the Grand tier boxes, there to ponder. The auditorium was superb for music and there on the stage was Lisbon as I had come to know it - the dazzling white sunlight on the buildings against a strong blue sky. I looked upon my work and thought it good. The dawn on board ship had been great fun to do too.

The following night was to present three hazards of which not the least was how to get in the place! Lisbon performances did not begin until 9-15pm. Returning after dinner (Pep had taken his earlier) clad in full tails and white tie I found the opera house was ringed with troops on both sides of the road. Wandering in and out over the weeks as if I owned the place, I had not thought to ask for a pass; nor had they thought to give me one. For a few minutes I thought all was lost. Visions of incarceration pending enquiry seemed all too realistic in this dictatorship; especially as a political jail was immediately alongside the theatre, forming a continuation of the backstage building, as had been pointed out to me earlier on.

Time passed. There was nothing for it: I pushed through the crowd, tapped the nearest soldier on the shoulder, declared firmly, "Je suis tres importante." and set out to cross the sanded road. I was not shot in the back or in the front. I probably owe my life to my 'midnight-blue' tails by Ellis of the Strand; I looked very smart. But not a patch on Arriaga de Tavares and my social interpreter: resplendent with starry orders and super sashes they were hovering anxiously with Bill Pepworth who looked, as he always did, large, droopy and relaxed. My entrance to the orchestra pit was breathtaking. Not for the audience, I hasten to add; but for me. The S'Carlos auditorium was lovely in itself; beautifully restored and lit, exactly in period even to retaining the line of boxes on the stage itself. In a sense the place looked its best when seen from the stage end. I could never get used to the large clock over the proscenium whereas the 'Royal' box slap in the centre at the other end was superb. Overall, hung a great crystal chandelier and along the box tiers crystal brackets. Not a single FOH spot had been allowed to intrude. The 1kW Stelmar spots were behind apertures, which could be closed manually in the 'dome', and four 500W spots (Patt.44s) were completely concealed in the column at the front of the stage on either side.

From the lighting point of view these were not as acute as might be, due to the boxes on the stage itself which meant that there was a permanent carpetted no-man's land forestage before the house tabs. These boxes had got Applebee's (and my) goat on our Sud Express visit. They were subject to argument upon argument, with and without the Minister. We had a considerable body of opinion in favour of their removal on our side. It was not a matter of losing seats as they were not accessible to the public. When I returned for the installation, the boxes were still there; we had lost and the architect had won. Today the words "I am glad to say" have to be added.

From the pit this auditorium filled with people, dressed as only a small country can, had become a fairyland with orders, sashes and bright uniforms abounding. It was a scene from an epic Ruritanian film and this was *my* night. This was what my whole career had been leading up to and would, only too probably, end with. It was to be savoured to the full, not a drop to be wasted.

After the Spanish ambassador had entered to a standing ovation, it was President Carmona's turn while the real master, Doctor Salazar, stood quietly to one side. No display for this, then, unusual dictator. One never saw his portrait hanging up anywhere in his country; thus it was that Carmona took centre 'stage' that night.

I cannot remember if there was an overture or a short prelude but I do know that when the velvet tabs parted (in disorder since the two halves were worked separately, each from its own side) the house lights descended only to half-check and stayed there. It was inconceivable that the dimmer had broken down as we had been asked to supply, as an economy, a manual board for that. A frantic enquiry of my 'hot line' alongside evoked his response that the house lights were never taken right out when his illustrious Excellency was in any theatre. He was much loved but it was a precaution.

Disaster impended: not only were there those night sequences and visions in this, the first act, but what about my lovely starry opening and slow dawn in the next? 'Hot line' was dispatched hot foot. After a while, the house dimmed to blackout. His illustrious excellency was not shot: that made two of us who were lucky to escape that night.

At the end of Act II Dr. Salazar sent a message of congratulation on my dawn via 'Hot line' (who else?), saying that it reminded him of those he used to see at Coimbra. Before taking charge of Portugal he used to be a professor of mathematics at that university - their 'Oxbridge'. He could not have known that the third disaster to avert had suddenly presented itself just before the end of that very act. My long dawn done, I was just relaxing when I noticed that sailors up aloft were untying ropes here and there and were just about to unfurl a very large sail. It would run right across the stage like the fore and after sails on a Thames barge. There was no sign or warning of this at the rehearsal. If one had wanted to intercept the spots on No.1 bridge and towers to give the effect of a patchwork quilt, this was the best way to do it. To select the appropriate tabs (stopkeys) took but a moment and a quick check as the sail came down and 'my' scene was saved.

Looking back over the many years at this production of *Don Joao IV* and the way it was put on, I have to say, in spite of all the intervening developments, there could not have been a better control and position than my Light Console in the orchestra pit. From there it was possible to see a singer oscillating the adam's apple or licking the lips before bursting into song. Instantly the circuit or circuits for that area were selected and the light gently increased as the mouth opened. A modern memory board would have been hopeless. My plot had only one line on it; the opening dimmer levels for the starry night on board ship. I wanted the tabs to open on this, so the levels had to be set without being able to check them visually. When as here you have a cyc with the three primary colours the mixture has to be precise.

An important feature of the layout was the setting of the spots to cover areas rather than the acting and the quantity of lanterns, and their numbers were low enough to be memorable. No question of reference to a plan or schedule arose. Leaving aside the fixed parts of the layout, like the twelve cyc circuits, the five 4-colour battens and the like, hardly any use was made of the men on the bridges and towers except to remove the colours. The closeness of console to stage enabled me to hop-up via the pass door and climb the bridges from stage level and set the lanterns exactly myself. Not, I hasten to add, during the show itself. Tails were worn very long indeed in the thirties. Like good theatre people anywhere, once the electricians had been shown what to do at the rehearsal, the odd wave and pointing from the stage was all that was needed during the performance. Backstage there were these few men, including of course Bill Pepworth, who knew how to get a show on. Language was not so serious, we could in large part read each other's minds. This was not peculiar to Lisbon but rather to Strand's role in theatre. We acted as both contractors and users, in effect. The reason was that someone from the R&D dept. had to be there to teach the way to use our more novel switchboards. Another reason was the supply (hire more often than not) of equipment specific to a production; the creation of an installation within an installation.

The Gala over, two clear days had to elapse before the next performance, in order, so I was told, to allow the de rigeur dress clothes to circulate. One more gap of two or three days and that was that. Three performances and except for the odd concert there was nothing to follow. The Italian Opera could not face the wartime journey. There was an interesting Portuguese ballet company in Oporto, but why they were not booked I do not know. Perhaps they were not experienced enough to dance on the very steep rake at S'Carlos. Something had to be done, so I played my colour music card. The records came from the very limited collection at the Emissora Nacional. The cyc was used but I had to have some white drapes which meant a visit to the Lisbon equivalent of John Lewis' just down the hill. I can still see the girl who served me. She wore a dark blue overall but with time her nipples had worn two holes in it so that her white blouse showed through. I invited her to the show but she didn't turn up so I had to make do with a dream or two.

I suppose the most substantial feature of these few recitals was the inclined plane that was constructed to mask the double row ground-row for the cyc bottom, there being no pit or trough. Back in England a few narrow flats propped up would have sufficed but here we enjoyed a formidable timber structure: built in sections to butt together, by those self same 'boat- builders'. The standard of craftsmanship was very high. All special bits required in the restoration of the opera house, and they were many, were made then and there on the spot. Great wood staircase balusters and the metalwork and all the rest. They also had the continental facility for cooking where ere they worked; hot meals, not just sandwiches. ('Old' Martin's biggest problem when we came to do the Palladium was to find somewhere to heat up his daily casserole.)

Bill Pepworth left as soon as he could after we opened. I stayed on to train Madail Rodriques in the operation of the Light Console and its maintenance along with all the other equipment. He and I became friends able to communicate, even to joke, using 'Notre Langue' as we called it. This was odd bits of Portuguese and English linked by very bad French. For a Frenchman to listen to it would have been torture; but we became very fluent as we did not have to bother about pronunciation or grammar.

Arriaga d'Tavares' office was down in Rua Boa Vista, and, as is customary over there, I was never invited to his home. Boa Vista was not how I would have described it, there was no view of anything but it could be fun nevertheless. On one of my afternoon visits, possibly about the Coliseu Oporto I had been to see, I rang the bell as usual. There was no answer however many times I rang. It was inconceivable that the office was closed. Suddenly the door opened abruptly and I was confronted by 'Heinrich Himmler' who immediately turned on his heel and left me to it. At the same time I became aware of much girlish glee off-stage. It was a well staged prank which we all enjoyed. The German represented a steel firm for which Arriaga was also agent. Apparently he had an office at the very top of the building and for a German to have to descend to open the door for an Englishman...!

It was nearly six months before I got a seat in the plane to return home; this time in the KLM Dakota which had been added to make a second flight each week. Applebee wangled this by pointing out that I was of military age. They failed to check my medical to see if I was worth bringing home, so home I came. I must say that looking round at the lit-up Lisbon on my last night I had a feeling that I was crazy to go home. All the more so, when on being shown into my room at the Royal Bristol (the Dakota was of course a landplane) I saw my window was covered over with brown paper; the glass having been blown out the night before. I rang Mother to tell her I had landed and she asked, with her usual concern, what I would get to eat on the train journey? My reply that I had a banana left over from the plane journey provoked: "Don't eat that! Save it for your sister," which I did, such things having long vanished from the land of England.

In contrast with the plane trip out, the one back (with a half and half crew of Dutch and British) had been uneventful - at least for the other passengers. About half-way I noticed that there was an altimeter at the front end of the cabin and that its needle had been censored by removing it. Unhappily it reminded me of the unwritten, and therefore well-known, law among us 'weak-chested' that an altitude over 5000-ft was dangerous. This thought had just registered when there was a sharp stabbing pain in the region of my right nipple. This followed at not infrequent intervals and there was no doubt about it I must stop breathing. This I did. In the business of landing and taking the taxi to the hotel the pain vanished. Once the brown paper window had been assimilated I realised that it was jolly cold. An immediate change to the warmer underwear, out of use since the previous October, was just the thing. Off came the Aertex vest and with it a vicious double-ended wood splinter *fully four inches long*; on cue the sirens began wailing but as I sat looking at it, what did I care!

It might be supposed that forty-two years in the same firm pursuing the same line of work could become humdrum, but it must be apparent by now, that there have been lacunae every bit as full of strain as a change of career. It is common to associate strain with overwork but to some of us boredom is the real hazard. My father-in-law ran the family bank at Neuteich before he had to up-anchor and move to Danzig and become a chartered accountant. Thanks to the Nazis he was to consider himself lucky to get the job of kitchen-porter at the Dorchester hotel. At the end of the war he moved to New York to play much the same role in a hospital. His long life, he lived to be ninety, spanned the whole range from an officer in the German cavalry in the First World War* to being one of those efficient continental nobodies who just get on with their lowly task, apparently without ambition. I never once heard him bemoan his lot. Nor had he been an easy-going man in his earlier 'incarnation'. For example, the groom who had been his batman had to come each day to clean his boots since the maid, who sufficed for all the others, was not considered good enough at it. I can only wonder at, and admire, this man's acceptance of the change of life.

As I sat in the train to town I know, though I don't remember, that there must have been a feeling of being lost - where was even a single familiar thread to pick-up for my kind of work to be found? A return to the Union Jacks and that blessed telescope could not be tolerated but how, with war in full cry, could there be any slot for me? Away for nearly half a year in a land of peace it was a stranger who reported to Jack Sheridan and Stanley Earnshaw; they had about as much idea of what to do with me as I had!

I wandered down into the basement and there was my lovely lighting theatre surprisingly intact, but not completely unused. On a table between the stage and the fixed seating area was a crude arrangement of lenses, retort stands and bits of bent tin. Vaguely it suggested an epidiascope. After a bit Frank Weston wandered in and told me in his intolerant way that some professor or other was mucking about with it for Mr. Corry of Manchester. At that time Percy Corry was mainly notable to me as the man who had re-printed some of the pages of my 1936 catalogue with Fitups of Manchester as a tailpiece instead of Strand Electric and Engineering Company. He had soon after started a Manchester branch, and as Mr. P. Corry, "Actor - Producer - Playwright," was introduced in the very first *TABS* ever: an issue neither numbered or dated, but known to be October 1937. A quote from the *Daily Express* said: "Corry is lean, dark and dry - does not look old enough to have been acting since 1911." He certainly looked dark in the photo alongside the *TABS* piece - the kind of smudge which became all too familiar in our national newspapers until their exodus from Fleet Street. His "Height of Ambition" in a fatuous last line, was "To sell a Strand Light Console!" With time he was in fact going to sell two and lots more of that ilk! Except for his regular articles as "Busker" in those very early *TABS* and

* Even in the Germany of that war, although he provided his own horses and batman, he could only be a warrant officer - because he was a Jew!

occasional visits, that was all I knew of him. The "Busker" articles can be seen now as the very first indication of the kind of journal *TABS* was to become. My own writing (we were all anon) was in contrast deadly dry and serious. My mission was to *convert* my readers!

If Percy Corry really did begin 'acting' in 1911, it was a nice coincidence because I began 'living' in that very same year and thanks to those lenses on the table in the demonstration theatre I was soon to get to know him very well. An elderly man came in and fiddled about and before very long - after a good lunch probably - Percy entered, with a tall thin lieutenant-commander RNVR and a couple of civilians, and said "Hullo" or something of the sort. Whether he added, "You may be interested in this," or not, I hung about; after all this was my theatre. The demonstration was feeble. There was little light, the image mostly out of focus and the amount of variable magnification nowhere near what they expected. Frank Weston and I became allies for the first time ever. He produced a 6-inch bi-convex lens from among his treasures and together we set about the problem. This was to project varying aspects and magnifications of a model ship so that pilots training to attack ships with torpedoes could do so while seated in a Link trainer which never did anything more than rotate and tilt within a great cyclorama.

How the trainer was to be connected to our projector and how the model within our epidiascope or its lenses were to be given their proper relative motion was for others. What had to be done, and quickly, was to show something optically impressive. The chronology and detail of the time is vague but I remember going to Bassett-Lowke's and buying some model ships and then inadvertently melting them with the amount of light I directed on them. Percy Corry had laid on a date to demonstrate our optical system to those that mattered; whereupon fate stepped in with two small bombs.

Returning from three days off to cover my brother's embarkation leave I went in through the Floral Street backdoor as usual up the stairs to my small office to find that the long corridor outside it, which extended over the theatre right through to King Street, terminated there and then with a temporary wall. I had had no warning; Jack and Stanley had thought it kinder to leave our family gathering undisturbed, which as he was destined to vanish (into Changi jail) for years, was just as well. The two bombs picked out my theatre alone, and the two floors above it descended gently into it, leaving the building at each end. The shock can be imagined; my theatre had gone. But the Light Console which had been moved under the balcony at the outbreak of war had survived, and so had the precious lenses of our optical experiment. They had got wrapped in the curtains blown off the stage into the auditorium. Before many days were out the experiment was demonstrated and given the go-ahead on the large echoing empty stage of the Adelphi theatre.

Percy Corry has described in *Sightline* (Vol.13 No.2) how he came to be involved in the T.A.T. (Torpedo Attack Teacher) first for the Fleet Air Arm* and then with destroyer and submarine variants for the Navy itself. The article is accompanied by three excellent contemporary drawings by Harry Rutherford the artist taken on by Percy to paint the sea around the lower part of the cyclorama. Fitups of Manchester had supplied scenery before the war; so the making and painting of it was a natural entry to the job for them. However, Percy Corry was not the man to play a secondary role for long and by the time I came in he was undoubtedly the driving force behind the whole thing; and this in spite of the fact that the idea had originated with a 'well-connected' RNVR Lieut-Commander. Coincidentally, Air Commodore Fellows ran the Link Trainer company JVW Corporation (of American origin), and it was he who had led the 1933 expedition which was the first to fly over Everest. This tribute to Percy's forcible personality is confirmed by the fact that although JVW were the main contractor on the original jobs, the Royal Navy made Fitups of Manchester the main contractor for the Destroyer and Submarine versions. In all cases Strand Electric were sub-contractors to Fitups - their agents in stage lighting!

The pilot scheme was to be at Crail on the eastward tip of Fifeshire just before it goes round the bend to St. Andrews. An attempt was made to lodge us at Kirkmay House in the village not far from the job. This was as dismal as it sounds. Of our trio only R.A. Mackenzie (born in Australia) did well with ample helpings at dinner and a hot-water bottle in his bed. All this was because he told the waitress she was wearing the Buchanan, or whatever, tartan. Frank Church, the third man, and I were genuinely puzzled at this esoteric knowledge. When quizzed, it turned out that the particular patch of tartan was immediately opposite that part of the Sussex Tartan Dive bar which Mackenzie had propped-up nightly in London.

A vote of two to one ensured that we upped anchor and moved to distant Elie where Corry, Fellows and McLeod lived in luxury (as it turned out). Wartime or not there was nothing to complain of with the food, accommodation and service in that sparsely populated hotel. This second Mac, Morgan McLeod, was to become important in the history of Strand, being the designer of the die-cast Patt. 23, the pressed steel Patt. 243 and much else before his early death in 1961. In the present instance he was JVW's engineer and responsible for joining their standard Link trainer equipment to the target projector which was as yet only a couple of experimental lenses. The Link trainer was a one-man aircraft with a complete cockpit and controls in a rudimentary fuselage. This was mounted on a pedestal and thanks to its vacuum motors (originally used for Pianola pianos) it would move in all directions without moving, so to say. It was a 3-wheeled 'crab' on the remote plotting table which traced the plane's course under the instructor's eye.

* Formerly the Royal Naval Air Service (R.N.A.S.)

What McLeod had to do was to get the two lenses to move the appropriate distance from the target model and relative to one another to give the vast range of magnification and sharp-focus required. The aspect of the model also had to alter and after the job at Crail this had to include the original sighting and steep dive before levelling out over the sea to attack. This kind of thing would be a matter of software for some standard computer or other today; but then mechanical action had to do everything. Keeping to the non-dive final attack only (at Crail) a second crab moved to correspond with the target and the instructor would set the course for that target and take avoiding action and so on. A thin rod joined the two crabs on the plotting table and the relationship of the two conveyed to the target projector action mechanism. Once the torpedo was dropped everything stopped. It was then restarted with the torpedo track projected from a small spot of ours mounted on the front of the trainer. These spots had been devised for the GPO pavilion in Glasgow 1938 and were featured, up the columns, of my now bombed-out King Street theatre. What we used was probably salvaged from there. The target ship would then sail on as it would have during the time the torpedo took to travel and they might not meet yet or the ship might go by and leave the track astern.

The T.A.T. (Flight Simulator), Crail 1942

Along with all this went a complete cyclorama colour-mixing installation, storm and fleecy clouds, wave effects, ripples and all. I devised a preset panel with a series of push-buttons labelled storm, mist, sunset and such. It operated a remote Mansell clutch dimmer bank and although the T.A.Ts were not theatres, the insides of their buildings came mighty near by the time we were done! We had a way of stealing the show with our effects. It was a precursor to the now common Flight Simulators used to accustom pilots, and crew, to flying particular aircraft without leaving the ground. The crabs operating in the way they did together formed an analogue computer of the type which was to precede the first valve types, then solid state and the now the micro-chip orgies.

One of the ways these trainers worked is to get the pilots accustomed, by sheer repetition, to the fundamental operational drill, so that it becomes second nature to them to go through a particular routine whatever the excitement or distraction. One of these distractions, which came just before dropping the torpedo was to "make your switches". There were five, as I recall, and were the equivalent of the safety catch on any gun. We had a grand, if not gala, opening for the show in Crail eventually. I think Percy Corry was the only civilian among the top brass around the plotting table on the 'bridge' above. On later jobs this became a separate room with very small observation ports through a 360° cyclorama. At Crail just this part of the cyc was cut-away which made the thing more like a theatre - we had an audience. We the workers (technicians?) clustered around the dimmer bank out of sight. The Commander Flying had the honour of being the pilot in the inaugural demonstration flight. We could squint round the corner of the cyc while the relays on the dimmer bank went into their sequence. Off he flew into the sunset, and as he went into the final phase we realised that he had NOT made his switches. Pressure on the joystick firing button would not project the torpedo track! Cyril Whitter (Percy Corry's foreman for the job) looked at me - I nodded - and he pushed the relay in by hand.

Cyril Whitter was one of the great, possibly the greatest, of all characters in Strand up-North, or Fitups of Manchester. It is difficult to disentangle Strand from Fitups or Watts & Corry which superseded it. Cyril had a penetrating Lancashire accent and a stocky, outward appearance which belied his active, fertile, eccentric inventive mind. Post-war Cyril and Percy used to take turn in representing the North at our very frequent R&D meetings. On one occasion, as his shining face entered, I could not resist temptation and asked "How's Bootle?" To which the reply was "We've got it!". Till then Bootle like Wigan was a target for the music hall comedians. I scarcely knew it existed, let alone that we were after its townhall re-equipment job.

Places like Crail were awful draughty and represented a constant hazard for pneumonia, pleurisy-prone me in the walks uphill or downhill from job site to officers mess* - I was too shy to cadge a lift. One night, warned of a strict alert exercise and armed with a special pass, I set off downhill for the distant isolated building which was the T.A.T. On approaching, out of the dark blue stepped a strangely menacing marine who promptly levelled his rifle and bayonet at me and challenged "Halt, who goes there?" Feeling an awful ass, I replied "Friend". To which the riposte was "Advance friend and be recognised." This I did holding out my pass as I advanced. As if on cue, the wind suddenly gusted and blew it out of my hand and right over his head, whereupon he promptly turned his back on me and ran after it!

The T.A.Ts became an industry: imagine it, the equivalent of forty or so large automatic theatre installations at a terrific pace with all firms, including Strand, already hard at other war work. There was no question of our orthodox suppliers. Comptons, who would have been ideal for relays and multi-contact pushes, had been bombed right out - all special tools and records destroyed in their North Acton works. Suddenly into all this noble war work, the theatre and my 'old' Light Console raised their diverting heads.

Stanley Earnshaw had been talking to Robert Nesbitt about our bombed theatre and the two of them dreamt up the idea of using The Console and dimmer bank for his show *Gangway* due to open that December in the London Palladium. Our first theatre job for the Light Console in this country and in the West End. It was impossible to do, but impossible to turn down. The Palladium meant George Black, whose eye we had been trying to entrap ever since the Console was inaugurated. We did not have much time and the Compton cross-relay had been somewhat damaged though the dimmer bank, cast in the Grand Master mould, so to speak, was of sturdier metal.

The fact that the work was completed well in time for the opening matinee on December 17th 1941 is a tribute to something that can only be described as the spirit of the Strand Electric - something connected with the fact that we worked for and in theatre. It is true that in Floral Street there was both the Hire department and the fitup team to do the wiring required for any special show (under Mark Stables and known as the "Black Tape & String"); but for the Works people it meant giving up their Sundays. They would already be working overtime on the other six days of the week. What is more, it was the same sort of work, since they were likely to be doing the T.A.T dimmer banks at that time. Nor was journeying to and fro easy for some of those based at the Talbot Road works in West Ealing. And here I must once again single out Paul Weston who daily, or rather nightly (since his days were so long),

* The Wardroom; Naval terms were used ashore. The liberty boat was a bus!

did the journey right across London from his parents' house in Ilford - bad enough in peacetime but with blackout, bombs and diversions it can only be imagined!

Anyway, the dimmer bank was dismantled and reassembled under the Palladium stage in what had been the band room and wired-up on the mains side to new outlets and some of the old; a complex layout for reasons which will become apparent later. The Console and relay were moved into the empty bacon-curing factory - known to me, and soon to everyone else, as 'Ham House' - which was next door in Floral Street. The atmosphere there was heavy; it was as if the walls were papered throughout with rashers of bacon; and not today's watery rashers but the genuine article when bacon was bacon. Somehow or other, 'Old Martin' our Lisbon interpreter formed part of our console team and after several Sundays the time came for a Ham House test. He disappeared down some steps to the dungeons with a temporary main and proceeded to connect-up. I stood at the top and gave the signal to the regions below to switch-on. From down-under came a big bang and a flash, accompanied by smoke and 'Old Martin'. Relieved to see him, I was nevertheless puzzled at what he could have done, since he had had only a couple of wires to attach and after all, he was an engineer of sorts.

Investigation showed we had had a narrow escape. There was a large ironclad 150-Amp switch - they made them large in the days to which it belonged. The baconers had left a cable attached and had merely thrown the bare ends up on top of a very large gasmeter nearby. Martin had left this cable on, assuming that it was part of the permanent installation and added his temporary one. Backed-up by a large fuse, it was the old cable which had to burn out, and did, on switch-on. Why the gasmeter was not ignited one can only wonder. Of course the rule with mains electricity has to be "Never assume anything!" (I lived for some twenty-two years in our house in Amherst Road Ealing before finding out that the Supply Company had connected-up their meter wrongly and live and neutral were reversed throughout the house. Fortunately, it was merely a tingle which gave me a warning at last.)

Curiously, it was the Palladium which had years earlier presented an even greater risk. Returning there after some years in sanatorium to show a couple of visitors around we descended to the dimmer room and I knocked-off the main supply over the door. Such a visit involved walking right through the centre of the dimmer bank with the 3-phase 400-volt busbars on one side and the dimmers on the other. We stood in there while I pointed out our panel wiring and dimmer construction. On going out through the second door into the tiny intake room at the far end I was confronted by large, obviously brand new, main switch. What's that I asked? It was the new main. No attempt had been made to label or remove the old main switch. Luckily my two companions had followed my rule of not touching anything during our passage of the valley of death.

As to theatre work itself, my lasting impression is of the sheer professionalism of the backstage staff at the London Palladium. The two balcony auditorium by the architect Frank Matcham has a very large seating capacity (2,325) and a proscenium opening of 47ft; but backstage the dimensions are very tight. There is really no wing space P.side and nothing much to boast about on the O.P. The grid was then only 54ft high and the rear wall angled so close to the outer revolve of the stage as to suggest a tangent. Any groundrow lighting in that area had to take the form of a long low bridge-truck spanning the floor that moved below. Yet this theatre under George Black was famous for its spectacular productions. The truth was that solid pieces, rostrums and staircases were all constructed to take apart, fold and stack away quickly. Our show *Gangway* thus relied on a combination of orthodox scenery and sets of drapes, taken from some of the Gaumont super cinema stages, plus clever lighting. Most effective of all was the song and dance sequence with black drapes and stage, lit in the main from three bars of 'my' Patt.56 acting areas hanging vertically overhead - about thirty in all.

The ex-King Street Light Console had only 39 dimmers mostly resistances but some experimental transformers as well. What it did have was the whole series of special contactors used to change-over from all the colour lighting in the auditorium to the lighting and special effects on the stage of that late temple. There was also the Palladium's existing installation, controlled from a Strand Grand Master on the P.side pros. perch. Thus such mundane things as battens (there were no floats) could be left to the G.M. and important items like the Patt.56s belonged to the Console. Some items were literally swapped between the two, using the change-over contactors, and specials, like the "Night and Day" spots, were patched-in remotely and discarded at will from the console. Such patching was only a wartime measure, and in 1949 all this was replaced, and the stage re-wired, when a 152-way Light Console was put in to enjoy, as it turned out, a run of twenty years.

It is difficult to put a name to a show like *Gangway* now. Perhaps, wartime revue is what sums it up, though it certainly was not 'revue' in the real sense; nor was it just a Variety show. Tommy Trinder, Bebe Daniels and Ben Lyon, Webster Booth and Ann Ziegler, Edmundo Ross and his band, and the Caroili brothers (the Blackpool Circus clowns) were all in the one tight-packed show complete with chorus and showgirls. Wendy Toye did the dances, Debroy Somers was in the orchestra pit and the whole show had pace and sparkle, tuneful music with striking lighting effects. This went on twice every day with three houses on the two or three matinee days each week. There were also a couple of acrobats who preceded a musical 'scena', with Booth & Ziegler plus chorus, called "My Paradise Garden" - a sugary item owing nothing to Delius! When we came to this at rehearsal, Nesbitt simply asked me to 'ad lib' the scene. It was never plotted and subsequently always vamped; which made it fun to do. Once Paul and I had handed the Console over to

The London Palladium, 1941

Hilda (Hilary Gould, who was to become the resident operator and marry Stanley Earnshaw one day), I often used to drop in of an evening and she would leave me to keep my hand in with this number.

A few seats had been given up at the extreme end of the Grand Circle for the Console and being separated by just a rail from one of the two exit gangways we were asked from time to time as to why no organ was heard during the show. The contact with both stage and audience from this position was marvellous. At the opening matinee Tommy Trinder began to describe how Nesbitt lit the show by just sitting in the stalls and calling "Mr. Bentham . . ," and so on for quite a bit, ending with, "and now for the first time on any stage, let me introduce Mr. Bentham." I really wondered what was to happen next, seated up there at the Console, but there was not long to wait: an actor reluctantly shuffled on, suitably dressed in a seedy overall. Trinder then went on to introduce Mr. Jeyes whose fluid was so extensively used in the theatre. I remember when dropping in via the stage door one afternoon some time later, I was greeted by an actor with the words "I have just taken your call" which flummoxed me for the moment.

One memorable morning I arrived late at the stage door to hear the Nesbitt "Mr. Bentham..," resounding - there was no other word for it - throughout the house. He must have turned the volume control right up. The entire cast in costume seemed to occupy the stage. Everyone, including George Black, was there but no lights; or rather none that mattered. There was no dissembling: I rushed on stage before dashing up to the circle. Nesbitt simply said, "Mr. Bentham we are waiting!" but he did not need to say more. Hilda or Paul could have done equally well for the opening number but they too had got fed up with arriving on time, to hang about for an hour before things started. They had decided that this time they wouldn't; they crept in later.

The acrobats were inadvertently to give me the chance to play a few minutes of Colour Music on one of my equally chance drop-ins. It was a front cloth act: something went wrong early, I cannot remember exactly what, but it was a case for an immediately blackout. I could just see the cloth fly away and the band went into *Paradise Garden*. The stage was sans girls, sans Webster and Ann: the stage was mine and full opportunity was taken for a solo on the Console until one by one the stage filled up. The Palladium was to remain a magnet for me long after emergency calls ceased. An unusual emergency occurred when the sound man from the balcony opposite deputised for Hilda one afternoon and pressed the manual keys so heavily that they rode over the wire contacts to rest on top of them. This meant that they were permanently on. I got there between houses but there was only time to get the back of the Console off. Hilda and I did a hastily vamped duet, on the stopkeys alone, to open before Tommy Trinder went on to provide the opportunity to get things right. The duet had been great fun and there was a temptation to continue this crossed-hands close-harmony with Hilda of whom I was by then decidedly fond.

The journey home; Oxford Circus, then hanging about on draughty Queens Park station, thence to South Kenton and a long walk in the blackout - gave ample time to cool off. The fact that I set myself this late ordeal so frequently confirms the allure of that corner of the Grand Circle. The atmosphere on three-house days was thick, but the packed houses enjoyed themselves just the same. This was an ideal show for a wartime night out. How the crowds from the last house got on the tube platform and away, is difficult to recall. The platform was by then lined with occupied bunks trying to get some sleep. What I do remember was gazing at a pretty young girl, until I realised that she was doing something to herself under her blanket that I did not think pretty young girls had to do for themselves! The sense of invading her privacy made me feel sad and embarrassed, but after all I had every right to be in her bedroom.

One night after a Palladium stop-over I alighted at South Kenton as usual and as I climbed the footbridge steps, I began to cough. It was one of those which persisted, and before long I was having to spit at regular intervals along the route. I was no stranger to expectoration, although not a smoker. The pleurisy period and the later pneumonia period had familiarised me with that hazard. The last third of the route was uphill and the first thing I had to do on arrival was to go into the downstairs WC and clear my throat before saying "Hullo," or whatever to Mother. It was blood! The pitch black of the walk had not prepared me for this. The thought that it was what I had been doing all the way was not helpful. How I managed to keep it from Mother and cope with the late supper she was bound to have prepared, I do not know. Bed and some hours quiet there, preferably not breathing, was what my engineer's logic indicated to me. But it could not be: I had to join Percy Corry, McLeod and others at Waterloo before 9 o'clock for one of our visits to the second T.A.T at Lee-on-Solent. And this I did.

The Lee-on-Solent job had been completed some time earlier but without the Dive part of the trainer. These day outings had become the regular thing. We used to occupy the first-class 'restaurant' part of the train. This service had long been discontinued but we found the tables useful to spread out our drawings and specifications. The key specification was my work. This was not because I knew most about everything - far from it. Our jobs were under M.A.P (Ministry of Aircraft Production) auspices and regular progress meetings took place with all of us - a couple of dozen or more - around a long table in the large building requisitioned from I.C.I at the North end of Lambeth Bridge. At one of these meetings the question of such a specification came up and from the blank looks around the very large table it dawned on me that there was only one person who had the slightest idea how to set about it; and that person would enjoy doing it. So I volunteered. It was back to the beginnings with Basil Davis except that in this case it was McLeod I trailed around with; and to Uxbridge at one end of the line to visit the Bell Punch company's factory and out to Barking at the other end to visit someone else's factory. Bell Punch is memorable because that is exactly what they made. The thing that all tram and bus conductors used to wear, and which used to punch out and store tiny coloured circles from the tickets. These circles had to be sorted and counted to check when necessary. I used to enjoy the visits to Uxbridge because of the then quite new Holden station, though lunch at one end of a nearby furniture store took some swallowing. I remember apologising for the untidy state of London by now, to some American officers who came along with us to one such pre-Bell Punch lunch. Graham, our M.A.P chairman, told me afterwards, "You don't need to apologise, you wait until you see their untidy cities." I was due to go out and supervise 'our' side of the T.A.T for Miami in Florida. Visiting that area for my Master classes thirty years later, it was difficult to believe I had missed a treat, but when I went ill the chap who stood in for me brought back a smart lightweight dressing gown - a present doubly appreciated in those years of illness and clothing coupons.

It was two Freds who made the journey to Lee-on-Solent and back that long day. Even then I was probably known as talkative in public, however shy in private; but nobody remarked on my rationed speech. Our farewells declared at Waterloo, the terror struck Fred took over from Fred Bentham for the rest of my journey home. A visit to our doctor followed next morning. He looked grave and I was off to Brompton out-patients the following week for X-ray and report. Things were bad to judge from the way a hush fell on the students as the specialist showed them my X-rays before turning to talk to me. These stage lighting biased pages are no place to go into detail: but two things stick out. One was, immediately after this shock, being told to report to the Almoner who probed into my financial circumstances. She eventually issued me with an out-patients card with NOT TO BE USED FOR BEGGING printed across it. Such were the Voluntary Hospitals before a National Health Service. The second thing was that I was completely unaware of the speed that T.B. got reported. Thus far I had not the courage to break the news to Mother and was trying to make up my mind how to do so. I envied the lone individuals in this respect; people like 'B' Bear. They could keep their troubles to themselves. At that time, a trouble shared was a trouble doubled - and there was my little sister, away at school, to worry about too.

Matters were taken out of my hands. There was a ring at the door while I 'rested' in bed in the little room upstairs just above that door. There was a prolonged murmur of voices, I crept out on the landing to hear Mother declare firmly that there was no T.B. in her house so the Health Visitor was making a mistake. I have a feeling that if there had been a couple of bare wires to hand, I would then and there have taken that way out. Memory is vague on all that followed and I have no intention of racking it here and now. The trouble about T.B., apart from the fact that it took so long then to recover from it (if one did), was that it is so infectious. Leprosy - a close relation - simply isn't in the same league by comparison. It is notifiable, hence that health visitor. And being gifted with conscience and imagination I was afraid of passing it on even at times when the symptoms were comparatively inactive. Other than Chopin and that ilk, the only one of my age who I had experience or knowledge of having TB was Jack Bennett, the other Strand Electric representative who had taken a long, long course of the fresh air treatment and returned to life only to relapse shortly after and die.

I still have a book on Papworth*, now famous for heart transplants, but then it was a kind of leper colony (or rather a T.B. village) where it seemed to me that I might hope to end my days as the lighting man in their hall and possibly do some colour music there. And I am not joking!

* *Rehabilitating the Tuberculosis* by Heaf and McDougall pub. Faber 1945. An aerial view of the Papworth Village settlement shows the village hall; it had, it would appear, a steeply hipped roof!

The only treatments in those times were based on rest. If just lying in bed for months breathing fresh-air did not allow the body to fight off disease, then surgical interference to prevent the affected part of the lung from *working* followed. The simplest was to inject air into the pleural cavity to collapse the lung. This meant a weekly or fortnightly top-up (AP or PP refill injection). If that did not succeed, then surgery of one kind or another followed. The ultimate being a thoracoplasty, in which ribs were removed to induce a permanent collapse of the diseased part. So it was off to Northamptonshire for me, to 'enjoy' months of fresh air in bed at Creaton sanatorium way up on a hillside. Beds were as precious in the War as now. As a result, there followed a return home after six months to Harrow, but to bed. The less difficult once a week journey by bus to nearby Harrow clinic for a refill was barred to me, because although our postal address was Harrow, we paid rates to Wembley who relied on 'distant' West Ealing's TB clinic. It was virtually next door to the Strand Talbot Road works at West Ealing; another coincidence and temptation which was not always resisted. Finally, a visit to Sir Geoffrey Marshall in Harley Street who showed me the X-ray and pointed out to me, as an engineer, what mechanically had to be done. It could mean a return to active life of ten years (or so I understood). But I must have got it wrong because that was way back in 1946 and the ribs, twelve ultimately, came out in 1947 - the year which began with the visit of the three merry gentlemen which opened this chapter.

VII: KING STREET AGAIN
Festival & Export 1948-64

"Had a delightful day at Yale. Lunched with the Rowing Coaches and was shown all over the Sports Associate Building". The date was 3rd May 1947 and it is not difficult to guess that the words were not mine. L.G. Applebee went on: "The main excitement was the Thyratron Board which is very, very near Bentham's Console, so near that I doubt if we would ever sell one of ours against this. The Inventor, George Izenour, is full of enthusiasm as much as Bentham, and it has been put over on a very good publicity. In 1939 the Rockefeller Foundation granted a Fellowship for the development, and installation of the Board at the Yale theatre. It was begun in 1939 and had to be dropped for 3 years during the war and therefore has taken 4 years to build." There followed in the letter a good (in the theatre sense) description of the control and what it set out to do. Full marks to Applebee; there was even this telling sentence which got overlooked in the excitement, "There is much heat given off by the valves but the temperature is constant whatever the load."

That letter was one of fifteen, varying from lengthy detail to single sheet, sent to Jack Sheridan during LGA's visit to New York. The fact that copies were sent on to me in Midhurst indicates the status of that patient. He had never stopped working for Strand Electric, even though work was, of course, strictly forbidden. It was the first thing the doctors thought of; 'you must rest,' declared they, with one voice. And Doctor Todd, who ran Midhurst, was a formidable dictator from Australia. By the 'thirties some doctors had got around to realising that you can't condemn people to do nothing and make them well. There was at Midhurst something called 'Occupational Therapy' which consisted, for men, in making leather gloves while propped-up in bed. There was also something known as Art Therapy which consisted of Adrian Hill's young daughter teaching the patient to paint water colours. My therapy was stage lighting and not only did I continue to do R&D for the whole of those long years but I devised and drew the Unit Board system which appears on pages 99 to 101 of my first Pitman book *Stage Lighting* (published in 1950). I also wrote the complete book there, including drawings, index and all. The index was a real test for me in bed in a room always opened wide to the elements, whatever the weather and the breezes.

It was obvious that George Izenour was on to something, even though I was convinced that large rehearsal levers did not make sense when put alongside mini-preset wheels which were set with a thumb-nail to match the levels obtained on the levers. By now Strand men, like Hugh Cotterill and 'B' Bear, had been demobbed and had been back at work for some months. Others had been taken on. Of these Bill Lorraine, McLeod and J.T. Wood, especially the latter, were to play roles which had been missing until then. Lorraine was a real theatre man who had been in lighting back in the days of Basil Dean at the St. Martins. He had been, so to speak, brought up on German Schwabe stage lighting, cyclorama effects and all the rest. He did not think of battens and footlights as others in this country were prone to do. While actively lighting shows, he pursued R&D within the firm, liaising with me in my Midhurst bed when necessary. I suppose he was really part of the Hire department as that was where the equipment he needed to light his shows would come from. But areas of activity remained ill-defined for most of the time in the old Strand Electric as we have seen and shall see.

McLeod was a contact made as a result of the T.A.T. project during the war of course; but he would not have joined (or remained) with Strand but for ill-health. He was a trained aeronautical engineer and he brought with him knowledge of light metal structures and mechanical engineering which was just what our R&D needed. He was also a disciplined thinker and had a way of getting one back to basics which made him an ideal colleague for me. The fact that one distant day I was actually going to enjoy the disciplines of computer software programming is attributable to working things out with this particular Mac. The other Mac in Strand's R&D was different; but then he was not a Scot, let alone a Highlander!

Jack Sheridan was by now well accustomed to the fact that some people did not have to come into the office each day to ensure that they went on working. So, before long, McLeod was based at his home in Nightingales Lane, Chalfont St. Giles; an address which evokes an image of his wife Rosemary playing a cello in the garden of an evening. This vision dates me, and anyway her interest turned out to be exotic breeds of chicken.

My image of Rosemary, who I had first met while she was in uniform at Crail and then at Lee on Solent, is of her sitting in the Midhurst Blue Lounge with McLeod at tea time. The fact that it was the area for guests did not stop the gangway down the middle being used for *theatre* traffic. It was a busy afternoon; stretcher after stretcher trundled to and fro. Rosemary's sotto voce "Here comes another Bod," exactly evokes the scene.

Nightingales or not, living out there did much to extend Mac's working life. As he had sat opposite me in my small office on the edge of the bomb abyss for some time during the war, it is necessary to remark that he was not suffering from my complaint; but from a rare disease for which there was to prove no cure in his case; fiddle around with expensive drugs though the specialists did from time to time. Mac had been against the idea of the National Health, like many others including the doctors, when it was introduced; but he came to admit that he had been wrong. Healthy people simply cannot realise the astronomical costs of new drug and surgical treatments. Memorably, only one visitor ever asked to see my own operation and that was Hugh Cotterill. With the four successive wounds curving from waist to nape of the neck and the three hundred or so stitch marks all still looking red and raw, to say nothing of the missing structure underneath, he got an eyeful. All this surgical interference and timeless dalliance was, as I suspected it would once I had got mine out of the way, replaced by drug therapy: but I must resist the temptation to quote Edith Piaff!

Cotterill had little to do with R&D post-war and Jack Sheridan held the occasional meeting. These were put on a regular basis by October 22nd 1947. That meeting was chaired by him and was attended by Earnshaw, Cotterill, Applebee, Jordan (Jim, the Works Manager of course), McLeod and McKenzie. On the agenda were notes in Cotterill's neat hand which show that I had been given the chance to comment beforehand. Even more to the point are notes of a meeting of October 15th circulated to the four directors plus Lorraine and myself only. The last item reads: "Mr. Bentham to report on thyratron control taking into account Mr. McKenzie's visit to Foster Engineering." This and other indications on R&D minutes from then on can be both puzzling and gratifying. I simply do not remember much of the detail except that I can clearly see myself working in my Midhurst bed and it is nice to come across some evidence that I am not just imagining it.

Thyratron control was, thanks to Applebee's visit to United States, the great preoccupation and, as it was to turn out, the great digression at the time. This is therefore the proper moment to introduce James Templeton Wood or 'Woody' as he was always known by everyone. Without his experience in Radar in the war we would not have had anyone versed in electronics. To the rest of us it was a strange world but not one which could be ignored. Woody, who used to work for Western Electric before the war, had met Percy Corry at that time and there had been some idea of his starting a branch in Scotland for Percy; but in fact when the time came to join him it was as the assistant manager to his Strand Northern branch. However that was not to last long and Woody was to be found experimenting with thyratrons in the chapel, disused except as a scenery store, alongside the Oldham Road premises.

The result was a 3-valve single dimmer which was taken to our temporary demonstration theatre in Floral Street on the first floor of 'Ham House' and shown on March 9th 1948. There and then it was decided that a 6-way prototype under construction in the chapel was to be "completed with all possible speed". The same

King Street, Covent Garden

minutes also said, "Mr. McLeod is to proceed, as quickly as possible, to investigate methods of remotely controlling potentiometers". In fact the agenda for the meeting had made a distinction between 'Thyratron Control (Direct)' and 'Thyratron Control (Indirect)'. In view of what was ultimately to befall the Strand 'Electronic' and the fact that some years later Siemens* were to adopt servo-operation (as it is more properly called) for their dimmer levers, this item is worth a passing note. It was, of course, me trying to get some essential inertia into an all-electric circuit.

As can be imagined my feelings during the period which had followed Applebee's Yale letter were, to put it mildly, mixed. Until then the prospects for my Light Console had, in spite of the cost, seemed good. Yet there was no question that in chopping the waveform a direct-thyratron system offered a great step forward which simply could not be ignored or opposed. The Strand directors under Jack Sheridan showed great courage at a time when there was bomb damage all around, and Europe had to be rebuilt. Our project was done properly. McLeod designed sheet metal racks for the valve dimmers, and an excellent control desk with moulded dimmer levers and integral 2-way and off tablet switches at one-inch centres with row masters. These were duplicated with a crossfader so that the levers not in use could be preset for the next change. Theatre people needed little persuasion - this was the control for them: the orders 'poured' in.

I had been home for some time now - my first R&D meeting in person was on 12th April 1948, and Stanley had collected me from Midhurst. As a legacy of that static regime I had to fight off sickness whenever we changed speed and had to ask him to take all crossroads at an even speed. Fortunately, there was not much traffic around in Spring 1948 and he was a superb driver so the 57 miles home were completed without accident - internal or external.

* Dusseldorf Opera 1956, and after

My complete rehabilitation was in the main due to two people and one building which as yet did not exist. Ilse and Stanley on the one hand and the Royal Festival Hall on the other. Stanley took me around London and not only was I able to get used to theatres and theatre people once more, but I also had to get on terms with the Expresso craze. These coffee bars, each one vying with the others to outdo the decor, were opening up here today and there tomorrow. Stanley took a delight in sampling the latest and off we would go for a late lunch adventure. The peak was in Chelsea somewhere when the manager came lisping-up and asked Stanley to remove his umbrella from *his* decor; the branches of a plaster tree having proved, till then, a convenient hanger. When in the streets on my own I still had this feeling of not belonging, of standing aloof, invisible. This feeling was to return when attending the East Berlin Staatsoper one evening in 1960. During the interval in the foyer there was this impression of being an invisible observer - a spy from a happier age. And they in their turn, although not yet separated by the wall, did not seem to see me.

Another impediment to my feeling really at home in Strand was that towards the end of 1949 I lost the battle to have 'my' bombed demonstration theatre rebuilt the way I wanted. I was not asking for the 1939 version - the temple to Colour Music - to be put back; but the notion of a half-theatre, which was adopted, was distasteful indeed. This "Demonstration Theatre with a Difference" was heralded by an article with a good drawing in *TABS* *. With Jack Sheridan as the neutral chairman, I think only Stanley was against it. All the rest (including 'B') were for this scheme put forward by Hugh Cotterill and Bill Lorraine.

The idea was that instead of a small complete theatre with ninety or so seats facing a proscenium opening of 13ft. as hitherto, the whole space except for a few stacking chairs directly under the existing balcony slab would become the stage. The left-hand wall of the entire space would be regarded as the centre line and an equivalent space, making up the prompt side, imagined beyond it. In reality the dignified premises of the Westminster Fire Office "Restored sensitively by Sir Albert Richardson"† lay beyond at the King Street end, and 'Ham House' at the Floral Street one where the party wall was constantly oozing salt. Some counterweight lines were installed in the alcoves along the right side. All this might just pass if the stage was lit by battens and floats only, but spotlighting had to assume, in the main, crossed beam techniques. Thus the spots for this half of the stage were imaginary, while the real ones overhead were to light the half which wasn't there! Apart from everything else, the very deep and tall but narrow space painted black was aesthetically unpleasant. We were not conditioned then to accept black slopped all over the place, as in the studio theatres to come. The other obvious

* December 1949 (Vol.7 No.3)

† Nikolaus Pevsner

trouble was the few seats that could be got in for lectures. The notion that our theatre would be for the odd customer or so at a time had proved incorrect in the original Seecol theatre in Floral Street. Not only did parties want to come to lecture-demonstrations but it was in our interest to foster them. There was nowhere else in those days to learn about the art of stage lighting.

The very first of these bookings post-war was for George Devine then at the Old Vic. It went on all day. The lecturers, who did not include me among their number, were exhausted. It was not just a case of two houses but half-a-dozen repeats. As soon as one party left, the next filed in. The experiment was not repeated, and the theatre was little used. Then the worm turned, or rather turned up. The timber used for this post-war teak flooring began to be eaten from under our very feet. The builder was ordered to take deterrent action and he coated the stage with creosote, which not only made us stink like a gasworks but refused to dry out. Weeks went by, but it remained tacky underfoot. Furthermore, the worm seemed to thrive on the stuff and before long little piles of worm-at-work dust began to reappear. The space was less use to us than when the bombs had opened it to the sky. At least we used to store the coke in bulk there! Eventually Jack Sheridan sent for me and asked me to take over, scrap everything and do whatever was necessary to give us a proper theatre once more - whatever the cost.

I don't suppose Jack actually could bring himself to utter "whatever the cost" but the signal was clear - a green light for Fred. It was typical of that chap that neither the restoration of the theatre that had been bombed nor any of the schemes, dreamt up as replacements during the sanatorium sojourn, held any attraction now. The stage had to go back to 1/2-scale of course; but I could not bring myself to scrap those half-theatre counterweight sets which would now find themselves out in the auditorium. Not only would they be useful to rig F.O.H. lighting and try out new lanterns but in combination with architectural piers at one side and beams overhead which had survived, I designed something which looked, and was, purposeful. This opened early in 1954 with a lecture by Philip Rose and L.G. Applebee. The rest of us had our work cut out fulfilling their needs from portable boards on the balcony. Inevitably men could not be taken from real jobs so the lighting part was very much a vamp.

This theatre was destined to survive for four years after Rank Strand left King Street for Brentford in the Autumn of 1973, thanks to the ABTT. Those 23 years of active life saw a procession of prototype Strand controls from the 1948 Electronic to the R.S.C's Stratford System DDM of 1972 - the world's first theatre control based on software. And there were the middle market systems and the juniors as well. It even saw in Autumn 1957 and Spring 1958 the return of the original Light Console for colour music recital at the suggestion of, believe it or not, some of the more recent members of my R&D dept. It had also to be said that one way or another this demonstration theatre played a unique educational and social role in our arcane world of theatre lighting; but that is for a later chapter.

As my work had been so bound up with the demonstration theatre I was in effect homeless while it was out of action in a form of which I could approve. An office did not suffice even though there was an optical lab alongside; and my pen was not anything like as free as it had been in my first years in Strand Electric. Hugh Cotterill was in charge of publicity, the catalogue and *TABS* as well as being a director and manager of the S.O. (Sales Other) department officially responsible for Export and non-theatre jobs at home. These latter ones could be summed up as those Applebee (by now a director) didn't particularly want his Theatre Lighting Department (T.L.D) people to get mixed up in! Although I did regular articles for *TABS* under the initials F.P.B. for Cotterill, we never got on with one another even when in December 1957 I filled the vacancy on the board caused by Applebee's retirement. As to the latter, we developed mutual respect and even in the earlier years when we did not see eye to eye as to the form a lighting installation and its control should take, our common interest in theatre bridged any gap. Cotterill on the other hand was never really a theatre man.

As will become clear later in this chapter my other love - the Light Console - seemed to be under threat. It was all very well for people to assume that it had a market for very large installations, but did I really believe it? Strand simply *had* to have an electronic valve system to challenge George Izenour's; by now taken up by Century Lighting in New York, and that meant for the middle range, the majority of first class installations, the customer would have the choice of a preset type of control. However, for the present, the wartime 'partial' Light Console in the Palladium was to be replaced by a complete one of 152-channels; and one thing was certain; if it suited anything (other than Colour Music!) the Console certainly suited the Palladium type of show. The year 1949 also saw an installation of 108-channels in the Palace Manchester and our second export one, in the National Opera House Ankara. The very end of that year saw the first bits of the Strand 'Electronic' arrive, far from complete, in Iceland to be put together by William Bundy* for the new National Theatre in Reykjavik. This 120-channel control was completed eventually and Bundy came back to England in June or July 1950. He then went on to install and service the (by now) quite numerous 'Electronic' orders.

However 1950 also saw the 216-way Light Console for Drury Lane take over *Oklahoma!* in the March. This Console, and the almost identical one for the London Coliseum exactly two years later were to constitute the largest 'one-man' controls

* See *Sightline* Vol. 17 No.2 for Bill Bundy's own account

for theatre anywhere until the Covent Garden Opera House broke the barrier with 240-channels in 1964. But by then, electro-mechanical systems had had their day and all-electric dimmers and solid-state devices were to relegate such things to the age of steam. Back at the beginning of the fifties there was a temptation to think that day had already arrived. Because everything had to be within easy arm's reach of an organist my use of Compton consoles automatically meant that I never had to worry about the physical side of the console design. Five foot square on plan would cover the operator and his desk no matter the number of ways. And this was just the amount of space we usually got. At the Coliseum there was certainly no room to spare, and to get at the back, the thing had to be pulled forward and it was a question of front access or back access; you could not have both. When we came to get it in, it could not go through the door and turn, so the top part with the stop-trays and three manuals had to be unscrewed from the bottom which supported it and which carried the pedals. The two parts were separated and there was just enough flex to allow this; provided Jim Pollard of Comptons, whose emergency brainwave it was, crawled along on all fours underneath to bear some of the weight and to warn as soon as there was any sign of tension on any cable. Other than the Lisbon unloading I can never remember anything as hair raising.

We were at the critical point when Sam Harbour, the well known manager of the Coliseum for so many years, came along. He misunderstood what was happening, got very heated and rushed off to phone Stanley saying that 'your men' were smashing up 'his' Console. By the time Stanley turned up, the Console sat proudly in its box. And what a wonderful position it was, just to the right of the left gangway at the back of the marvellously raked stalls (there was no dress circle overhang). Another superb room was in the old Stoll theatre in Kingsway. This had a row of seats with boxes behind in a mezzanine under the front edge of the Dress Circle. We were given the last box before the central projection room. Originally to be the London Opera House, the Stoll had spent its between-wars life as a cinema. This 176-way job was completed early October - in time to take-over the last two weeks of *Oklahoma!* which had transferred there to free Drury Lane for *Carousel* in the June.

There could not have been a greater contrast between the two changeovers. At Drury Lane, *Oklahoma!* had a run of nearly three years behind it; but to us, with a new control and entirely new lamps (due to the change over from DC to AC power) it was a new show - another first night. There had only been the time from curtain down Saturday night to 10-am Monday to put the old board out of action and put in the new one. The only place to put my Console - designed specifically to operate with a view of the stage - was in the Prompt Side scene dock. So Paul Weston could only see part of one cue in the show, and that was a bit of stray light which escaped through the wings onto the top of the scene dock wall. Conditions could not have been worse; and this for our largest ever job in London's most famous theatre. Joe Davis was in the stalls doing the lighting in his usual precise way. It was a full dress rehearsal with everyone wondering what all the fuss was about. My role was to worry and to be on hand as Paul's 'assistant', should anything go wrong. Apart from the fact that my doctors had warned me not to indulge myself in the late theatre hours, it was not in my nature to perform lighting by others, I fear, and certainly not if one could not see the results. At Drury Lane, even when at last the old switchboards had been finally cleared out and the Console went in that room, all it gave the operator was a very limited extreme sideways down-stage view across the orchestra pit via a small window with a fire shutter. There was a coil of flexible cable under the Console to allow it to be taken out to the stalls cross-gangway for rehearsals; but it was never used. Jack Miller, the resident-stage director, typically for an ex-stage manager did not want the thing out-front and Prince Littler said he always gave his man in charge the final word.

At the Stoll his manager had agreed that the Console should go out-front. This, plus the fact that we now knew *Oklahoma!* and its lighting cues, made the change-over sheer delight. Paul was again at the Console and Joe sat in the row just outside our open window. All we needed was a couple of hours in the afternoon before the show; no cast, no stand-ins - relaxed and friendly. Standby at the Stoll could have involved me in violent exercise rushing from Console to the dimmers; one did not want to sit in the dimmer room at the ready, of course. I never had another dimmer room as close as at Lisbon where it was only a matter of popping through a door from the orchestra pit (very fortunate since I had to play and do standby there at one and the same time). The Stoll was the very opposite. The journey to the dimmer room involved setting out from the front of house, through the pass door right across the deep stage and through the scene dock, up to the top floor by lift to a room alongside the ballet rehearsal room. Recollection says that the equipment was very reliable however, and so was Ken Thompson, the Stoll operator. Indeed when in time the Stoll Opera House was demolished, Ken and that Console moved to the London Hippodrome to control Nesbitt's *Talk of the Town*

My roles in the Stoll productions around that time indicate the disciplines I had to impose on myself during a period when I still had to regard myself as a convalescent. I wanted to do so much, but how much ought I allow myself to do? Real theatre work, especially stage lighting, always meant late, even all-night, work in those days. The 1951 Festival Ballet season which followed *Oklahoma*'s short sojourn at the Stoll is a case in point. This touring ballet company was headed by Anton Dolin and Alicia Markova, and I was expected, though I am not sure by whom, to be doing the lighting. Ben Toft, the stage director, acted as if it came under him. But the stage manager was the man who saw things in practical terms of simplification to make things work night after night, once I was out of the way.

I did a layout for that season which if recall aright consisted of three bars of Patt. 56 Acting Areas pointing straight down, with Patt. 50 Pageants high up to provide side-light from the wings. There had to be plenty of white light because the place was haunted by "full-up white no colour" for *Beau Danube*. The other colour was blue (probably 18) for *Giselle* and other night work. The theatre's own magazine battens would have been 4-colour. I was determined to work the console for the opening night which consisted of *Nutcracker* as two acts, and *Beau Danube* after the second interval. Paul Weston would take over after the first night and train the theatre's own operator at the same time. But what about rehearsals? Under my own health discipline I never saw the end of any of these. As far as *Nutcracker* was concerned, only the first act had anything important and I would, and did, vamp the rest. As to the *Danube* that was just full-up white - yet that was to be the one item which came unstuck.

The trouble that night was distraction. Just as the tabs were flown-out, into our control box came two people. One was instantly recognisable as Godfrey Winn, a newspaper columnist (then very much in the limelight). Known to me from black and white photos only, it was a shock to see him in person and in full-colour. At that moment the phone went and the S.M. asked if the Console had broken down as the FOH spots had not come in. Hardly had I started to remedy this when the phone went again. It was Anton Dolin demanding to know why I was ruining his ballet? By then the stage was full-up anyway. I had been creeping in the missing lighting as gently as possible - to bash-up all that extra light might have put the solo dancer off his stroke or whatever. One first night was my medical ration so I could not do the *Giselle* rehearsal the next morning; but did attend the show itself as standby. I itched to make changes to Ben Toft's lighting. In particular, as midnight struck, his Wilis* certainly gave them to Paul and I. Although they had used low-voltage torch bulbs to imply the dancing of these ghostly sylphs here and there among the scenery, they appeared blinding against the low-check blue lighting. We could do nothing about it since they were switched on from the prompt corner. At the very end of the ballet, with the first light of dawn, I would have liked to apply a tiny ray of sunlight to the prostrate Albrecht; but as I was not at rehearsal I could not be sure which spot would hit him. Strange how these little 'might-have-beens' haunt one.

Anton Dolin narrowly escaped apoplexy during a memorable matinee of *Petrushka*. As the wintry daylight faded in the square, enter a lamplighter. Purposefully, he stuck his taper-pole up the left hand side lamp-post, whereupon the lamp on the right hand side lamp-post lit up. Needless to say when he got to the

* Ghostly spirits of young maidens who had died of grief, due to one thing or another on the part of their lovers, before their wedding bells had chimed!

other side the reverse happened. As so often when these Light Console installations went in, opportunity was taken for Strand Electric to rewire the whole stage; a process which might take many weeks. Here was a fine example of cross-wiring due to lack of time to test. Fortunately Dolin had his back to the stage and the audience was too well behaved even to titter. We were standing among the empty rows of rear stalls, under the balcony at the time. Why we three were there I cannot recall. I know that the third man was the manager of the Stoll itself and he enjoyed the same view as I, but of course did not let on. Robert Nesbitt soon followed at the Stoll with another *Square*, a *Rainbow* one this time and he expected me to do the lighting with him. This I really enjoyed. It was very much my kind of thing and had echoes of those *Gangway* days at the Palladium. There was only one scene *Rainbow Square* itself - designed by Georges Raymond. The buildings forming it were completely encompassed by a cyclorama from floor to grid. Equipment once hung and positioned could not be moved or focused. Lighting therefore was a matter of selecting the appropriate stop-keys to paint the stage with light - real Light Console stuff. There was a particularly fascinating cue to do in which the stage had to build from the first light of day to full sunlight as the Square gradually became populated. It began with the faintest overhead wash from the blue and white battens only; but need I go on?

By now Ilse and I could relax with Stanley and Hilda in the stalls for the first night and afterwards at the Ivy restaurant. The timing was perfect, another couple of weeks or so and the evening dress Ilse had made for the opening of the Royal Festival Hall earlier that year would no longer have fitted - I was happy to know! There was only one shock in the show. We were gazing at a full-up fine day when a large white sheet (somebody's washing?) blew high up right across the Square. In those hand-painted mica days, part of the 'Photopak' on one of the fleecy cloud discs had peeled off. Always on the alert, Ken and Paul managed to identify it and fade out that disc before it came round again (would a modern computer memory system have done as much?) Mention of the Festival Hall reminds me that it was another case of a dimmer room a long way away up aloft involving a journey by lift. It was an annexe built on top of the roof. Also, being accessible from an almost external staircase meant our men could go on working during the inevitable strike before the place opened. However, what the RFH was particularly memorable for, in our context, was the Console room only 3-ft front to back to include operator and desk. This mere cupboard was to survive until an MMS memory system replaced the Console some 25 years or so later. Then they had to build a special room at the rear of the stalls way back under the balcony to fit all that in.

'Our' room was certainly cramped, but the end of the centre cross-gangway was a much nicer place to be: one was part of the show and of the audience too. It was as good as our Palladium balcony. As I have probably said elsewhere, I don't like being shut away behind glass; nor do I approve of large control rooms. The tight cockpit of the fighter pilot induces theatrical concentration. You don't have to gather up your thoughts and you have to keep paperwork to the minimum. The Royal Festival Hall was a piece of luck for me and the perfect rehabilitation job after my years of illness. It had everything, both mental and physical challenge and social stimulus. There were plans to be made, circuits to design and draw, new people to meet and battles to be fought. Physically when I started on the job the building was only one storey high, and as it grew, so too did the number of steps to be climbed.

This job suited me perfectly, and my amalgam of engineer and artist perfectly suited the L.C.C* engineers with whom I had to work. It is not too much to claim that I was theatre consultant to the job, unpaid though I was. But that was very much in the old Strand Electric tradition, and I have no doubt that it paid dividends in those days. Besides I was hooked on the Festival Hall. Ever since I had heard about the project for the new concert hall, the only permanent building on the 1951 South Bank site, I had wanted to get involved, but how? The L.C.C. called in Strand to do any dimming and platform lighting, so not being a theatre that meant Cotterill and his department and no hope for a one man band like me! Cotterill passed it on to one of our outside reps, Jim Murray. Jim has already appeared in chapter 3 and was a very good man for those who liked a casual approach. This was just right at the early contact stage. He got us the Ideal Home Exhibition jobs and the pre-war 'Queen Mary' and 'Empress of Britain' ships, or rather any theatrical lighting in them. But as soon as technical detail surfaced he was sunk and knew it.

So it was that having quoted for some acting area floods over the platform and a simple automatic dimmer bank, he thought he had better show off the Strand prowess at the Palladium and asked me to go along with him and the delegation from the L.C.C. on January 10th 1950. This I enthusiastically agreed to, and as soon as the party gathered around the Console Jim Murray vanished through the stage door to the Marlborough pub† and the job was mine thenceforth. There was, of course, at that time no question of a Light Console for the new hall, the main purpose of the visit was to see a Mansell clutch bank in action. At that stage the big worry was the dimming of the cold cathode fluorescent tubes in the ceiling coves. There were to be nine coves and each was to have two 6-ft and three 7-ft tubes, while under the balcony there were to be six 6-ft plus one 7-ft. There was also to be 45kW of tungsten lighting - downlighters and other such to be used with or without the cold cathode. That was easy, as were the thirty Patt.76 acting area floods over the platform. For these floods, an 18-way remote panel (based on the *1934* Covent

* London County Council

† Now the 'Dog and Trumpet'

Garden principle but with a motor) had been quoted in June *1949*! Up to that time the correspondence shows that Hugh Cotterill had been personally involved.

The great thing to bear in mind about the Festival Hall is that unlike the later South Bank 'masterpiece' the National Theatre or the Barbican Centre in the City across the river, it had a deadline date to meet. It had to open, and did, on Thursday May 3rd 1951 and the Festival of Britain opened the day after. It wasn't the case of going on for years and opening parts of it when ready - a bad habit, not peculiar to this country alone. Mind you, not all was smooth sailing although I do not remember any trouble with Gunnersbury, though our factory had a lot of work on. The difficulty was to get the dimmer room completed so that we could put the job in. There was no question, as at Lisbon, of doing it as a series of complete banks; everything had to come apart at the works and be reassembled on site. The room had to be completely finished and the builders out before we could come in.

At the regular Wednesday morning site meeting of March 14th I put my foot down, spoke up and told Holland & Hannen & Cubitts that we could not be ready unless ... ! I think I went on to declare that in my opinion we were not the only people that were being held up. Anyway, an emergency site meeting was called for the next morning and somehow news of my non-servility got through to Cotterill and for the first time he came to the meeting and sat alongside me, presumably to ensure that I behaved myself. He did not utter a word the whole time - how could he, as he did not know a thing about it by then?

Officially Strand were sub-contractors to Cubitts, but I felt my first duty lay with the L.C.C. Engineers Dept. and in particular to J.G. Hunter and his assistant Clarke, way up on the 6th floor of County Hall. They were acting both as consulting engineers and client as I saw it. But the truth is that I got so completely involved in 'my' side of the hall that I had no boss. The engineers were my colleagues and the architects were the enemy. And they had a secret weapon which they were not loathe to deploy - the acoustics. These were in the hands of Hope Bagenal whom I had met at the time when the Royal Albert Hall had to take over from the bombed Queens Hall. He had hung an acoustic canopy over the orchestra there which set problems in lighting. He was an easy going man, prepared to listen, but by the time of the Festival Hall he had an assistant Peter Parkin, who went around seemingly draped with instruments and a revolver. "Parkin says no!" was the architects' weapon when all else failed.*

What they objected to was holes in their decor, every blessed aperture had to be fought for. There was a wonderful space right along each side of the hall, above the top row of boxes, labelled "lighting gallery" on the architects' plans but what they

* Parkin himself enjoyed this tale of mine when I related it at a lunch hosted by Derek Sugden of Ove Arup umpteen years later.

would not agree to were apertures in the wall and panelling to allow light to get from there to its likely target. And there was no question of hanging anything up there in the open in those civilised days. All spotlights had to be concealed. When I arrived on the scene four apertures each side (at ceremonial box line) had been agreed provided they were closed when not in use. By the time I had finished, a further seven a side towards the platform had been added and sixteen spots in a housing on the circle front. Over the platform a further twenty-two acting areas and a cyc flood bar were thought necessary and above all, everything was under the control of a Light Console. Forty-six of the lanterns were fitted with remote 4-colour change, largely to help keep down the number of apertures required.

Why all this for what was to be purely a concert hall? For months I was a lone voice though it has to be said that the L.C.C engineers were early converts to my theory. It was the architects who opposed it. Their brief was to design a concert hall and from that they would not budge. On the other hand I knew that the hall was bound to be used for theatre and other productions sooner or later. Wherever there had been a concert hall, theatre - and spectacular theatre at that - was bound to follow; whatever the difficulties of staging productions there. The idea of using my console did not occur to me for some time. My first idea was a panel "of oak 24 inches wide by 16 inches deep," with "55 pushes laid out diagrammatically as the platform lighting. The lanterns selected by these pushes (Compton luminous stop heads, of course) are controlled from a set of nine engraved Raise, Dim, Preset, 3 secs speed, 7 secs, 15 secs, 30 secs, Blackout and Dead Blackout." To quote the specification of 8th May 1950. In addition there were to be a further eleven pushes to control the auditorium lighting one way and another.

This idea I eventually dropped in favour of a small one manual Light Console and it became more and more clear that theatrical productions would take place. The appointment of John Shove as General Manager confirmed this, as he was determined to stage ballet in the hall during the weeks when the Proms season was on at the Royal Albert Hall (and could be assumed to be the focus of musical attention). Here I came in conflict with 'B' Bear for the only time on any real scale. He had, unknown to me put forward a scheme in which the complete ballet installation, portable switchboards and all, would be *hired* from Strand. Playing on the architects prejudices I was able to counter with the gambit that such a fit-up with lanterns hanging everywhere would mess up their beloved brand new auditorium just when everyone would see it. It is necessary to stress that for that first season there was no question at all of the horrible makeshift temporary pros. stage which was to disfigure the place from 1952 when the Festival Ballet became the regular visiting company. For 1951 it was Mona Ingolsby and her father's International Ballet on the open stage and quite well it worked as lit by Bill Lorraine.

Royal Festival Hall in the 1950s

The opening of the Royal Festival Hall by King George VI was very memorable in a number of ways. Ilse and I had marvellous seats in that terrace which runs along the side of the front stalls. An excellent position to see and enjoy both the audience and the concert on the platform. Hugh Cotterill and his wife Sue sat in the pair of seats immediately behind us and during the hush which preceded the entrance of the Royals she asked him, presumably gazing around in wonder, "What part of this did you do?" - he remained discreetly silent! We had a close view of the ceremonial box and the King looked very drawn. The rest of the party, particularly Princess Elizabeth, looked by contrast in the pink.

The concert was fine, the sort of occasion which suited Malcolm Sargent. By a quirk we two heard most of it twice. Arriving early I had scorned the queues standing in the cold outside the main entrance, and gained entry via a side door through which, fortunately I noticed John Shove was slipping with two of his guests. We therefore sneaked into the auditorium during the last items of the rehearsal. All that was very well; it was after the show that we came unstuck. At that time we lived out at Harrow with Mother and I had hired a car to convey us, dressed-up as we were, there and back rather than the usual bus and Bakerloo tube to Waterloo. The driver had gone off to the particular distant car park allocated to him - all the rest of the South Bank site being occupied by the Festival of Britain due to be opened by the King the next morning. The wonder is that we were not still there for that ceremony! Chaos reigned. Officially one presented one's car ticket to a chap in a little office and he would summon the appropriate car. This was besieged anyway and when at last one got to him the phones weren't working and there was no idea either where the car was or how to get in touch with it. The South Bank is a draughty place at dead of night in early May. There was nothing for it but to lurk inside and make the occasional foray to see what if anything was happening. In overdue course a long procession of cars snaking away into the dark crawled up and past the main entrance; in those early years at the side towards where the Haywood and the N.F.T.* now stands.

Getting sick of waiting for 'ours' Ilse and I set out along the procession and just before we had given up all hope, there it was. We had certainly earned our Zadok and Hallelujah etceteras that night. Thirty-one years later we were to attend the equivalent ceremony at the Barbican in the City of London. But I have to say that I had nothing whatever to do with it or its equipment. Still it was nice of them to invite me; especially it must have been well known by then, that of its architecture and planning I did not approve. There can be no doubt at all that give or take a lighting aperture or two the Royal Festival Hall as it opened that May in 1951, it was an architectural masterpiece, a landmark in the housing of live entertainment in this country. Apart from the remarkable feat of deciding to build it and getting it built in those immediate post-war years, it was quite notable for its influence on many of the German opera houses and such which were to be rebuilt or built.

The next night was the first concert proper and although provision had been made so that at concerts the steward or stage manager could operate the console remotely to bring in appropriate combinations of lighting, I elected to sit at my console all alone out front in the little room and do it myself. The nearest to a real lighting cue was when the choir rose for choral finale of the Beethoven Ninth and I dimmed up the lights over them. This was the sort of thing of which Sir Malcolm thoroughly approved. Sir Adrian Boult who had shared with him the conducting honours the previous night would have been shocked. A real shock that night was when just before the interval a man hurriedly left the stalls in front of me to be followed by immense crash of shattered glass. Apparently he had spotted the 'WC' sign he needed so urgently and dashed through the wall of glass. These clear glass unframed doors and partition walls trapped some nine or ten people this way in the first weeks. By day it was particularly hazardous and even I, who came to know them well, nearly went through one. The trouble was that your eyes were caught by

* National Film Theatre

the marvellous view across the Thames and therefore did not focus on what was just in front of you. Some ten people and an L.C.C inspector actually walked through the glass before a solution was found.

The Royal Festival Hall has a lesson for us today as I write after the abolition of the Greater London Council (for party political reasons - the same reasons which caused the enlargement of the London County Council into the G.L.C. in 1965). Given the Thatcher test, instead of Herbert Morrison's enthusiastic approval, it would have been quite wrong to spend all that money at that time on a showy architectural concert hall, to say nothing of the rest of the 1951 Festival of Britain outside. However I know from personal experience what this showplace meant to just one firm - the Strand Electric. If I had been the hall's theatre consultant in all but name (and professional fees!), I now became one of its P.R. guides. It is impossible to say how many people I had to arrange to meet at the stage door, conduct along the extensive catacombs lined with pipes and cables for the formality of meeting the building's chief engineer before taking them to see what I thought important. Mind you, these meetings took place in the very impressive boiler house, or rather the balcony overlooking it which housed the switchgear, dials and all the rest. The then rather pioneer gas-fired boiler, instead of oil or coal-fired, plus the experimental heat-pump installation made this item fascinating of itself to some of my engineer visitors. To me it seemed to impart a soupçon of coal gas to the taste of the tea I drank down under.

This tea was made by the 'Dial & Knob' man as he monitored and twisted with evident pride, seemingly stuck down there all hours of the day and night. The chief engineer and his assistant only kept their desks down there. Their work took them all over the building, inside and out. My query to one of these two as to how the 'D&K' man put up with being shut away sans daylight but avec that atmosphere, was answered by, "He worked in the Gas, Light & Coke Company for over thirty years". As to my own breathing, common-sense suggested that after this experience we should take the lift to the top of the building and work down. Up there the first thing was to go on the roof-terrace and look across the Thames to the City and St. Pauls. Blitzed it certainly was, but not fouled-up with high-rise. This view and the one across to Westminster from the corresponding west roof-terrace showed that this site on the bend of the river was the true centre of 20th-century London. A centre hitherto cluttered with warehouses and other relics of private enterprise among which only the shot tower of 1826 stood out. So much so that it was rightly retained for the 1951 Festival of Britain.

Admission to the auditorium needed care, at any rate during the mornings, due to the incessant use for rehearsals. Though it was of the nature of this large hall that one could usually sneak in to give it a look. Demonstration of the Light Console needed the lunch break and during one such occasion it had its most unlikely visitor - Queen Wilhelmina. Two surprises here; that she wanted to see it, and that she could sit at it in the eighteen inches between it and the wall in that tiny room! This room was so small that we literally had to remove the partition wall between it and the auditorium to get access to the otherwise back-less console. Four screws had to come out for the purpose but these we were not allowed to remove. Thus Paul Weston and I often found ourselves hanging around in a frustrating manner until a member of the carpenters' union, or whatever it was called, dropped whatever he was doing and took the screws out. We had to be jolly careful not to fall foul of any of the unions. Once the hall opened things became more relaxed. Fortunately, as already mentioned, our dimmer room was way up on the roof, accessible by some back stairs which were only known to initiates. I cannot remember the provision for the original Cotterill/Murray dimmer bank; but by the time the cold cathode cove dimming had been properly worked out, and the platform lighting had become a stage lighting installation, a special room had been necessary. It is not unusual in building complexes, however large, to have difficulty finding space for technical equipment. The struggle to get a satisfactory range of dimming for the ceiling coves in 1950 can readily be imagined by the technically minded. Normal filament lamps, whatever their wattage, were easy, but any type of lamp involving an electrode at each end of a tube was quite another matter.

The Claude-General would be supplying the lamps and auxiliary equipment and their base was on the Wembley Trading Estate i.e. the site, and most of the buildings at that time, of the 1923 Wembley Empire Exhibition. Living in Pebworth Road Harrow, it was a matter of catching the 92 bus and a short walk the other end. Doing this for the first time I was surprised on nearing my destination to be waved at from a stationary railway train. Entry to these 'offices' was however via the Claude-General factory alongside. The episode does give some idea of the building makeshifts that were around at the time the brand new concert hall was conceived.

The range of dimming demonstrated at Wembley for cold cathode tubes was 4 to l: since tungsten stage lighting at that time was 300 to 1, its inadequacy was obvious. To get a cold-cathode discharge tube to strike was quite a different matter from just heating up a tungsten filament. It was to remain a problem, at any rate in economic terms, for a decade. In our case money was more or less no object and the solution was fifty-five circuits each with its own resistance dimmer, suitably ganged together mechanically or electro-magnetically. A hell of a lot of effort just for decorative cove lighting. Even then the dimmers had to be specials with 130 contacts instead of the usual 100. This was because a ratio of 600 to 1 was found necessary since the gentle delay inherent in filament warm-up and decay was absent from a discharge tube. The result was both excellent visually and very reliable. Whatever else was subject to criticism, it was never the cold cathode cove lighting; but I did suggest that it should not be used at all when theatrical productions were staged. The tungsten downlighters etc were more than adequate and gave a more intimate feel to the hall.

Discharge lighting was to prove an infernal nuisance when around 1950 Thorn Lighting solved the problem of dimming hot cathode tubes; a form of lamp with whose introduction and manufacture they were such pioneers. To their Dr. Strange, once these lamps could be dimmed, here was the elixir of light for the stage. To Strand Electric it represented unwelcome competition and to myself something evil indeed. Here were people such as Percy Corry, 'B' and I who had at last put over the idea that a basic stage installation need not rely on battens to flood the whole stage with one colour wash or another, when enter up-stage a novel invention, whose only merit was that it could do just that! There was nothing for it but to attack the idea at every opportunity. One such occasion was a talk and demonstration to the I.E.S. and I can still remember Hugh Cotterill pulling at my jacket in a vain attempt to get me to sit down during the discussion on Dr. Strange's paper. These Atlas tubes and the inevitable colour-mixing battens Thorn were trying to sell were the last straw. R. Gillespie Williams, with his post-war 'Delicolor' under the Furse banner was out of our hair as he had joined Century in New York as Rollo G. Williams by this time. So the question now posed was would the great Thorn publicity machine succeed where the relatively small Furse firm had not. It is a matter of history now that fluorescent lamps made little impact on stage lighting outside the large German cycloramas. Looking at my own I.E.S. paper presented to the society in November1960 one can see from the discussion that Dr. Strange was still not convinced*. According to him I referred to these lamps "in an unnecessarily disparaging way," and this was not an attempt to get back at me - he was much too nice a person for that. It is worth pointing out in this context that the very same year Strand Electric itself, in the shape of Applebee's department, had put into the new Royalty theatre (on the old Stoll site opposite Magnet House Kingsway) an installation the greater part of which was based on flooding from battens. As soon as Joe Davis appeared on the scene to light the first production there, Durrenmatt's *The Visit,* he had them all replaced by spot-bars. Colour mixing flooding had of course been ideal for the stage drapes and concealed cornices of the super cinema in the twenties and thirties.

Thanks to the Compton connection, the Royalty had a jolly good lighting control - a direct descendant of the Light Console. This system known as 'CD' represents the peak of what can conveniently be thought of as the steam age of lighting control. It owes its invention to a combination of electronic unreliability and the needs of television studio lighting. That is the way it actually fell out but even if Strand had been able to stick to thyratron dimmers we might still have had a form of system CD. Some means of holding dimmer levels without constant energisation from dimmer levers was essential if the ever larger lighting installations were still to be

* *I.E.S. Transactions* Vol. 26 No.2

controlled by one man at a compact console or desk. This was the key to lighting in my belief and I loathed the sacrifice of that ideal in favour of any extra facilities however sophisticated. Radio City Music Hall, New York, with its 5-scene 314-way all-electric control in 1933, and others over there around that time, had shown how large such control boards could become no matter how small the levers; but I never thought to see a whole room whose walls were covered with them as was to happen in the New York Metropolitan Opera House in 1966.

The remark earlier, "if Strand had been able to stick to thyratron dimmers," is crucial to that time. The thyratron was what has become known as a 'chopper', and this has been the basis of dimming for a quarter of a century as I write now. It is in effect a high speed switch allowing part or all the AC waveform to pass with consequent effect on the voltage to, and therefore the brightness from, a lamp or lamps. The thyristor which does this today is a solid state device without moving parts; but its predecessor, the thyratron, although without any moving parts did require a heater filament. It was another member of the great thermionic valve family but designed to cope with much heavier currents. The filaments would take about 30-watts and there were three valves per dimmer in the Strand system which meant over 10 kW for medium to large installations. This load had to be on all the time so that the valves could go into instant action.

Apart from this wattage as inefficiency, it complicated the crucial matter of ventilation - the valves were sensitive to temperature. One way and another valve systems were not satisfactory and were discarded in USA and Europe as soon as something better turned up. Strand's three valves gave an incentive to discontinue earlier which was not present in the two valves used by others. Sunday the 5th of October 1952 saw Paul Weston and I in the Saville theatre gazing at a main switch before using it to liven up the stage lighting. It was not the switch but the neutral cable that claimed attention - it had undoubtedly got very, very hot. In a 3-phase system the neutral, as its name implies, is the under-worked cable, its job is to take out-of-balance current. I remember a chance remark by a member of the Works' test room team (I can see Cassel now using it as an exit line as he paused in Jim Jordan's office doorway), "the neutral gets bloody hot". The job was one of Percy Corry's, the Theatre Royal Hanley, and Cassel had just come back from servicing it. Here was a clue to be followed up immediately.

After a morning collecting ammeter readings at the Saville, it was back home to Sunday lunch and study of the figures. There was no doubt whatever we had all been blind idiots; but we need not be too ashamed for the same mistake was to be made in Los Angeles by an American firm thirty-three years later. And they could have read any editions of my book* from 1955 on. In a way, Woody, as the inventor, had

* *The Art of Stage Lighting*, Pitman

dropped into this ambush rather than steered himself into it. Unlike George Izenour he had to use three valves instead of two, in order to cope with 2-kW at our higher voltage and to use what was then obtainable here. That there were *three* suggested putting them across the 3-phases and thereby balancing each dimmer; instead of locating each phase to particular areas of the stage as normal. In this orthodox practice the nearer to full load, the better the balance and that in any case the neutral would never have to return more than the load of one phase at the very worse.

The defect that stared out of the figures that Sunday afternoon was that as each thyratron was a rectifier passing current one way only (say the top half of the AC cycle at best) the only return was down the neutral cable. To have this revealed all on one's own, with the knowledge that by now there were several large installations already working in UK and one in Iceland, can be imagined. The solution was to feed the dimmer banks from a star-delta transformer (or a static-balancer) installed as close to them as possible. In this context pages 80 and 81 of the 1950 and 1955 editions of my book which describe "Electronic Dimmers" carry a message for those in the know. Most of the text is the same but not all of it. No, not all of it!

One way and another, and including the fact that, like lamps, one day valves needed replacement, this pioneer preset control was by no means as inexpensive to purchase and run as had been hoped. But the preset desk had been a revelation - a foretaste of things to come - for theatre people whose ideal control had been a Grand Master. Reliability was a serious problem in some installations but there were some, notably the one in Iceland and that in Stratford-upon-Avon, which saw many years of service. The latter was not replaced until the end of 1971 when the new installation went in for the 1972 season.

A substitute for electronics had to be found quickly, and position control of Mansell clutch was a must. McLeod had already designed a revised version of the latter which was in use on the Light Consoles in Her Majesty's and the Adelphi theatres. Due to the tight space for the dimmer rooms it had been essential to reduce the horizontal dimmer centres. Quite when the TMC* polarised relay turned up in our lives I cannot remember, but it made the commercial application of the well-known Wheatstone bridge servo-circuit practical at long last. The relay seems to have been developed during the war and was as compact and responsive as a thermionic valve, but of course far more robust. The 144-way early electronic in the New theatre, with which by then Donald Albery (previously an enthusiast) had become very discontented was taken out and replaced by an almost identical system 'PR', as we called it - a desk and of course clutch-operated motor-driven dimmer bank. Although it was still a double desk, it had a feature not possessed by its predecessor, namely that the levers no longer needed to be used to hold lighting in

* Telephone Manufacturing Company

use. Once dimmers had been driven into position they stayed there. In consequence one could set two lighting changes ahead of that in use, instead of one. To combine this with the stop-key selection of a Light Console was logical, and this turned up as system 'CD' that Christmas in the Palace theatre*.

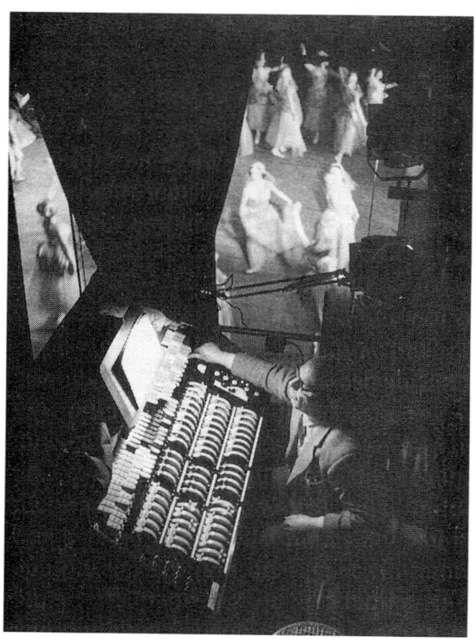

"So we had to make do with the perch actors' right"

We were both lucky and unlucky at the Palace Theatre. There was no position out-front for the CD console so we had to make do with the perch actors' right. The perch itself was quite spacious and as such sites go it did offer the operator some view of the stage from the wings. The operators there invoke happy memories, especially the first one, but they were all good and the control was trouble free. The first man subsequently went to Australia but while at the Palace he found the CD real fun, and once cues were established he would devise novel ways of working the more complicated ones which he would show off to Paul or me. This was all the more interesting because being the first CD for theatre and for Emile Littler into the bargain, it had minimal facilities. I can easily recall the hubbub when I dropped in for the first time the console was really being used. Emile was doing the lighting during his dress-rehearsal with the band. As if that was not enough, there was no communication system with the backstage areas. It seemed to be a matter of shouting across the band. Be that as it may, he went on to order a similar CD for the Cambridge theatre which he was running at the time. Not bad for a man who when Stanley and I first went to sell him the idea of a CD console for the Palace in his office next door to the Coliseum, declared that what he really wanted was, "a couple of second-hand Grand Masters."

* The system was called CD. This contains an essential clue to its antecedents. CD, according to 'B' Bear stood for "Corps Diplomatique" ie. pro-Console. On such whimsy did we base our marketing! System SR stood for Saturable-Reactor; but LC stood for Len's Choke, hardly descriptive but he (Len Leggett) devised the transistor preset circuit!

Although we were to do many CD installations for theatre, the system had been devised to serve the needs of live television. Historically that is fact; therefore the subject is dealt with in the next chapter. Meantime the Light Console did very well for spectacle in the larger theatres. It was also exported to Ankara, two for Caracas in Venezuela and one, the last of the line, for Warsaw's Theatre Polski in 1955. By then there had been sixteen installations, representing a total of 2,088 dimmer channels, excluding Strand's demonstration theatres and the Ideal Home hire job. "Not altogether bad," as 'B' might have said, considering those times.

In 1954, the original export job, the S'Carlos Opera Lisbon, resurfaced, and even I, who had easily resisted any travel temptations the other jobs had offered, could not resist this one. So off I went to Lisbon, in the novel Viscount turbo-prop this time. It was a question of up-dating the installation and adding more dimmers. From then on, "business and pleasure," as the USA visa puts it, trips were to provide all the travel and adventure I needed world-wide. And from time to time Ilse came too; not purely on social grounds as at conferences; but as a jolly good interpreter. And what about our two sons when we were both travelling? The answer was often no less a person than 'B' Bear. However for my first visit ever to Germany in August 1956 no such luxury was possible. After all, Freddy was only 4½ and Jeremy was 2½. Jeremy posed something of a problem for me on that tour. He was very fond indeed of his daddy at that time and had to be sent plenty of postcards. Thanks to our Sunday trips from Ealing to Kew Gardens on top of the 65 bus via Brentford along the Thames, he had developed a passion for gasworks. Neither gasworks or postcards of them seemed to be a feature of Germany, but for some reason oil and other factory installations were; so I was able to get by with a certain amount of deceit.

The Aula Magna, Caracas, was a prime case of one job leading to another. Their original enquiry was passed over to Strand by Philips in Eindhoven to which it had been sent. It asked for a quote for a similar stage lighting installation to that of the Royal Festival Hall for the new concert hall to be built as part of the university. Similar it certainly could not be. The only place for any front-of-house spots was around the rear wall of the *fan-shaped* auditorium. On such a long throw these had to be our new narrow-beam Patt.93s and I used 32 of them, if I remember aright. The Light Console was a single manual with 94 channels instead of the Festival Hall's 84 and unlike that job there was plenty of space to build it on standard organ lines with roll-top cover and all. Once quoted, *nothing* more was heard for months, when suddenly there came from Venezuela an urgent order for the whole lot as our quote. It happened at just the right time; we needed work at Gunnersbury and here it was. Stanley brought Jack Hylton along to see the completed masterpiece on test and orders for 152-channel 2-manual Light Consoles at the Adelphi and His Majesty's theatres soon followed.

Despite damage during delivery due to our misguided packing methods (or rather lack of any, to judge from Paul Weston's report at the time) Strand nevertheless received an order for a 2-manual 121-channel Console for the new Plaza cinema in Caracas. This and Theatre Polski in 1955 were the last of the keyboard consoles. Theatre Polski had involved entertaining in June 1954 a delegation of three engineers from Warsaw plus A.N. Other. The latter represented the Stasi, or whatever it was, and kept a strict eye on the three human beings. A bottle of port and Jeremy, who was then only six months old, played important roles when Ilse put on a dinner for them at our home in Ealing. Stasi enjoyed the port so much that glass after glass was tossed down in the Vodka manner. Next day he was out of action and our, by now, three friends enjoyed a day-off his leash, which they put to good use, we gathered. The third engineer was the theatre electrician. Communication with this electrician who only had Polish was difficult indeed, but as a grandfather he and our baby Jeremy got on fine. For much of their stay in London we were loaned a young woman on the staff of the RSC as interpreter. We did of course take them on a day outing to Stratford, where chance ordained that on the lawn in front of the theatre, Morris dancers were carrying out their eccentric ritual, ponderously waving handkerchiefs and legs in the air, which must have modified the Polish image of we English somewhat.

Theatre Polski set up the strangest of chance encounters. On their last day we returned with them from lunch to the office so they could collect up their things. As was not unusual I was intercepted and by the time I rejoined them it was obvious our RSC interpreter was in need of the ladies' room. I escorted her along the corridor to the staircase at the far end, telling her that at the very top floor she would find it and I saw her no more. So what, the reader may ask? Well, the scene changes and it is sixteen years later in the new Ottawa Arts Centre in far off Canada. I am wandering that morning in the main foyer when down an open staircase from the Ladies comes..... You've guessed it, and my remark, "My word you have been a long time." I simply had to put it on record here. Not really surprising she had got a job there; but that we should meet at the bottom of those particular stairs after all those years - amazing!

While on the subject of coincidences, here is another. Not unnaturally my work saw me making, like it or not, a lot of flights. The one that is really memorable came late in that career. Returning from Glasgow to Heathrow in a crowded plane, I found myself sitting on the gangway side of a smart business woman who did not even exchange a glance to see what had landed alongside. Time passed without a word until we were approaching Heathrow. Out of the blue, literally, she turned to me and said, "Do you mind holding my hand?" She went on to say that she was scared stiff of landings. To which I uttered reassuring words while enjoying contact - she really was quite attractive. Descent began, nearer and nearer to touch-down; when suddenly with a roar, all engines full-blast we shot upwards. As we circled the voice of the pilot apologised that the previous plane was not yet clear of the runway. So there it was, an all time double, never before or since has either happened to me, let alone both together.

A narrow escape of another kind may not be out of place here. This time it was an electrical trap that we in R&D fell into. But for Fred's intervention it could have had serious consequences. That Fred was not me but our elder son when he was aged five or so. Strand was in great need of a connector-socket to take a standard 3-pin 15-amp BS. plug. It was a version of the 2-pin of DC days with an earth contact added that had been in existence for many unsafe years. Also there was a 3-in-line 'Bakelite' pair of connectors; but it was time to replace them with something up-to-date, strong and safe. A die-cast bath-shaped affair with 'Bakelite' shuttered insert was devised, approved, and five-thousand die-castings ordered. One of the first-offs I took home to try out, in the course of which I explained its safety measures to Freddy, who even at that age was fascinated by such things. He took it away and came back ten-minutes or so later with the query. "If .... then, why can I do this?" He had found a way of forcing in one sort of plug which had not occurred to us in our disciplined tests. The outer metal case *could* become live if..... There was nothing for it but to abort the project. Wandering around Woolworths not long after, I saw the very thing which would do the job, lying in a heap on the counter. Thirty-three years later it is the direct descendants of that Woolworth connector which still dominate our stage lighting installations.

My first tour of Germany is best seen as 'Three Men in a VW' or *'Three Men on a Bummel'* perhaps. Woody and I flew to Munich and from then on we were in Gerd Ohlmer's hands and his Volkswagen car. Being Munich we soon found ourselves in a bierkeller, several in fact. At first encounter the shock was considerable. They seemed awash with beer from overflowing 'steins'. Our pubs seemed positively gentle; mind you that was 1956. Anyway Gerd's target-for-tonight was the restaurant not the 'kellers'. The memory of the taste of the fine freshwater fish served that night lingers on, though not in name. The other memorable first encounter that night was with the word "Umleitung" (diversion). Thereafter the German landscape and

Woody and the Listening Man

townscape was littered with Umleitungen. No sooner we had set course and got up speed, than one of these diversion signs would appear. This was natural since large chunks of autobahn needed restoration after the ravages of war. One could see the reason, but in the cities "Umleitung" seemed to arise from sheer perversity; like being 'verboten' for a pedestrian to cross a road without a car in sight, simply because the signal was red. At Munich we had to drive all round the map to get from a theatre, we needed to visit, to our hotel on the other side of the square. As we did this Gerd would keep saying, "There's the dome," when all I could see was some spires, first to the South, then to the East and so forth. His English was so good that it was days before I rumbled that the word was 'Dom', i.e. cathedral. Bed was the stage for my first battle with a duvet or more appropriately 'Steppdecke' as the Germans call it. Fighting with it that night, little did I think that not only would I grow accustomed to its face; but would come to prefer it to blankets and sheets at home!

After a whole morning with the Munich TV people we set course for Vienna, intending to stop overnight on the way. This overnight stay, Gerd had declared, would be easy as there were plenty of 'zimmer' and no need to book ahead. The result that night resembled the quest of Harris, George and 'J' in 1889* except in our case it wasn't Datchet but Bad Ishl. We too were forced to return to our earlier fastidious rejects of hotels one by one, only to find them now booked solid. In the end Woody and I shared a small bed just as we had given up all hope, and Gerd made do with an armchair and his feet on a chair across our door. Luckily the room was on the ground floor and I was able to make use of a bush in the garden rather than disturb him during the night. The next morning after a detour we found ourselves drinking coffee by the lakeside at the "White Horse Inn" - yes, it was THE "White Horse Inn". We didn't manage to make Vienna that evening but stopped at Baden nearby. Thanks to that we were able to see three aged couples tottering around to the strains of a 'valse' from an almost equally aged nickelodeon in an ancient ballroom deserted but for us. Truly in Vienna, always they dance!

Whether those aged pairs got much sleep that night, we three certainly didn't . Our rooms overlooked an inner courtyard and after we went to bed the place livened up and we were tormented by the racket as more and more inebriated persons sought out the 'Damen & Herren'. Not only did they make chatty progress to and fro but the doors of their respective relief-stations sprung closed with a loud hygienic bangs deep into the night. It would be nice but incorrect to say that we slept well in Vienna itself the following night. Fate ordained that we chose a hotel with a welcoming look in a quiet part of the city, only to become aware much later that it enjoyed an excellent turnover in nocturnal red-light business. It is improbable, but true, that virtually every night wherever we stopped some strange disturbance interposed itself

* *Three Men in a Boat* by Jerome K. Jerome

between us and slumber. At one date in a small town we actually managed to obtain three small rooms lying alongside the wall of an indoor bowling alley night club. The next night, at Worms, we took jolly good care to choose rooms overlooking the cathedral square about which hung an all pervading reverent hush. We should have guessed; not long after midnight, teams and transport arrived to erect the stalls for market day, or maybe it was the 'Saint Wormsfest'. Anyway it inspired me to greet a sleepless Gert and Woody at breakfast with the words, "In Germany they either play with their balls all night or have erections in the square." This remark of mine was destined to endure. I am sure that some of those who had to listen to either Gerd or Woody retail the tale over subsequent decades, thought it apocryphal; as indeed some of the other remarks attributed to me, are!

It would be a great pity to convey the impression that our version of the Grand Tour was an ordeal, it was not. It was a great adventure with two companions who could not have been bettered. Gerd had perfect command of English, having spent some time, between the wars, at the County school just across the railway bridge at the top end of the Watford Road in Harrow, a school well known to me by sight. He was a man of culture and if we had time we never passed by anything of note still standing or rebuilt without going inside. One such detour took us up the hill to Heidelburg castle to be greeted suddenly, as we turned the corner, with a great banner across the gateway proclaiming "Genuine Ohio Popcorn" - a lesser known peril in the American zone. As to Gerd's own war record in the German army, he seems to have spent most of his time in occupied Norway and the fact that he so frequently went back there afterwards to stay with one friend and another was surely significant. Another aspect of his character was provided by pre-dinner drinks in his flat in Brunswick. An abiding memory is of his care in preparing a dry-martini that James Bond could not have faulted.

One of the trips over there provided two opportunities to see the Hamburg Opera House in action. The first night from the backstage switchboard perch and the second to enjoy *Cosi van Tutti* from prime seats out front. The control was then an AEG thyratron/reactor job; but it was the opera (whose name escapes me) set in the Ireland of legend that provided the big thrill. The famous stage, the only part to have survived our bombs, was set as a giant rocky staircase with, as a result, a perilous precipice up-stage. At spear-point the heroine, or prima donna at any rate, was driven back and back up them steps by a brutal man with untidy whiskers everywhere and horns sticking out of his helmet. From our perch Woody and I could see the real disaster backing her backside. Without a glance, back and back she went and there was no net to catch her. At the critical moment two sturdy stage-hands could be seen (by us) shoving upwards a giant pair of tongs to grasp her round the waist as the lights blacked out. An example of legendary German precision if ever there was one. This was more than countered in Act-2 of *Cosi van Tutti* the following night. Shortly after curtain-up the singers found themselves competing with a loud tape relay of something far from 'Cosi'. After a couple of minutes the noise came to an end with a sigh of relief from everyone; only to restart even more violently a bit later in the scene. The Maestro stopped the band this time and the singers with gestures of resignation sat on the edge of the large circular dais which was the feature of this set. Search parties set out presumably. German backstage areas are large indeed, and some time elapsed before the noise ceased and the all-clear given.

November 1960 saw we-three at Helmstedt about to cross the border with all the visa rigmarole that entailed, including rationed time to drive along the lonely road across the Russian zone to Berlin itself. Timing at our Theatre Colloquium target was, as is not unusual especially at an international one, also critical. Although not scheduled to speak on stage lighting or anything else I simply *had* to, so that I in my role as editor of *TABS* could report my own 'contribution' in full. By sitting on the edge of a chair in the front row all day I was able to report,

> *"The meeting on stage lighting, which shared a day with Stage Machinery, Sight Lines, and Acoustics, was opened by a commendably brief and pungent contribution from Joel Rubin (USA) to make a basis for discussion. However, M. Leblanc (France) reverted to the long descriptive dissertation favoured by so many speakers. Furthermore, the papers on Acoustics and Sight Lines intervened and by the time a few minutes was found for Stage Lighting discussion Mr. Ruben's points had vanished into the haze. Frederick Bentham (Strand Electric) managed to obtain the floor for the last five minutes of a long day and what he said to the punch drunk audience was more or less as follows: . . ."*

However, I need not go into that here. Anyone really curious can seek out *TABS* Vol.18 No.3 December 1960 where Fred gave *himself* 740 words and the rest of the Colloquium 400! At that time our circulation world-wide was nearly 17,500 so the exercise was well worthwhile.

There was much to see in West Berlin of course. Indeed the problem with all my visits to Germany is to avoid mere name dropping; though they are of places not people. I liked the Schiller theatre which had just opened, *inside* whose stage lifts and revolve we technical delegates like children were given a ride. Gerd and I went to the Kroll Opera house that night for a performance of the opera *Xerxes*, Apart from the fact that it was the first time I had ever seen Handel staged, it was a strange experience to be sitting there in what had become Hitler's Reichstag after his

Reichstag fire. But it was passage through the Brandenburg gate to the East Berlin Staatsoper that provided real excitement. Our two visits were both after dark; the first as delegates to see over the building and stage. Somehow we lingered behind and lost our party. Without our guide we found ourselves out in the road at the back of the building. Looking both left and right, there in the ill-lit misty distance was in each case a small group of uniformed men with rifles slung over their shoulders, evocative of shots in the *The Third Man.* Back through the exit door we dived. It was the second visit when Gerd and I went to *Eugene Onegin* there, which provided the odd feeling of being part of the foyer crowd and yet not; as referred to earlier in this chapter. As to the opera itself, it was most enjoyable and as a bonus was also a rare example of tactful televising of a show. It was all done very discreetly. There was no distraction at all. But for the fact that our seats were front row stalls, we would not have been aware of the cameras in the stage boxes as we turned to go to the foyer for the interval. There did not seem to be any supplementary lights either.

Gerd Ohlmer

What needs filling in here is something on Gerd Ohlmer's career in Strand Electric. There is every reason for singling him out from among the several unique European characters to which Strand owed so much; because of all the places in the world to which we might export stage lighting equipment, none seemed more improbable than Germany. They had been the European leaders in that field since the early years of electric light. It was a Siemens who over in England first devised the dimmer control for our Savoy theatre in 1881. And unlike GE and Westinghouse in the USA where they dabbled in theatre technology for relatively short periods, Siemens and AEG were firmly in control. It was to become true that with the passage of time AEG was to give up; but not so Siemens, who in 1987 were actually able to seize an order, from under Rank Strand's very noses, to put their latest lighting control system in OUR Royal Opera House. So my R&D department's early thyristor dimmer-banks of 1964 in Covent Garden found themselves under German mastery!

Post-war Gerd Ohlmer had found himself travelling around Germany dealing in distilled water and other 'apothecaric' items in the repertoire of the family firm of Diedr. Buschmann in Brunswick. His interest in theatre especially opera and ballet established a need for stage colour-filters. In 1955 he wrote to Strand therefore and was "appointed agent for Germany, importing on his own account and risk.

Extensive travels under the technical assistance and advice of Mr. Wood and other experts from London," followed. The words are his; and one of these early "travels" was the balls and erections affair above. At the end of that same year Gerd started an official branch under the name of Strand Electric-Hessenbruch. At the same time he moved to a large house nearby in Salzdahlum. It had a largish male population which was neatly summed up on one occasion when at teatime Gerd invited Ilse to pour out saying, "Since you are the only real woman present, you had better be Mother." On my own first stay there, it was obvious that as the only Englishman I must make the early morning 'cuppas'. One door was locked against my delivery of it - that of the only woman, a retired elderly ballerina. It was amazing how Gerd built-up that firm to become a real power in his land and, "to scout the lost European market with various English engineers; Prague, Budapest, Warsaw etc" to use his own words. Even after the Rank takeover in 1969 he never had a signed contract himself, yet he had to be the sole signatory for all German contracts - including one of DM13 million. Even after his retirement he had to return for two periods, "until everything was legally arranged for Heinz Fritz (the first employee he ever engaged) to succeed him." Born in 1912, he died unexpectedly in 1986. One year earlier he had come over for Woody's funeral service at Littleton Parish Church.

Gerd Ohlmer was a fine example of the kind of agent Woody seemed to attract, though whether by lucky chance or design it would be hard to tell. People like Torsten Hammarlund in Sweden, Carlo Casagrande in Finland and Fred Larsen in Norway, to name but three, soon came together as friends. And this kind of thing seemed the basis of so much in the old Strand. Whether it was common in other small companies in those distant decades I know not; certainly after the Rank takeover the atmosphere changed, even among those who managed to survive for any real length of time. I don't like the expression "team spirit" in our context. It has an air of drill and discipline about it. Our people got together on the job from a common interest. A good example is *My Fair Lady* at Drury Lane in 1958. There had been predictable trouble in the case of Peter Brooks' *Tempest* there a few weeks earlier and a meeting followed in the stalls one morning, between Prince Littler and Binkie Beaumont on the one hand and Stanley and I on the other. Joe Davis would only light *My Fair Lady* if I would undertake to sit by his side in the stalls for the many lighting rehearsals. I declared that I would only do this if Paul Weston was the Console operator and he, in his turn, stipulated that Mike Wooderson should be his standby.

We had no faith in the Drury Lane staff at that time; they were too used to sleep-walking their customary long runs. The rehearsals went on for nearly a month; but proved fascinating as we had the talented understudies as stand-ins and they sung and went through the routines and lines with enthusiasm whenever necessary. I had been put off the show by all the advance publicity from the States; but those understudies soon had me hooked - for ever! As to my own role, I do not remember doing anything except turning up after office hours and sitting alongside Joe, drinking Guinness and eating Lyons chocolate biscuits - appropriately named busbars (Buzz-bars, actually). It was an odd way to light a show: under the contract Joe had to use Abe Fader's original Broadway lighting and plot. This did not work out at the "Lane", of course. So up would go 'cue x' and there would follow a process of de-lighting item by item. Then Joe would proceed to add lights as necessary. Joe should have had control from the first; as no matter what the contract or anyone said, it certainly became his lighting. Ilse and I attended the first night in the Dress Circle. Even then I cannot say I made any real contribution, for when Ilse asked me to identify some of the notables in the Rotunda during the interval, all I could point out was Lady Docker!

VIII: WEMBLEY, GOLDEN SQUARE & RIVERSIDE
Television Takes Off ! 1954-64

Modesty is not going to be a feature of this chapter, as it deals with a time when I was really allowed my head. The impending launch of commercial television in 1956 and the competitive stimulus this gave the BBC made it something of a walk-over when compared with the battles to be fought to get theatres to purchase sophisticated control installations. Mind you, how we, or I, would have got on without 'B' Bear is another matter. Recently on a now less rare visit 'backstage' to a couple of the BBC TV Centre studios someone tapped me on the shoulder to remark "Ah, those King Street meetings. I shall never forget them!" or words to that effect. Indeed, much the same thing only more so, had occurred at the summer meeting of the Society of Television Lighting Directors at a restaurant in Windsor. It is possible that such a society, of which 'B' and I were made Hon. members, would never have come into being but for B's idea that we in Strand should hold an all-day meeting in 1957 in our King Street theatre for the TV Lighting people we knew. By that time he, at any rate, knew everyone, to judge by the noise as they all assembled like an old boys' reunion in our lower showroom. The food - wrapped sandwiches as purchased by Henry Myers at the Lyons teashop alongside the Arts theatre - was certainly not the draw, nor the morning lecture by myself. But 'B' saw to it that they did not go thirsty and it really was a reunion - for they all had been in the BBC before seeking their fortune in the new ITV companies.

'B' and I had our eyes on television right from the start of Alexandra Palace in 1936. When purchasing gramophone records for our Light Console Society recitals we would watch the Saturday afternoon transmission on the great mirror-lidded Marconiphone set in the basement of Remington Van Wych's shop, before returning to Floral Street to rehearse. Then, as already pointed out, early in 1938 I had purchased my own 405-line Murphy TV.

Identifying 'firsts' can be difficult to establish as my brother was to find in 1979. Hurriedly commissioned to do a Golden Jubilee slate tablet to be fixed to the one time Baird premises in Long Acre declaring the 'First Regular TV Transmission in the World', or something to that effect, he had just completed it when the call came to alter 'World' to 'Great Britain'. And slate is not an easy material to muck about with. That Baird system was the old 30-line low-definition dead end which I had seen in Croydon. In 1936 it was the 405-line Alexandra Palace Emitron studio that was going to be the important one. Into this, and the Baird 240-line studio next door, Applebee shoved a couple of 35-way Grand Masters. The only thing special about these obstructions on the studio floor was the use of mercury switches (instead of the usual knife switches) to reduce the noise. I was very annoyed about the use of Grand Masters and the odd visits I made out there were all the more vexatious because they found they could seldom waste precious light by using the dimmers and fades were better achieved by using the camera controls and just switching the lights on and off!

I could easily have designed them something neat taking up no space for this purpose with a 'Hold' circuit or some preset, for the same money or less. A chap called Stephen Thomas used to rub this in by saying that they had the perfect dimmer on the camera and dimmers had no future in television. Since I had a notion that television was going to be a good outlet for my Light Console one day, this was irritating to say the least. I have never been at all clear about the background of Stephen Thomas. He first came into my life when I had to design special flush mounting ceiling spotlights for the ceramic display in our Government pavilion at the Paris Exposition of 1936 and later when I did the cyclorama lighting and cloud effects behind the globe in the Government pavilion in the Empire exhibition in Bellevue Park Glasgow in 1938. Obviously he had some connection with the then Department of Overseas Trade.

Around the time Alexandra Palace went on the air, in Autumn 1936, I had to meet Gerald Cock (who was then head of BBC Television), Stephen Thomas and the Dean, in Westminster Abbey on a secret mission. This turned out to be none other than the televising of the crowning ceremony of King Edward VIII. The rest of the coronation service would be sound only; but vision would be added direct from that part of the Abbey under the crossing, known appropriately as "the theatre". The question to be answered on the spur of the moment was how would I set about it? There was no one else there to butt-in and as far as memory serves I suggested 100 of our Pageant lanterns to go up *somewhere* in the triforium. These to be cabled back to a couple of the liquid dimmer banks we had in Hire stock. The purpose of the dimmers was to bring in and take out all this extra lighting on *very slow* checks so that the congregation would not be aware of what was going on. In retrospect I am sure that many would have nevertheless experienced a sense of elation which they would have put down as Divine in origin. All this was 'not altogether bad', as 'B' would have said, for straight off the cuff.

In December 1936, not long after this meeting, Phyllis took me to a small dance academy one evening. It was somewhere just off Shepherds Bush Green. I think they may have hoped for some advice from me on lighting. Anyway we sat among the audience as a single row around a square. An attractive slim girl in a suitably ambiguous Oriental costume danced a solo. Between the movements of, probably,

Luigini's *Ballet Egyptien* she held a pose with arms upstretched within a couple of feet of us, whereupon her bare midriff gave vent to a positive cadenza of tinkling sounds which echoed around the hushed room. I expect she remembers it as I do to this day, whoever she was and wherever she is. The other memorable thing about that evening was the adjournment to the lounge after the show for coffee and the radio. And there I heard Edward VIII deliver a 'farewell message' to his country which I 'decoded' as: there would be no role for me and our pageants and liquid dimmers in the Abbey. I was right, because although George VI allowed his coronation to be filmed in the Abbey, television was limited to an Outside Broadcast from Hyde Park Corner.

We now change the scene to 1953 and the 'Lord Ranelagh', the pub just up the road from Earls Court's Empress Hall. 'B' and I were in consultation. He had summoned me from home one Saturday morning to see what was the matter with the control which we were loaning one of the two Radio Show BBC TV studios - the other studio was equipped by an opposition firm. They were both simple saturable reactor dimmer types with small 36-way panels upstairs in their respective control rooms. Ours may have been borrowed from the demonstration theatre. Be that as it may, it had gone berserk. The lights in the studio never came higher than half and this was achieved at both the full-on and off ends of dimmer lever travel; in other words the lights did a half-hearted dip as the levers were moved from top to bottom. With the opposition next door, an air of unconcern adorned our faces while the brain went to work inside. The two 18-way dimmer racks still hummed with electricity even when the phase fuses were removed. The contractor, Mole Richardson, had got phase and neutral reversed on one rack so that we in fact were doing a phase change with the levers. Needless to say one did not diagnose this at once - and when corrected the levers still did not bring lights to full. Goodness knows what made us take a look in the studio at last, but when we did there were the lights blazing away - the windows of the control room were glazed with the then rare grey tinted glass!

What happened, and exactly when, is difficult to remember, but a brief account of Strand's entry into the TV world as 'B' and F.P.B. saw it in 1964 did appear in the Jubilee *TABS**. What that article could not make clear was that it was not 'B's job to sell TV lighting controls. He had neither the Strand Board's sanction for this, nor for the pricing policy we adopted. As a result of pressure from the directors of the two departments whose concern *was* sales of equipment I, not then a director, was taken to task by Jack Sheridan who had a schedule of the contracts carried out or on order at the time. He was appalled that some of them had our official profit margins cut to the bone. There was an inquest and although 'B' was not yet the

* *TABS* Vol. 22 No. 1 March 1964

corpse, someone obviously had poisoned the atmosphere so that he would become one! I well remember standing there and insisting gently again and again that in total there *was* profit. With that admitted at last, I went on to insist that it was a good profit. This was true. Such was the skill deployed by 'B' and FPB in 'playing' even the most lukewarm customers, that Strand adverts (written by FPB) were able to claim for a number of years that we had supplied all the controls for both BBC and Commercial studios. Actually, I would have liked to have added "except One Small One". This was in Aston Birmingham where Applebee's department demanded to be allowed to tackle it - and lost it to Major Equipment!

Back in 1953 at Earls Court 'B' had been operating well within the ambit of Strand Hire department (where he was then assistant manager to Jack Madre) in arranging with 'Grump' Mayhew of BBC to hire controls for nothing or next to nothing. But by January the following year negotiations and contracts produced a request from H.C. Nickels of P&ID (Planning and Installation Department) that a demonstration be given to a BBC delegation. This took place in our King St. theatre and was followed by a visit to the London Coliseum on March 11th specifically to see the 216-way Light Console. Now it is a fact that our first order for a remote lighting control for BBC TV was for one of my beloved Light Consoles. It was to be installed in the Shepherds Bush Empire where Phil and I as boys had sat in the front row during the Great Carmo's circus and had for the first (and only!) time stroked a pair of lion cubs brought down from the stage so to do. This variety house by Frank Matcham was a stone's throw from that other boyhood rendezvous, Frank Verity's Shepherds Bush Pavilion. The Empire was about to become the BBC TV Theatre and in view of the success of the Console in the London Palladium its choice would seem a logical one, a world away from those idiotic Grand Masters of Alexandra Palace; but I did *not* want to supply it!

In considering the lighting of television shows it is necessary for the reader to remember that they were transmitted live. Only the Sunday play went out a second time, on Thursday, and even that was live. This explains why television studio production was a combination of cinema studio and theatre techniques. The better cameras post-war allowed dimmers to be included once more. 'B' thought that in the time available we should concentrate on these dimmers and their control, and made arrangements with 'Old Man' Page, who ran Mole Richardson over here, that we were content to leave the rest to them. There was nothing in writing, it was a 'Gentlemen's Agreement' over drinks, of course. Here is yet another example of the way so much of my career has involved retracing again and again my own footsteps, in this case Mole Richardson were in Chase Road, Acton, a little way down from Compton's factory on the opposite side of the road. Mole Richardson's equivalent of that firm's 'Jim Pollard' as far as we were concerned was S. Lewis ('Johnny') Johnson. From then on Johnny, 'B' and I were often seen around as a trio.

In the event the permanent installation at Shepherds Bush did not go ahead at that time and the BBC turned their attention to two old film studios they had acquired at Riverside just by Hammersmith Bridge. These were to go into action, as soon as possible, as properly equipped studios. In so doing they would act as a useful test ground as to what should go into the new White City TV Centre - only the scenery workshops had by then been built. There were to be two studios at Riverside and although my specifications were dated February 21st 1955 and we issued the orders on our factory on March 11th (which stated "to be working on site mid-October"), as far as studio R1 was concerned the only real item settled at this time to remain unchanged was the price; £16,857 nett. Included in this sum, my notes include £250 "desk foolery". We issued a heavily revised specification on August 15th, but in January 1956 there were new delivery dates; R2 on site by February 9th and R1 by March 16th.

About this time another character entered our TV scene. He came from South Africa via BTH Rugby and his name was Ackerman and he became an assistant to Nickels in P&ID. To tell the truth, he might be of assistance to Nickels but to 'B' and Bentham he certainly wasn't then. The trouble was that, although a qualified illuminating engineer (he was to become IES president for 1974/75), he was busy trying to *learn* about television lighting techniques as quickly as he could. So he was no use to us in our task of filling up the gaps in our knowledge. However, before long Ken Ackerman was our P&ID contact for 'our' jobs. So much so, that when he was away on holiday in South Africa, the manager of that department (known to all, seemingly, as 'Uncle') asked me to meet him at the Langham opposite Broadcasting House. There we collected our drinks and indicated to onlookers that we were *Going Dutch* (no possible corruption) by each waving our arm with our own money over the bar counter. This was Uncle's instruction to me and he was dead serious. That hurdle cleared, we got down to business: his problem was that our equipment as being supplied seemed to differ so much from the specification. Of course this was so. Because we were all learning at this time, there was only one real rule - Strand must keep to the price on the BBC order. I wish I could name the many friends we made at that time. One was Bob Anderson, soon known to us as "Breakages Ltd." As another member of P&ID he had a gift for fault-finding. The most remarkable occasion was when on a visit to Gunnersbury works to report progress, he went over to a bracket-handle board nothing to do with the BBC. There it was poised with its test label, ready for despatch. For no reason he pulled out that very circuit fuse with the test label and behold - unlike the rest, that fuseholder had no fuse wire in it!

It is an odd thought that if anyone had told me then that one day Bob would become the proud owner of our canal cruiser 'Peter Sam'; or that Ken Ackerman and his wife Joan would enjoy regular days out on 'Peter Sam' during the twenty years we owned it, I would of course said that they were talking nonsense!

The BBC committee and working party discussions (and there was somewhat of a divide between those who planned and those who used - or rather would use) did cause delay but they were valuable for 'B' and I to take part in. After all, this was when the BBC was *the* source of all knowledge as to practical studio working - albeit based on rather makeshift converted premises, as at Lime Grove (immediately behind the Shepherds Bush Pavilion!) It is no good overlooking the fact that I was the only one who could talk about and provide sophisticated lighting control which would work and be reliable in UK in the 'fifties. This was confirmed by the big turnout, including Sir Harold Bishop and Alistair Maclean (the BBC chief engineer and his deputy) when on December 12th 1957 I gave my paper* in the old, and much more impressive, lecture theatre of the Institution of Electrical Engineers at the bottom of Savoy Hill. Opposite which the BBC were housed at no. 2 in my boyhood days and where that other influence, ELMA the lamp ring, had once kept a curb on any too bright ideas in spotlights.

I think the thing that most impressed me about my first IEE paper was to see P.P. Eckersley sitting at the end of the front row - a great name in the early years of the wireless. Awe inspiring the BBC might be (until one got to know it!), the real zip came from the Commercial companies. Those in charge of lighting were all BBC trained but there was neither the time nor enough of them in each company to get involved with meetings. One sold an idea and was left to get on with it. Consequently the main lines of control with the Commercials were established and even installed by the time 'B' and I began to discuss any real detail with the BBC. Discussion, if any, tended to centre on lantern suspensions, studio grids and the like; but that was Johnny Johnson's province, and right well he ruled it. And so did we ours.

Associated Rediffusion's studios 1 and 2 at Wembley, on the edge of what had been the Empire exhibition of 1923, were the first this side of the Atlantic to have lighting controls designed specifically with TV in mind. Although the dimmer room was just the other side of the control room wall we were determined that there must be no repetition of that Ally Pally Grand Master nonsense. We had no idea how much Rediffusion would be prepared to spend, so two versions of the control desk were dreamt up. The more expensive, system B, appeared as a detailed line drawing in a red 'book' with photos of the Ally Pally Grand Master, the Drury Lane Light Console with operator, the New Theatre twin desk and appropriate clutch-operated servo dimmer rack and thyratron valve rack. The last had a small 38-way jack and cord patch as an integral part. Goodness knows what that had been for. One thing is certain, none of the photos were of TV jobs - except of course the

* *Electric Control of Stage and Television Lighting* IEE paper no. 2424 U 1957.

'dear' old Ally Pally one. Equally certain is that we had no intention of selling that type or the 'Electronic' for TV. Strangely enough that was just what we were going to be forced to in the latter case by the BBC of all people. A third version of control, system C, "designed for the large television studio in which an exceptional number of lanterns are hung to avoid waste of time in rigging. The control problem is to discard the lanterns unwanted for a particular production so that large numbers of control channels do not lie idle."

Patching, the flexible selection from a larger number of circuits to a lesser number of dimmers, so common in American stage lighting; had scarcely been practised over here. But television studio work in those days, when dimming was so much more expensive than switching, was bound to need something of the sort. Cord and Jack type and later Cord and Jill when a female was needed so that the dimmer could be moved to circuit sockets, we did set out to make. My own obsession was with remote switchpatch and this I am surprised to find I described in the very first edition of our TV red book. In due course the BBC were to adopt it for the Riverside I; but it never got any further than that, as we shall see later. It was a good idea derived *obliquely* from the extension principle used in cinema organs to provide several stops in various pitches from a single rank of pipes. Most brainwaves have their origin somewhere - no matter how improbable.

Before getting into Riverside we must get Wembley out of the way. It had seemed sensible for Mole Richardson to act as main contractor, so we had quoted them for 'System A' and 'System B' alternatives, but they still had to be sold to Associated Rediffusion and this we set out to do one afternoon. Already cowed by our first encounter with Musak in the lift, 'B' and I met Johnny in an ante-room where he passed over our quotation as retyped on their paper to include their profit. The shock was terrible, our lips went dry; we had been alarmed at our figures especially 'System B', but to have to sell these! The door opened and in we went. There sat the director a Mr Gabriel and the chap of theirs we knew, rugged and friendly Eric Vast. We talked and I held forth on the merits of system B with the instant group memory based on their latching crossbar relay and their luminous stop-heads - none of which we had a hope of selling. The handing over of the quote could be put off no longer. Gabriel read it carefully, turned to Vast and said "I think we had better go for system B".

This was a landmark indeed, from then on it was a fundamental part of the equipment and operation of any TV studios of any importance. Long before electronics could take over and extend what is now known as RAM (Random Access Memory) we had it thanks to a relay designed by Comptons in 1930 and part of any de luxe version of their pipe organ console piston action - and therefore my Light Console! Subsequent to this although we worked very closely with Mole Richardson we both quoted independently and avoided any discount uplifts.

So far this chapter has been written without any particular stimulus, but the remainder follows the 50-year anniversary celebrations of the opening of Alexandra Palace. These, as far as I was concerned, were conferences which took place in Bradford at the end of September 1986 and Savoy Place in November almost to the day of the first high-definition television broadcast. The venue at Bradford was the Museum of Photography, Film and Television and since it was a STLD conference it was more fun as one felt at home. Also it more than made up for the relegation at the IEE of lighting to a mere 20 minutes on the last afternoon of its three days. I was asked to be one of the four opening speakers at the evening launch at Bradford. This I much enjoyed. As usual on these occasions the sound amplification played up and even managed to include from time to time some inter-taxi talk from outside. As Leslie Bridgewater and Bob Gray gave their talks sitting at the table, I decided since there was no platform that it was better to stand. Furthermore, I would stand and move around in front of the microphone and not behind it. This gave me full control of my audience and I went over big, as one might say. My only regret was that I made no mention of the Chinese gynaecologist in my reminiscences. All the more so as he, Ron Koplick, was present in the audience. They would have picked it up at once as it was it was the joke of all jokes which brought the house down when he likened himself to a member of that profession as he gazed with his head on one side in bewilderment at what I was demonstrating - system KTV or 'Klonk' in King Street. All this was back in April 1959 when the STLD was 'our' society and we had to show off our first Thyristor dimmer. We were on the way to Dimmer Memory controls albeit using punch-cards. For the desk a system known as 'Shift' was devised to scan and activate part of the installation at a time. It does show my profound aversion to single channel numerical call-up, because this would have been both cheaper and less difficult using the same means at the time. But I had rejected phone dial and uniselector back in 1930 in favour a playable 'organ' console, so I was hardly likely to change my philosophy now. All this is really irrelevant here as *we* ('B' and I) had no intention in going ahead with system KTV - hence its full name Klonktechnischewerk a fake German portmanteau word and the art of using it, Klonktechnischebunken. All of which was shown to the TV lighting designers at the demonstration. One result of which was a query by a high BBC administrator over drinks afterwards, as to why on earth I had given the system a German name?

Jack Sheridan also seemed put out when sometime after he queried why we had not sold any yet. To which my reply had to be that we did not want to. The fact was that the writing was on the wall for electro-mechanical servo systems and it was not sensible to get really involved. The new solid-state thyristor dimmer meant that we were bound to go all-electric sooner or later. The next step was Strand C/AE in which all-electric thyristor dimmer banks were operated via a relay and contactor array which automatically *parked* channels brought-in. Compton group-memory was retained and in consequence the number of levers as presets was much less than otherwise would have been needed. We stuck to two presets for television and Associated Rediffusion's Wembley 5 was a good example. This was a large twin studio with movable sound barrier walls in the middle. For some reason only the CD servo-system in one half, or rather one side, of the divide was replaced by a C/AE all-electric. A number of these were installed including a couple in BBC White City. However as with most things for them by then they departed from the *pure* intent of the originator*.

Another example of this, but for the theatre, was Covent Garden. By 1964 it was more than time to remove their pioneering and unique 1934 Mansell remote control and replace it with the latest system available. The result was a 240-way C/AE in the Summer of 1964 and along with it Strand Contracts Department did a new electrical installation. The control desk was not exactly as I would have liked. Instead of my three sets of preset levers each with its own set of 40 Compton group memories as quoted, Bill Bundy, then their Technical Director, insisted on four presets *without any increase in price.* So there was nothing for it but to cut the Compton to two sets, covering presets 1 & 2 and 3 & 4 respectively, to cover the cost of the extra set of levers. This made an arrangement which took rather more getting used to and put further strain on the very limited space in the new control room out-front at the back of the three-row deep Grand Tier. This was a very good, almost centre, location, but it was only a converted ventilation shaft. So tight was it, that we were never able to photograph this important job on site for publicity purposes, and relay gear had to be housed in a sort of attic above our ceiling, access only by cat ladder before the main cable set out on its long journey for the dimmer room under-stage right. We were only on the edge of the solid-state micro-chip age then, of course.

The Palladium in 1966 was a good C/AE installation. The regular ATV programme, "Sunday Night at the London Palladium" in that theatre made the 152 ways of the 1949 Light Console too few, both in number and wattage. There was no question by then of putting in an extra servo-dimmer bank and substituting a 3-manual console for the old 2-manual one, as might well have been done some years earlier. With some regret, the end of circle position was given up for a behind-glass room at the rear of that same circle. There were two presets, one under the fingers and one as an adjacent wing. Each had its own set of forty Compton group-memories. The remote control colour-filter change being very important in Palladium shows, a row of stopkeys with their own group action, was therefore provided on this console.

* For somewhat more detailed descriptions of the Strand-Bentham Era control systems see Appendix.

The Palladium was also to become a good example of the 'change for changes sake' our takeover brought with it. Such marketing sees every customer as a sale no matter whether he has something similar of yours which would do him as well already. This was not peculiar to Rank - it is the 'glory' or disease of our time. It goes on everywhere; cars, cookers, cameras, videos and all the rest. Every now and then, in the engineering or ergonomic context, there is a real breakthrough which cannot be ignored and one has every right to draw the customer's attention to this and try to make a sale. Where, however, as in the case of the Palladium C/AE, what had been supplied was doing a very satisfactory job and the system you propose to replace it with had already had a run of some years (and in terms of the rate of electronic development the firm's R&D must already have the next advance well on the way), it is positively dishonest to make the sale. It is not as if, in this kind of equipment, one is dealing with stock in store and where one is, there is always the well recognised principle of the "Sale". All this is to say that I did not think the Rank Strand modular system MMS was good enough to justify its replacing the C/AE. Were it not for that ill-timed change there can be no doubt that the Palladium would have had some years earlier a really compact control of a number of channels and a flexibility for using them better suited to the requirements of the productions staged in that period. Of course it is all very well for me to write in this manner from the safety of my retirement where the question of sales figures or the sack does not arise. And in any case in the Strand Electric of a large part of my time I was in the happy position of being responsible for the 'specials' and the R&D behind them and the literature and 'PR' to stimulate or *restrain* our customers' desire for the equipment.

Which gets us back to the example of 'Klonk' - the control to show that Strand were 'with it' and thus give authority to our advice *not to have it.* It was a fine example of playing for time. I wish I could say that it has a happy ending but it didn't. However that is a story for the next chapter. The word 'happy' can also be applied to the jobs themselves, the venue, the people one worked with and the equipment supplied bring back happy memories no matter how hard the work may have been. The Palladium and the Royal Festival Hall are obvious examples but what about television studios? The answer has to be BBC Riverside, especially R1.

Len Leggett at 'Klonk'

Riverside was another of those jobs in an area very familiar to me. There it was down by the river in the shadow of Hammersmith bridge over which this OTC cadet had broken step in his youth; and just up in the Broadway itself was the tram island which used to launch me homeward to Harlesden after school, once I had given up the Addison Road/Willesden Junction train. 'B' and I were in at the beginning of the Riverside pilot schemes and by then had some practical experience behind us thanks to the rapid take-off of commercial TV. There was not the same urgency behind the BBC as they had Lime Grove and Alexandra Palace. The main rule at the time was, once quoted we had to stick to the price but there could be considerable modification within that. For example R1 was intended to have a similar rotary patching system to that supplied Associated Rediffusion's Wembley 1 & 2. This was based on rotary selectors as used by Kliegl in the States. It was, so to speak, a copy at long distance since we had only seen catalogue photographs at the time. Our visit there to see such installations for ourselves did not take place until March/April 1955.

The journey itself was quite an adventure. I had got a hint of the new jet age with my 1954 post-war visit to Lisbon in a BEA turbo-prop Viscount to service and advise on extension of S'Carlos console installation. By comparison the BOAC Boeing, a version of the wartime Flying Fortress, was noisy and slow with its four piston-engines. One thing it did have was a bar 'downstairs' which, since my two companions were 'B' and Johnny Johnson, did not close on the long overnight journey. I had been told that, contrary to expectation, it rained a lot in New York and in consequence we were all armed with umbrellas, but mine was destined to be left behind in Cleveland Ohio, a city not on our itinerary. Heathrow was a village of huts as far as passengers were concerned then. Not one of the 'gorgeous palaces' or cloud-capp'd towers had appeared, let alone faded. But the service was out of *this* world - except for very VIPs I suppose. The baggage was taken from the taxi by 'footmen' and we neither touched or saw it again until New York's Grand Central station - the unscheduled destination the fates had booked for us.

Having crossed the Atlantic in the pitch black we put down in darkness at Moncton, a remote airport in the far north, or so it seemed, of Canada. Anyway, it was a land of snow and ice nowhere near anywhere. It was far from lonely however. Plane after plane had been diverted there before ours, and yet more were to follow. Somehow or other as each party was decanted they were served breakfast. There have been two occasions of the many when landing over there that I have felt like jumping back into the plane and returning home there and then. One was Montreal in Summer 1967 when my targets were the Expo and the Colloquium and the other was this, my very first landfall there. At Montreal it was the humidity that hit me; stepping out of the air conditioned plane I really thought it inconceivable that I should be able to breathe and move about. It is amazing how soon a body even with my rebuilt chest adapts. In next to no time there we were taking off our jackets to go out and putting them on to cope with the air-conditioned cold inside. Back in 1955 it was the white bread revealed under the glare of the raw fluorescent lighting which struck terror. I am not being funny - it is a near accurate evocation of the shock. It was not a question of health food theories, but simply that we had become unaccustomed to its face. The war and rationing had accustomed one to colour and texture. I do not remember public demand for the return to snow-white and the multi-slices. Maybe I am wrong; but then, does anyone recall public demand for the modern bacon rasher? We may have had a tiny ration of bacon during the war and for some time after, but it was real bacon oozing fat into the frying pan not water-foam. We were to encounter much good food on this trip, though portions could be off-puttingly large. It was not until my next, in Spring 1961, that freeze-food made its first impact. Having landed at Idlewild, as Kennedy was then called, a meal in New York followed. Across the table, Percy Corry, whose first trip over there it was, looked to Fred the *expert* to advise. With succulent memories of Super Jumbo Shrimp (*outsize* prawn) Cocktails, they had to be the starters. Whether there would be room for something else, time would show. They arrived and we weighed in. Mine proved to be made of rubber and defied both teeth and taste-buds to make any impression, nor was I alone in this. Percy was gazing across at me as if it were a practical joke of mine. From then on that trip was a sequence of tasteless tough food - virtually everything was the same. Lettuces like half a frozen cabbage glittering with ice crystals. Only one item remains memorable for flavour - the dire taste of root beer, the only thing on sale on the Canadian side of Niagara Falls the morning we were there.

We were told that the weather was responsible for that first encounter at Moncton with whiter than white bread. However, before too long we took off again and managed to make Boston; the journey to New York would be completed by train. A mad rush by taxis across the city followed. We boarded the 'Whatever-it-was-Limited' without even a minute to call our own. The de-luxe Pullman, into which we three were ushered, or rather precipitated, was fun. One glance around removed the notion of friendly American welcome. Nothing but hostile glares met our eyes. This was no mass movement, as each lounged in total isolation on a personal pivoted pedestal screwed to the floor almost out of earshot of his neighbours. The chairs resembled dentist chairs and the general effect was that of a barber's shop without any barbers. The sound and any fury outside signified nothing, so complete was the insulation. So oppressive did we find this that we spent much of the four hours journey on the platform at the rear end of our coach. Anyway the number of stops was far from 'limited' and these gave us a series of brief encounters no plane could have provided. So enjoyable did I find the journey that when Percy and I had to visit George Izenour's 'adaptable' Loeb Harvard theatre in 1961 I suggested we went out to Boston by train and planed back to New York that night. A happy result of this is a vivid image of Percy gazing at his choice, a toasted sandwich, but served on a plate swamped in a bath of dark brown gravy. The solution came later when two ladies joined the train's dining car at the next stop and ordered loud and clear two sandwiches and *no gravy*.

Back on that very first train, it deposited the three of us in Grand Central station around midday without any real luggage whatever. This made us uneasy until we were able to collect it in the evening. New York is an ideal city, or was then, to get to know by walking. A block or two away from our Wentworth hotel was Times Square all lit up with, as it should be, a host of small sign lamps and chasers. All on the move, one could sense a live warmth. Broadway had none of the aloof withdrawn effect of the cold cathode fluorescent signs which had afflicted post war Piccadilly. (To get a taste of the real thing in London then it was necessary to go and see *my* auto-changes upon James Gardner's 'Lumascope' at the end of the lake at Battersea Park). With 42nd Street nearby, theatre was no problem but television studios were another matter. Somehow or other out of the blue (but in a lurid red hat) there appeared first thing next morning the guide supreme - George Gill. He had been, one gathered, Kliegl's 'B' at a time when that firm had been at its most active in equipping TV studios. He was then with Metropolitan, who had recently entered the field with their Lumitron system based on magnetic amplifier dimmers and a control desk with dimmer levers like the tone sliders of a Hammond organ. Ned Lustig, the designer, actually had and played one of these organs very loudly in his home, as 'B' was able to tell me after his Sunday visit there. This experience I was spared since I used the occasion to inaugurate a New York routine of mine, a visit to Ilse's papa out at Washington Heights. The Lumitron control desk had its points assuming the ten presets essential with all-electric dimmers. We saw an 80-way one in NBC's colour studio at Brooklyn and preferred it to the Century-Izenour control in CBS 72 (a theatre converted for TV colour). This was not due to the latter's thyratron dimmers but the layout which made most of the levers on the preset wings inaccessible to the seated operator. It was not the extra 20-ways. The Lumitron principle was altogether more compact; besides all its levers were the same size. I was against the Izenour thumb-nail reset when I first read of it and was able to put it to the test when taken to a convent school theatre where they had a 5-preset version. Setting a simple colour mixture effect on the large manual levers I asked my Century escort to duplicate this *exactly* on a preset. This neither he nor I were able to do, even in this haven of peace with no one and nothing to hurry us.

By then New York for us was complete as far as TV studios were concerned and it had been intended that we should go to Los Angeles and see the new Burbank studios - the latest thing. However, as far as equipment was concerned, as an in-house Strand report of May 1955 confirms, we had seen all there was to see and talked with most people that mattered. So on learning of a convention on the subject to be held at General Electric's famous illumination HQ at Nela Park in Cleveland Ohio we decided to opt for that instead. In fact I was not to find myself on the West Coast until Autumn 1976! Before we go any further it is essential to counter the hostile impression we got from Boston-New York train. Wherever we went and whoever we met could not have been more pleasant or helpful. At the higher (executive?) levels that is. Lower down such a thing as service seemed unknown. I never expected much in this line but 'B' did, and was disappointed! This did not apply to us only, as I was to find when alongside our host Ed Kook at a special lunch he laid on for us one Saturday afternoon in a top hotel. Nothing he had ordered or was to order came out right. The lunch party was a largish one with Jo Mielziner, Abe Fader, Sol Cornberg (NBC), Carlton Winkler (CBS) and others such. Among them was one familiar face - Rollo G. Williams now of Century but better known to me, of course, as Gillespie Williams of Holophane and Furse. After lunch we all adjourned to the deserted Century premises there to sit in a large semicircle with 'B' at one end and me at the other, with Ed Kook behind his desk facing us as chairman. Predictably, 'B' soon began to nod off and there was nothing I could do, save raising my voice and trying to draw attention away from his end of the semicircle while blaming myself for lack of foresight in allowing us to become separated. Come to think of it, these rib-jabs were probably the only physical contacts we ever had, certainly we never shook hands; but this applied to others 'in the Strand family'.

Years later when this involuntary snooze became recognised as narcolepsy, Ed and I were reminiscing and I got on to this occasion and how embarrassed I was. To which his reply was "I *knew* you were." What did we discuss in that deserted building that afternoon? I cannot now remember; it must have been the art of lighting in theatre and television practice, what one could and should do and *might do* one day. If we did get onto this latter subject, one thing is certain - we never could have got anywhere near the integrated circuit and software reality. Anyway the occasion was very American and fun to take part in. What *was* the most fulfilling event of the first New York trip has to be the visit 'backstage' at Radio City Music Hall. Even then in 1955 this was a monument to a pioneering past. 'B' and I were taken all over by Eugene Braun, himself 'part' of the building and a *TABS* enthusiast. The peak was the ascent to switchboard pit, out beyond that of the orchestra. As one poked one's head up, there it was - the great multi-preset GE thyratron reactor board 1933. Looking in the dim light just like its photograph in the first edition of my book - and every edition since! In size and its wall of multi-preset it was as different from my own Light Console of that time as possible, except for its location in full view of the stage. But of course anyone with knowledge of thirties electrical engineering must hold that control's electronics in awe.

We also saw a show in Radio City Music Hall. It was very much what one had been accustomed to in our super-cinemas before the war; organ, orchestra, stage show and film. But on a much grander scale. After all, it seated 6000-plus and the stage was umpteen Rockettes wide and reasonably deep to match. Although I was a plain-surfaces for colour-mixing man when it had opened, photographs of the auditorium in the press did not meet with my approval nor did the reality twenty years later. My trouble was that I saw, and still see, lighting as variations played upon an architectural or sculptural form no matter how abstract. The concentric curves here only allowed change of colour. They cannot evoke an atmosphere of, say, a cathedral or a forest or a mountain-top simply by a change of how the light falls, or where it comes from.

A touch of cathedral out-front would have suited the particular stage show we saw. This, the *Easter Show,* can be imaged by anyone who has seen a Christmas show anywhere. Large doses of sugar and sentiment presented professionally. Easter infected New York in a way we only experience at Christmas in London. Organ music Wurlitzered around the lofty spaces of Grand Central when we went to book train tickets for Nela Park. The organ console was tracked down eventually on the balustraded balcony which ran the length of the concourse. It was deserted up there. As we stole up the organist twisted round on the bench as if to take a call. It was large lady in a large Easter bonnet. The visual shock was exactly that of the organist in the Noël Coward Film *Brief Encounter.* One wanted to laugh, but there was nothing for it but a quick retreat.

As can be imagined Nela Park was impressive to see after all one had read of it. The TV convention, as with any conference in which I did not have a speaking role, has not left one iota behind in the memory. It was another organ console which provided the event. Oh, and the girl in the box office at an open stage theatre who rang her manager to tell him that "a couple of limeys" wanted to see him. The console was in Cleveland's Severance Hall and operated the stage and auditorium colour lighting there. I was not able to see the colour lighting because an orchestral rehearsal was in progress and maestros do not appreciate lightseers; but I was able to examine the console itself. It dated, like mine, from the early thirties and it was nice to confirm, what I had always suspected, that it was not really based on the organ principle of select and play. True, the controls occupied a console (a grand organ not a cinema stopkey type) but it was largely an affair of rotary-knobs with some pedals and other echoes of organ practice. Fortunately there was published a good detail description at the time it went in and the interested reader does not have to rely on me*. The dimmers were Westinghouse saturable-reactors but the console was very much a special one-off.

* Transactions, IES USA, April 1931 p.331 et seq.

The importance of the Severance Hall in my context is that it confirms the preoccupation of some of us in the Thirties with a larger palette for the art of Colour Music than just a screen or stage. This was well summed up by Stanley McCandless*, a consultant on the job, in the above paper, "I feel that picking three primary colours to get a variety of any shade or tint in the spectrum is important, especially if we are going to accompany music. I think we probably will have to go though the process of learning to play the light organ just as much as the organist has to learn to play the organ. It is going to be rather unique if we accompany the music successfully the first year or two.... It is a very expensive job....". This was part of the discussion: in the main paper Dean E. Holden said in his introduction, "No attempt is made to develop a theory of colour music for Dr. Luckiesh has proved this futile as far as can be seen at present. It is MOOD lighting only, that is proposed. By this is meant an almost subconscious play on the audience, the lighting effects in colour being felt rather than seen".

I only came across this very detailed description when seeking, as expert witness early in 1986, prior art to invalidate a servo-spot patent. Recollection said Severance Hall had some but that is not evidence so much documentation had to be sought out. Confirmation of like thinking on Colour Music from over the decades was a happy by-product so to speak. Alas, we have no equivalent over here to Mr. John L. Severance who "provided funds for the construction of a permanent building, a memorial to his late wife". America seems full of concert halls, theatres and arts centres bearing the name of whoever put up the money whereas in UK such names all too likely mean that they only chaired the odd committee - Odd's Lytteltons and Cottesloes!

In due time we set out to journey back to New York, accidentally leaving my umbrella behind in the process. That process being plane whereas on the journey out it was an overnight sleeper. There were only the two of us, I think Johnny had opted for Burbank California rather than Cleveland Ohio. We landed at La Guardia near enough midnight to be met by two surprises. One was George Gill and the other was the contents of a paper bag he was carrying. These were muffins or rather what *we* would call crumpets. George insisted that we sampled them there and then. Even he realised that they could not be eaten raw and a toasting facility had to be found. La Guardia's night life did not seem to include any such facilities. However, it required more than 'B's oft expressed distaste for the project to abort it. George at last dug out a staff canteen buried in an area obviously dedicated to non-public activity. Once there, cups of coffee appeared and toasters went on duty. The verdict was up to me, 'B' wisely drew the line at crumpets whatever the source at that hour. This was a Gill activity divorced from lighting or television; we were *not* making a

* Author of *A Method of Stage Lighting*, pub. Theatre Arts, New York 1932 and seemingly forever after.

commercial! What I was donating my expert opinion towards was a money-making hobby. Seemingly common USA practice and maybe a wise one for those in any calling of uncertain durability.

It would be true to say that only one item we saw over there exercised any influence on any *equipment* I was to be responsible for from then on*. What I did take away was the 'Queen Mary' coming into moor, as seen from a committee room window I happened to be facing high up in some building. To go down to the waterside later and almost stroke her prow underlined the skills behind reports of the captains taking in the great liners under their own power during the occasional tug strike. The Hudson was not really wide and there was a right-angled turn and deadstop, so to speak, alongside each pier in order to avoid hitting the quayside. Then there is the memory of 'B' being ticked off by a cop for carrying an *unlighted* cigarette in his hand as we moved towards the subway exit. As to TV studio impressions there was NBC 8G with 100 Century 2kW Fresnel spots adjustable for height, direction and focus from a joystick on a movable pedestal. The sequential selection of each number could be aggravating. That was in Radio City itself. More impressive still was the NBC Home studio with windows on the street level. This was Sol Cornberg's idea - where the daily *Home* show originated. Centre overhead a remote control camera on a much pivoted arm could reach out and focus on a series of sets around the studio. These sets were a kitchen of course, an interview area, office desk etc, plus any topical special. Sol was to come over to England to advise Sydney Bernstein on the new 4500-ft^2 studio he was building in Manchester for his Granada circuit.

Purpose-built studios were something of a novelty in those early days of commercial television, it was more a matter of conversion of old film studios or Variety theatres. Anyway, before long 'B' and I found ourselves seated around a conference table in the Golden Square H.Q. of Granada in London awaiting entry of the C.O. himself. There were some like Reg Hammans the chief engineer and Sol Cornberg with whom we were already on terms; but most of the others were strangers. Except for a brief encounter with Cecil Bernstein at the Granada Tooting over the side lighting of stage drapes before the war, Granada had not come my way - youthful attendance at the Granada (formerly Empire cinema) Willesden always excepted!

Upon the dot, enter Sydney Bernstein. It was quite a shock; I was totally unprepared for his height and that nose. It was large and had that bashed-about look of a prize-fighter. Hammans introduced me, whereupon out shot the question: "Do you crimp?" I hadn't an idea what he meant, but assuming it must be a question

* Immediate replacement of the traditional D-clamp for hanging spots etc, by simple Hook-clamps.

of engineering rather than of morality, I replied, "Only when appropriate," or something equally ambiguous. Apparently he had just returned from United States where instead of muffins at midnight, he had encountered crimping. This method of joining small wires was the latest thing and has become commonplace long since, but at that time the soldering-iron and Compton testboard were well suited to our wiring needs. The rest of that meeting has left no other memory behind and I never met Sydney Bernstein again.

However I do recall that Percy Corry's firm Watts and Corry did do the scenery for Granada Television (including *Coronation Street* while it was inside) for a considerable time. It was taken for granted that Strand would do the lighting control for the new studio and by then that meant a standard system CD/TV with 100 channels and 50% dimmers. On which Granada, however, did make its mark and on *all* CD consoles thereafter. Someone, in the architects department probably, wanted a more up to date styling of the wooden desk itself and made a suggestion both for the shape of the ends and the finish. This Comptons made, and it was a great improvement; though for other jobs the ebony finish tended to lapse into Methodist oak again. Looking back, it is surprising that I had not taken this aspect in hand myself earlier. After all I was very fussy as to the way everything Strand did, be it lanterns or literature, looked. Indeed I had got some 'modern' woodwork for the special Festival Hall Light Console in 1951, although it and its operator were to be stuck in a tiny cupboard.

Lighting Director at Riverside 1

One's attitude to the ergonomic design of television lighting controls was greatly influenced by the fact that, as already pointed out, the shows were then always transmitted live with at most one repeat. This meant that the lighting director could do his own lighting using the control itself instead of instructing an electrician as in a theatre. This view seemed to coincide with the BBC plans for Riverside and before long was endorsed by an official hands-off technique in which the camera controls once balanced for the show, using an attractive girl perched on a tall stool as target, were not touched and adjustment of picture quality or effect was left to the lighting. Our control would be upstairs in the production suite and an "electricians panel" on the floor of the studio would be used when rigging the show. The Electricians' Trade Union thought otherwise however and much argument followed. The climax was a trial before three independent judges, or whatever they were, in the council chamber of Broadcasting House. It was my privilege to be invited to give evidence on behalf of the BBC. On arrival that morning I joined a dozen others in a small waiting room hastily studying their notes and licking their dry lips. Creative conceit ensured that I was not nervous and needed no notes. I *knew* we had right on our side and did not imagine any sensible person could think differently. I was called early and was escorted to a desk, stage centre. Almost alongside but at right-angles to mine was another at which sat Frank Haxell; easy to recognise as he was then very much in the news as the ETU firebrand. In general the place looked rather like a lofty court and there were a number of others around whose role remains a mystery. I suppose I was asked some leading questions by the pro-BBC 'counsel' and then it was over to Haxell for the attack. I had noticed that he had a copy of my book open on his desk and recognised the page. I knew what he hoped to shoot me down with. So just as he got going I interrupted with "Its no good you quoting that stuff of mine at me; it is about theatre not television," or words to that effect. I was certainly on the ball that morning; it was a gift. The BBC won the battle of Portland Place. Granada and some others also went in for lighting director operation but others gave away. This was particularly noticeable when some years later the Thorn 'Q-File' replaced our 240-channel system Cs in ATV's studios C and D at Boreham Wood. Q-File being just a desk panel, it could be put in the same room as vision control. But alas the unions could not be allowed to mingle, and an incredibly crude 'cardboard' partition was built so that in no way could one man do or see the work of the other sitting immediately alongside.

In the theatre, at any rate in the Strand-Bentham era, we did not suffer much from union problems except when rigging exhibitions. While Sol Cornberg was over here we showed him several of our theatre installations and he was staggered at the

A Present from ATV to B and B

way I could demonstrate the controls myself. As he put it, "on Broadway every switch and lever seems to have a bell to summon the union man, the moment you touch it." This was one reason for the survival of the temporary 'piano boards' for so long over there. Of course Unions are not the only ones to erect job barriers, the legal profession immediately comes to mind with the veto on a solicitor pleading his client's case, no matter how simple, in court instead of a barrister. I was destined to encounter union problems when appearing myself at Riverside as an "artiste" on March 7th 1960 in the same programme as John Neville and Patrick Moore.

Unlike the latter with his *Sky at Night.* I did not get another BBC date on TV! The studio was R2 and when we came to rehearse my "Theatre Item" we hit a snag right away. The trouble was that I opened my item by describing and showing two lanterns, the Patt 23. Profile spot and the Patt. 123 Fresnel. Unfortunately I had had a brilliant idea, the two spots were specially made half-lanterns. I had only to pivot them through 180° on their stands to show the optical system inside each. After performing this demonstration, the director's idea was that the camera would track through and show some effects, in black and white then, on the set behind using this kind of spotlighting. Finally I would be seen on camera seated at a system CD desk supposedly working the lights, while John Neville asked some questions. This last part was easy since the CD did not have to be connected up to anything except a power supply to allow group movement of the stopkeys from the pistons. The lights were worked out of picture from R2's own 'Electronic', cross-cut with shots of R1's clutch-operated system C dimmers filmed the previous Saturday. So what was the difficulty which caused all work to cease shortly after the start of my rehearsal? It was simply the question as to who should move the two spots on their stands out of the way of the camera when I had done with them?

It was not their weight or fragility that constituted the problem, it was a matter of deciding *what they were.* The ETU claimed they were *spotlights* and it was their job as electricians to move them; but NATKE* said they were *props* as they did not light up and therefore their members should shift them. Believe it or not, we had to adjourn upstairs to the smart 'Festival of Britain' style canteen for a premature tea-break. This interlude became more and more protracted, until at last we were told a compromise had been worked out; the two spots would not be moved, the camera would track around them. Whether or not some scenery had to be moved to enable it to do so I can't say, but that wouldn't have presented any difficulty, as everyone knew scene-shifters shifted scenery! All this childish behaviour was for one item only in a children's magazine programme called, rather appropriately, *FOCUS* which went out on Mondays at 5.10pm. It was a nice quirk that they used R2 for my

* National Association of Theatre & Kinematograph Employees (later to include an extra 'T' for 'Television')

TV item, because that was the very studio with the Strand 'Electronic' that I had not wanted to supply. It went in because Alistair Maclean had caught the bug on his latest visit to the States. By then Strand had decided that thyratron valves were too unreliable and the installation in the New (now Albery) theatre had just been replaced by its servo-preset equivalent; which meant we had a second-hand desk in stock, so to speak. 'B' and I decided that Maclean should have the New theatre's cast-off. With some trouble we persuaded our works to refurbish it rather than make a new desk - more childish behaviour?

The BBC decided to split our contract as it would be cheaper for them to buy the 360 thyratron valves direct from the makers, STC. This was a grave mistake on their part as it was impossible to tie down which firm was at fault in the inevitable string of troubles that followed. Paul Weston and I would meet BBC engineers brimful of ideas and enthusiasm at 9.30am. After a while we would slip out of the R2 dimmer-room and set course for Strand's Gunnersbury factory a short drive away. After a happy day testing the latest servo installation before dispatch, we would return to the R2 dimmer-room to find the air hot with thyratron valves and thick with tobacco smoke and despondency. In contrast, the rather larger studio R1 evokes nothing but pleasurable memories. After some months of life among the engineers and engineering I was walking down the ground floor passage, probably to call at the Gents, when I had a strange encounter. Coming towards me was a scantily clad young girl. What on earth was she doing here in Riverside was my instinctive reaction. Then I realised that *she* represented my first glimpse of the real reason why we engineers had all been working here for so long.

This spotlights the divorce between the planners and the television shows their installations were there to serve. We in Strand's R&D could at least feel ourselves part of theatre because not only did we have our own small one to run, but also could find ourselves working a show in the real thing. In television it was quite different, we were creating something for others. In no case did we find ourselves working a show. This is why the fact that all shows went out live at the time was so important. It was possible to think of them, to some extent, in terms of theatre one-night stands, or where the same format would come back each week, then it was like playing in repertoire. If in those days it had been possible to record shows in relatively short-takes as now, then I don't think we would ever have got into television or attempted to. The primitive lighting control of film studios would have dominated. For the live exceptions such as News and Interviews a few minimally equipped studios would have sufficed. Except in the BBC I do not recall much coming together of brains, as committees to ponder and deliberate. Riverside committees are recalled as composed of power engineers and planning engineers with the lighting *user* as a lone voice - fortunately that of R.de. B. McCullough.

I must say the ten years 1954-64 represented a most enjoyable time during which adventure spiced our undoubted control of control. 1964, as my next chapter will show, was to be the turning point, however. Meantime Strand's compact playable console philosophy with its seated operator had made a good foundation on which to build for television. There was one fundamental difference. TV's main concern was switching cues whereas theatre's was dimming. Thus theatre channel switch relays were normally held on and selected for off; whereas in TV they were normally off and activated for on. This was due to two things. One, that the camera would only be looking at part of a studio at one time and the other that cameras needed a lot of light at that time so mains load was a major preoccupation. Group memory was not so much there for the Art, but rather to look after the Cash!

This concern over cost dictated the need for some form of patching. This was something common in theatre across the Atlantic but something we had scorned over here, plenty of dimmers was our rule. It is significant that we did not have a word for it. It did not appear in the Ridge and Aldred book nor in my 1950 *Stage Lighting*; but by the second edition of 1955 there it was, and also in our TV red book

Brian Legge jacking-up at Associated Rediffusion, Wembley

of the same year. Many studios, notably ATV Elstree, ABC Teddington and Granada Manchester did not use patch-panels as such but had rather a large number of socket-outlet channels equally spread over the suspension grid above the studio. The lighting units were fixed to 'telescopes' devised by Johnny Johnson for Mole Richardson. These could be positioned and their height individually set as required. The BBC used instead a system of short 4-circuit motorised bars complete with socket-outlets. The general idea was a saturation rig with appropriate units already hanging there. This was where the patch-panel came in, for there the circuits were sorted out, grouped and given dimmers as necessary. The obvious solution was a jack-plug for every circuit and pairs of sockets for the dimmers. Such panels rivalled the hated Grand Master switchboards for size, especially as I had decided to be kind to the ETU and make large jacks to handle each day rather than tiny ones to finger. By the time the TV Centre jobs came to pass the Jacks had became Jills so that the lesser number of channels would be moved around rather than the very large number of circuits. But the only system I liked was the one I got them to put in R1. This was a remote patch operating banks of Government Surplus (G/S) relays 175 ft distant. At the control end there was a series of vertical selector switches - one per dimmer. These were of our own make and had seven positions and off. Sixteen such levers would control the patching for 28 circuits to seven dimmers. In all there were 348 circuits and 166 channels to Riverside 1.

Reading my spec. of 2/8/55, I am struck with wonder at my ingenuity which put all those patching relays under control from such a small compact wing panel. The far end was equally innovative because the G/S relays were connected on the dimmer side by busbars equivalent of the Compton cross-relay. This obviated the complicated tied-out cabling we had to make for A.R's Wembley 1, 2, and 4 direct selector-switching patching. And this vast improvement to make and use was devised only a matter of weeks after Wembley; the pace of inventiveness surprises - I warned that this was not going to be a modest chapter! I intended the remote patching system to operate by areas of the studio. Unfortunately the manner of 3-phase balancing insisted upon by the BBC engineers made the patching principle rather more difficult to grasp and use than it need have been.

One could not imagine then that the dimmer would one day become relatively so inexpensive that it would be sensible to have one in each lighting circuit and patch their control lines so to speak. If we in R&D seldom found ourselves working shows on our control system, this certainly did not mean that we were shot of them after hand over. The phone at home could ring at almost any time and anything from a short lecture on likely faults to hasty departure for the West End was possible. Sunday dinner all dished up and steaming appetisingly on the table when the phone rang. Joe Davis speaking from Her Majesty's. Couldn't believe it, so treated the voice as a prank on the part of 'B'. But no, Joe when challenged declared he was Joe and so he was. I had to tax my brain there and then as to the layout of their console to judge whether the operator was right or wrong in denying him a particular cue. Joe then went back to his rehearsal and Ilse and I back to our dinner.

It was just as well that we had chosen to live in Ealing at that time. Some key workers lived nearby in West Ealing, having moved there to be near Strand's wartime factory. We had no car then so it was search by taxi to see if Arnold Turner or whoever was available to shoot off to the London Coliseum to replace a damaged jockey-sprocket - yes, there really is such a thing! They played a key role on our electro-mechanical dimmer banks. Then there was that *Carousel* rehearsal another Sunday at Drury Lane. I was the only person they could contact so it was off to town for me. This threatened to become an all-night standby, until Stanley after some hours, managed to locate Paul Weston to take over. I remember the Lane and Her Majesty's Theatre as the most troublesome, but there were certainly others. One such was on Christmas Eve. A pressing invitation over the phone late afternoon to go at once at Riverside 2 simply had to be shared with Paul. I got there first from home having, unlike him, given our office party a miss. When he did turn up he was not in prime engineering condition. We managed somehow, but what it was we managed escapes me. Anyway we did eventually depart leaving peace on earth and goodwill shining around.

As the number of our type of installation increased, a rota was devised for on-call nights at home. A sum of £1 (free of tax) was the reward and £2 plus expenses if it meant going out on the job. Once a year I used to be on-call officially, so that the regulars could enjoy their special party. There was to come a time when this amateur service ceased to be a practical solution and for many, many a year Fred Brown became the name for the distressed to invoke.

While on the subject of maintenance it has to be said that, given reasonably reliable equipment, TV studios did not need as much cosseting as theatres. They had real engineers working there, theatres did not. This was highlighted by Nottingham where, at last, the Playhouse CD control of 1963 was replaced by a memory system. The local amateur society, having acquired it as it was thrown out for their own theatre, had no difficulty in reassembling it and making it work. The truth is that compared with the sophisticated engineering many earned

Fred Brown and Wembley 5A C/AE

their living at, this one-time-machine-of-mystery was a piece of cake. Another nice touch; the dimmer bank went out-front in what had been the projection room in this one time cinema. It was the console desk that went backstage on a perch - the operator wanted to enjoy the fun of putting on the show together with his friends. No solitary confinement for him in a room with a good view far away of the professional!

IX: SOUTH STREET
Convent Garden to Brentford 1964-73

The special treatment accorded a visit from Royalty in Britain is well known, even today. Things are spruced up, the best clothes (your own or Moss Bros.) come out on parade. There are tales of whitewashed coal heaps and so on. I have no difficulty whatever in believing these stories because our own experience in Strand Electric was exactly like that, when the King's youngest brother - Prince George, Duke of Kent - visited us on April 30th 1936. Officially, it was in the role of a factory inspector; but of course, the factory was by then in Gunnersbury, and Frank Weston's workshop and the Strandsigns "works" on the floor above were out of the question. So what HRH saw was a recital of colour music in the Seecol theatre. It is typical of the Fred Bentham of that time that he does not appear in the photograph of HRH standing with Phillip Sheridan alongside my Light Console. I thought it proper to retreat among the small audience. The thing that had to get the limelight was The Console, not its inventor.

All this may seem a long way from South Street thirty–three years later. The visitor to Strand Electric then also came to inspect, but he came as a conqueror. He was John Davis and much the same aura of unreality as we'd experienced with HRH was attached to this visit. The streets of Covent Garden to be traversed by him and his car were not mysteriously cleared of traffic and *sanded* as they had been for HRH, but Davis' chauffeur had rehearsed the route the day previously and what to do with Sir John, as he later became, was carefully planned; or at least the part that concerned 'B' and I in the lower showroom and theatre was! Any idea that our visitor would be content with the regions below was knocked on the head when, having entered 29 King Street to be greeted by a ready and waiting Jack Sheridan, he promptly decided to see upstairs.

Down-under there were the drinks and a superb lunch masterminded to the last detail by 'B'; but it was to be up-over instead. This might have just worked if only J.S's office (our boardroom) had been the destination. But it was not to be so. What John Davis wanted was the grand tour, no less. Even with careful advance planning this would have been difficult, but with no planning at all such a tour was bound to end in disaster - and it did. Struggling around the pile-up of buildings and piled upped offices and stores, they crossed an overhead bridge from one to another

- part of a fire escape route - to be stopped by a door which would not open. It was jammed by a pile of packing cases in the store beyond. So there they stood, high up in the draughty open air before a fire door which would not open! A messenger was despatched from on high, but some time was to pass before they could continue.

Meanwhile, 'B' and I were already in the lower showroom wondering whether, in view of the delay, to make a practical test of some of the aperitifs. But we were not to be left unmolested. Ed Chilton, the boss of Rank Audio Visual (of which we were to become a part), rushed in and said that he had forgotten the Chairman's cigars. He always smoked Montecristos and 'B' went out to track them down as nearby as possible. Much to his surprise he located a box in the small tobacconist's just opposite the office door end (Cranbourn Mansions) of the London Hippodrome. It was a miracle that 'B' had sufficient money to cover the vast cost involved in this transaction. I do not recall the figure, but in any case inflation would have removed the punch from the line.

John Davis had very specific tastes - La Ina sherry and Chivas Regal scotch, for example - and they just *had* to be there. When at length he did descend to our level, all went according to plan. We did not have the Blue Room, that famed resort of sybarites in the last years of King Street, (it had to await the infusion of Rank wealth), but the vagaries of our early dimmer memory controls, like 'WHZ' and 'IDM', had got us skilled in staging a buffet back-up. The large game-pies usually cuisined for us by Mrs Bessinger (Stella) of the 'Lamb & Flag', around the corner, were out of this world. I am not exaggerating when I recall the disappointment when she could not oblige 'B' and we had to go to Fortnum and Masons instead. The greatest tribute ever paid to B's catering was to come at the end of that very lunch.

J.D. was put at the head of table with Jack Sheridan on his right hand and I was opposite on his left. Who else was there I do not recall, but I do know that Ed Chilton put himself safely at the far end. When, at last, the coffee, brandy and that box of cigars arrived John Davis remarked in an aside, "You do yourself well, Sheridan." It was a fortunate circumstance that I was there to overhear, to pass on to 'B', and to record here for all time. Jack caught my eye, as well he might, and we could both see J. Crow bearing his master's daily sandwich from the Round House along with a cup of Nescafé he had just made.

John Davis never visited King Street again and, but for an annual day out for we 'executives', I would never have got a chance to talk to him again. And this in spite of the fact that I had been in Strand ever since 1932 and was such a well known name in the esoteric business of stage lighting. Sir John and Ed Chilton at least had a tenuous connection with stage lighting though the Rank chain of cinemas, most of which had at some time in their life some stage lighting equipment down at the screen end of the house. In the Rank Organisation these places were referred to as 'theatres' and some had large if rather shallow stages - a legacy of the cine-variety days. If Sir John and Ed were familiar with the vagaries of the entertainment industry this certainly did not apply to the 'executives' taken on by Rank Audio Visual to run Rank Strand, as we had now become.

Having paid six million pounds or so, largely for the goodwill, it was obviously stupid to change the name which would put us in a different part of the phone book and other directories. At the very least to keep the firm's name would have preserved it as a package for re-sale if necessary. And it is significant that as I write, when any organisation's future is by no means as assured as it was in the early takeover years, the Strand part of the name has been brought out and stressed.

The name of the firm was not the only thing that changed with takeover; everything and everyone changed; not once, but every few months. We were organised and re-organised with fantastic frequency. Nor was it just a matter of re-shuffling the court cards: such changes involved heads falling. Nothing and no one could regard his job, in the sense of what he was doing, as secure. At the top end with his head in the firing line he could find himself out at a few minutes notice; with handsome compensation maybe, but out of a job he had just begun to master and removed from among colleagues he had only then got on terms with. Others might find themselves transferred within the firm to totally different work - dealing with sound equipment instead of stage lighting or with export instead of the home market - having to cope with customer resentment at the removal of their familiar contact man, plus no knowledge whatever of that country's language and arcane technology.

The only thing that remained unchanged was the requirement to write a period report every four weeks. The Rank year consisted of thirteen months! My reports, of which I still possess a large number as I write, again and again stress the need to leave us alone to allow the team to settle in. But no, along comes yet another upheaval. It is now many years since Rank and I parted company but during those years there has been some direct evidence that the purge principle still rules. At a lunch at Brentford, to celebrate Paul Weston's forty-five years with Strand, our host is missing having departed with others the previous evening. When collecting slides from time to time an air of strain over all could be felt. Nothing was said to me, but something was up and sure enough by lunchtime there were the gaps.

Talking of gaps, the extraordinary thing is the way things did expand and contract within our part of the organisation right from the start. On Rank's arrival at King Street in the bleak mid winter of 1968/69 the first thing they did was to expand into the buildings to our east. Out went our tenant Ellis the greengrocer, whose rent seemed to be Jack Sheridan's last buffer against bankruptcy of Strand, and in came a mass of new offices. The house telephone list grew greatly and there was provision for personal secretaries almost everywhere. The sight of all these young girls leaving for lunch down the King Street staircase each day was really something to see - especially as there was so much to see in that mini skirt era. Of necessity, King Street was a menage of individual offices; but at Brentford, in the Art Deco ex-toothpaste factory of Macleans (to which Rank Audio Visual had just moved from Goldhawk Road), it was 'open plan'. Now it was one thing to decimate the population at King Street and leave a trail of empty rooms; but quite another when at Brentford the survivors clustered at one end of a wasteland, or passed through one corner of an entire floor without trace of human occupation. Although not entirely without trace; for the vast fitted carpet, and line upon line of phone/electric terminal boxes sticking up at regular intervals, reminded one that this had been a land of bells, belles, typewriters and rubber plants, plus an occasional male doing, at the very least, his period report. To me, the evocation of the war graves in Northern France was inescapable.

Nor was this the first time something of the sort had come to mind. In the Autumn of 1973 the latest of our managing directors, Andrew Taylor, decreed that King Street and Floral Street should close and their functions and staff transferred to Brentford. This enabled his regime to receive a credit of a million pounds* at South Street, and in theory the move benefited the export trade as well, since all the customers had to do was pop off the plane at Heathrow, take a short ride along to the toothpaste factory and then pop back onto the next plane home. As Taylor had no experience at all with theatre people it did not occur to him that inspection of equipment was just an excuse to see what was going on the heart of theatreland - the West End. In the old Strand the seeking out of suitable shows for our visitors had the highest priority and Stanley Earnshaw was master at obtaining house seats for house-full hits. Actually, Taylor had hoped for a million and a quarter, but in the battle for the books, Sir John, as he was by then, knocked him down.

My department was the last to leave King Street. We had a farewell lunch down in the basement of the deserted block of buildings - in the Blue Room of course. Above, and all around was empty office upon empty office; their phones with their secretary extensions at the ready. Even then in 1973 the notion of the great evacuation before the nuclear holocaust was never far away during that farewell lunch. This place had been a hive of stage lighting activity and mini-skirts, and now except for a distant unanswered telephone bell, nothing stirred. We were the survivors but, like the five survivors in Conan Doyle's *Poison Belt*, in an hour or two we would have to emerge - the oxygen tubes would not last for long.

We had a jolly nice lunch and much to drink, but not too much. Bill Crisp, the one genuine Rank man allocated to my department after takeover, remarked that he

* Before the great inflation take off, of course.

regarded his four years with me as a sabbatical - a high compliment. I like to think that our work and way of working had been fun. Not through our efforts to make it so - rubber plants, socials and such - but because of what we had to do. Compliments are not easy to pay. Taylor failed utterly when he presented 'B' Bear, Twynam and myself each with an expensive leatherbound volume of the complete works of Will Shakespeare. My copy has written on the fly leaf the date, 12th September 1973, and, "To F...... B ...... On the occasion of the 100th edition of Tabs. Congratulations from Andrew Taylor and Rank Strand Electric." Coming from a man who had never read *TABS* and did not know Strand Electric, this had to be a meaningless formality. Compare the Earnshaw Sheridan presentation of the watch way back in Christmas 1935 or the presentation in 1983 at the hands of Robert Nesbitt of the first ever ABTT fellowship certificate. In neither case did I know that any such thing was in train, though of course in the case of the ABTT I did know once the decision had been made, otherwise I might not have turned up that night!

The key is the sense of direct appreciation from knowledge. Formal awards, especially if, as with the fellowship of the Illuminating Engineers Society it involves filling up a form and obtaining sponsors, removes the surprise and excitement. Membership of the I.E.S. - that was exciting when J.S. Dow (their first Secretary) had picked young me out after my contribution to Applebee's Cavalcade paper back in 1934. But fellowship, although entitled to it much earlier, I left until Applebee said that I really must apply and that he had asked Dr. Walsch of the NPL to join him as sponsor.

Like H. G. Wells, who was said to regret that he was never asked to become a F. R. S (Fellow of the Royal Society), I would have liked to have been offered something from the IEE (Institute of Electrical Engineers). After all, they had two important bang-on-target papers, and one near-miss out of me on my speciality. No, the last one was not a near miss, it was an off-day ill-prepared affair in which I tried to get over the complex story of my career in lighting with too little preparation. Then again the lecture started one hour earlier than I thought, and cut in half my preparation time to sort slides to a mere half hour or so. However, my first lecture in the old IEE hall in 1957 was quite another matter. The television component in my audience was really something. Those were the early days of the fifties' television explosion when I could write at the bottom of our BBC tenders: "To carry out the intent of your specification" and get away with it!

I have only used a script at a lecture twice, or at any rate when talking in public, and that was on the two occasions when I was asked to give an address at a funeral. I was scared that I might make a joke. The trouble is that I cannot resist following up a lead the occasional word or combination of words may give.

Of course, some of my shows have been very elaborate and have involved much rehearsed demonstrations or colour music but for lectures, the sorting of slides just before going on is sufficient. What, looking back, I find curious is that I never had standard lists of slides for my various subjects. It was only in later years when, in my retirement, trotting over to Brentford and sorting through, on my own, the very large collection of 35mm slides in the room upstairs (located past the war graves!) that I at last made a list. Literally in the King Street days there would be Brian Legge at the boxes sorting out a subject we had done many times before, while I walked up and down. The fact is that I have always hated doing the same thing twice. Except, that is, in colour music. I could never rehearse or play a piece enough. The all-time record must be held by the first movement of Tchaikovsky's *4th Symphony* on the shadow set of 1935. Played that June as part of the inaugural recital on the Light Console in the Seecol theatre, I never tired of it over the years, and it was the finale to the show which closed the King Street theatre as the Rank demonstration theatre. We had a packed house and I can remember my surprise when seated at the switchboard (an LP Preset, not a Light Console alas), I was conscious at the end of the audience rising to their feet as they applauded. My first and last standing ovation. I had hoped to close the theatre with "Our revels now are ended ... ." from the Tempest and Joe Davis was to bring John Gielgud along to do this but his rehearsal went on longer than expected so Tchaikovsky 4th had to stand alone.

As it turned out, this occasion was only to mark the departure of Rank Strand because the ABTT were able to continue using the King Street theatre at a modest rent payable to another part of the Rank Organisation. During this time we staged colour music recitals each year to coincide with Peter Daubeney's World Theatre seasons at the Aldwych. There were other such shows including use by Rank Strand from time to time instead of their Brentford showroom, plus the use by the ABTT of the place for training and their 'last Friday of the month' members meetings. The last of which took place on Friday January 29th 1977. Appropriately, if sadly, this took place a few hours after most of us had been to B's funeral, or more memorably the Wake that he had arranged for us in the pub across the road from the crematorium. Everyone seemed to be there in the large room which his brother had taken for the purpose. He had by then suffered from heart trouble and was subject to emergency departures to the Middlesex Hospital; but as far as possible he did not let it interfere with his way of life - including going off to the Isle of Wight to attend Jack Madre's funeral two days before. He had an arrangement to call the Middlesex hospital when an attack came on. The drivers had strict instructions from him not to use that foul wailing siren on such occasions. This time the phone in his flat was out of order.

The last occasion I had seen him was the evening of January 13th 1977. We had been to another funeral, a Strand man of a younger generation John Corne, and Paul

Weston had dropped us at B's flat in Russell Court, near Queen Square where I had an AWG meeting at 7 o'clock. We relaxed and he suggested a drink. As an economy measure, since our retirements, we usually tried to make do with Foster's lager; but he turned to me, and said that he had some of the "real stuff" that night if I would prefer. I did, and he poured out a couple of large scotches. Few words were spoken and before long I departed for the Guild, where it was Master's night - Arthur Bultitude, "A Bowmaker's Tale". It had been summer 1935 when Stanley Earnshaw first introduced 'B' and I in the bar of the Palace theatre for *Anything Goes* by Guy Bolton and P.G. Wodehouse. It had been scotch for him then, but not for me. I was a ginger beer T.T.

More than anyone else 'B' embodied the spirit of the old Strand Electric. To say he had no other interests but Strand, and the theatre people in the stage door pubs, would be incorrect for he was well read and politically aware; but he never looked forward to a weekend off, or took a holiday from Strand if he could help it. This proved to be his undoing, and his keenness to return to work after his serious illness got him the sack from Rank Strand earlier than need have been the case. The latest purge had his name on the hit list, but Rank did not sack people who were ill. Presumably they were covered by insurance. I was tipped off from high up that so long as he stayed away he was OK. A lot of concern was expressed about this and the personnel manager, who was by no means one of *us*, went to the trouble to ring me one Sunday lunchtime in an extreme move to see if I could get 'B' to stay away. But no, although he was far from recovered, back to King Street he had to come, and with his return he was given a month's notice.

The King Street lunch was not our first with John Davis. That had taken place shortly after takeover. Like Dubcek off to Moscow about the same time, we set out for South Street to be greeted at the door by Ed Chilton and taken up the stairs to the first floor to join Graham Dowson for drinks. The drinks were large and the conversation seemed designed to make us small. It was of yachts, both Chilton and Dowson *had* seagoing cruisers of a kind that can only be imagined. My companions, Jack Sheridan, Phillip and Ken Mould, *had* nothing. I wasn't thinking of, or even had by then, 'Peter Sam'. My experience of boats was limited to an interrupted week on the Fens at the time of the first takeover battle earlier that year. I am not sure whether the other Rank subject - women - came up then. If it had, we would not have been in that class either. It certainly became a de riguer component of any Rank executive get-together in our King Street Blue Room.

My first encounter with the genus Rank Executive came with a request to go and see Ed Chilton at Rank Audio Visual in Goldhawk Road. After a bit he took me to the man who was obviously going to run Strand for Rank, although Jack Sheridan was to continue as Managing Director under the new regime. This is the way things are done when retention of some of the old directors is part of the bargain. Changes at the next level below render the top brass impotent in all but name. They may stay on for a while but in the end the golden handshake wins. J.S. was to survive as MD roughly one year. The man Ed took me to see was John Ball and he was the only other being in the building, all the rest had departed for the toothpaste factory. Ball was a stern ascetic looking man with rimless glasses. He had been with Rank some time and was obviously dedicated to the methods and Methodism of Lord Rank. Strict adherence to office hours and no drinking until after 6pm.

I returned to King Street and warned 'B' that our working life style was in for a severe jolt. He took the warning and as both he and I thought that Rank money was the only means by which we could recover from our parlous position in advanced lighting control, *Monastic days* ensued. The unmasking of John Ball came very early on in the brand new Blue Room. The distinguished customers having departed (whoever they were), 'B' was about to put the brandy away when John suggested another round and late lunch extended well into the evening. The longer this went on, the clearer our vision became, and it is not too much to claim that from then on life in Rank Strand had its centre on the Blue Room. Many a fruitful business exchange, many a first intro. and many a last farewell was held down there. Among all these an annual lunch for the 'expensively-departed' developed. At these we hung photographs around the walls chosen from the vast range taken of each person for publicity purposes at the time of their appointment - sometimes barely a year before dismissal. By Autumn 1986 the latest managing director Marvin Altman was the eleventh to occupy this Strand post since the Rank takeover eighteen years earlier. It must not be thought that only the Man. Dirs. (General Managers, call them what you will) were vulnerable, anyone who appeared by name on the upper part of an organisational chart was identifiable and therefore at risk. Thus in May 1971 there was in addition the marketing director, production director, chief engineer, personnel manager, admin. manager and financial controller. Just below there were the market planning manager, product manager lighting controls, product manager auditoria, sales manager export, market manager home, and PR & Technical Liaison manager - this last being me. All in all there were twenty-two names identified as managing something or other on this particular set of charts, and I have left out the factories. And this was just stage lighting. About this time 'we' also 'did' drapes, carpets and seating. Such side dishes (including sound) were added or subtracted from our menu as the particular Rank reorganisation dictated. I certainly found myself writing jolly telling stuff about the advantages of all-over fitted carpets as floor covering in theatres and places of entertainment. I never was required to do it for sound equipment I am happy to say.

In a sense I found myself warming to the Rank idea of a comprehensive package. Perhaps it was an internal flashback to my early days running the Seecol demonstration theatre with Hall and Dixon stuff to cope with, or even earlier to the idea of G.E.C. for "Everything Electrical". In the event, of course, no Rank package was left long enough to mature. Something that did stay around for quite a number of years was architectural lighting as a logical branch of stage, or rather theatrical, lighting. But even there things did not work *my way*. Probably in 1966 and certainly while the Arts Council were still housed in St. James Square before the move to Piccadilly, I was sitting opposite the chairman of the Theatres Advisory Council and gazing, as was not unusual, at the fine mirror behind him. As there was a second mirror immediately behind me and a lit crystal chandelier hanging above us, what I saw was a line of these stretching to infinity. Musing on this, one fell to wondering on the expense and the labour intensive cleaning of these delightful luxuries. What would be an equivalent today if one wanted to make a similar show? The answer was my 'minilabra' as I called it. A candelabra whose arms ended not in candles or candle-lamps but Minispots.

On return to King Street I set about it and it went on the drawing board right away, and as usual I myself wrote the 8-pager to sell it. Of course, crystal chandeliers sparkle and this sparkle we got by leaving the lenses exposed. There were to be three types of minispot: mini-fresnel, mini-profile and mini-effects projectors. The Fresnel version was 3 by 3 by 4½ inches deep, which was very small and neat for a 100-watt spot in those days. The Profile had the same body but with adjustable gate in place of the lens. The single lens, or two for wide angles, hung from rods out front in much the same way that had been Schwabe practice years and years ago for their giant scene and effects projectors. Used the other way up and with other mods the Profile became an effects projector. Here Eddie Biddle entered enthusiastically into the project with mini-discs for storm or fleecy clouds, snow or flames, but his masterpiece was the disc and set of glasses (plastic in fact) for the Mini-Kaleidospot. At this time the notion of "psychedelic" lighting (i.e. lighting patterns on the move) was just beginning to creep in. Or I think it was. It was difficult to be sure for the Minispots were a development from inside as so much of our (my?) ideas in Strand were. One thing led to another - it was not a matter of what did 'they' outside want. Moving colour combined with patterned glasses was a common feature of the optical effects range for decades so it was quite natural to try the same thing with a mini-projector.

The whole philosophy was the use of these Minispots in quantity. The table in the Blue Room was lit with three 5-way 50-watt lamp Minilabras on a dimmer. Outside in the lower showroom, by then the theatre foyer in all but name, there must have been a couple of dozen Minispots at least. At one end focused on comparative theatre plans which formed the wall decoration, while at the other end they were mini-effects projecting *slow* changing colour patterns. In the theatre, ten 6-way

▲ Pollard, Paul, 'B.', Brian, F.P.B., Sheppard, Maestro

◀ Blue Room: Minilabras at the ready

100-watt lamp minilabras formed the auditorium lighting, a great improvement on the anonymous downlighters which had, perforce, preceded them.

To get this idea firmly established outside our theatre and television sphere of influence we needed an up-market firm of fittings people. I had in mind Merchant Adventurers. Unfortunately Rank after takeover made an arrangement with the firm of Concord Rotaflex who had an extensive range of their own to flog for architectural lighting. Downlighters and the cylindrical equivalents, based on reflector lamps, to hang from 'Litespan' tracks and that kind of thing. It was not until Thorn's "Camera Spot" of Autumn 1984 with its 50-watt lamp and compact transformer that I have seen anything approaching what I had in mind. Although not focusable they are certainly being used in quantity, as for example in the foyers on the new Stoke on Trent theatre-in-the-round of 1986. Minispots survived in the Rank catalogue for some years after I left and sales were reasonable enough to justify this, but outside 29 King Street they were never used as they could have been. As for psychedelics, the eye-jabbing that went on in the seventies in that direction had about as much in common with my own notions as the present flashing pop lighting had with my hot rhythm on the Light Console in the thirties!

All this is to anticipate. How and why were we taken over by Rank? Strand had until Spring 1968 been left very much to itself. Except that is for one attempt early in 1958 of particular concern to me. At the end of 1957 L.G. Applebee would retire and needless to say there was speculation as to who would replace him on the board of Strand Electric Holdings and the rest. Anyway to keep it short, I was able one evening to walk into 16 Ravensbourne Gardens, pour out a couple of sherries and demand that Ilse and I drink to the Strand directors, something she was a bit hesitant to do. For some years it had seemed certain that Jack Madre would be next director but by this time, I have to say it, it simply *had* to be me. Not only was I running R&D but I was also in charge of publicity and had become editor of *TABS*. Of course the King Street theatre was 'mine' and I was well known as a writer and lecturer. With a marvellous department of enthusiasts, each a character maybe, but just right for his or her role. Outside, so to speak, was 'B' and outside, in fact, was 'T' James Twynam of Twynam & Oxlade* and many others on whom I had come to rely.

However, few of the Board of Directors could be described as Bentham enthusiasts, but I had Stanley's backing and he told me that Applebee made a passionate plea for me to occupy his vacant chair. This was nice to hear, after all back in my early days in Strand he and I were very much on opposite sides of the fence, although not when out on jobs together. We had so much in common when it came to Strand and stage lighting in the widest sense - what is better summed up as *theatrical* lighting - the title chosen of course for that very first 1936 catalogue of mine.

Here we see something which was to become so different after takeover. Keeping to Board of Directors and management level, though it is not really necessary to do so, there was a common bond between us and theatre people - our customers. Even Henry Myers, our company secretary, had previously been in C.B. Cochran's office. In a sense Jack Sheridan our chairman and joint managing director was the least at home in the theatre, but as Phillip Sheridan's son he must have been brought up in an atmosphere saturated with *theatre*. In any case it was just as well for us to have someone at the top who had not become too friendly with his customers and could view things with some detachment.

When we had become a public company in 1936 two of the four directors were

* Later to become Twynam Publishing Ltd.

'City' people but first Tillett was replaced by Myers then F.L. Blow by L.G. Applebee, and JS became chairman as well as managing director. Until Rank came on the scene, the few replacements and additions to the board were individually chosen from people we knew and confirmed at the next AGM. A ceremony at which not more than six, if that, shareholders were likely to turn up. Even with the odd pressman plus we directors, an AGM was the thinnest house we ever used to see in our King Street theatre. All in all I was able to 'enjoy' nearly eleven years as a director in addition to my other roles. However, within only a few weeks of my appointment to the Board it was to seem that an enjoyable future was not to be.

A thundercloud suddenly arose on the horizon in the shape of a takeover. The details elude me three decades later, but I know Ed Kook of Century was mixed up in it and Mole Richardson USA. The all-important finance was to gush from an oil tycoon. What chance would the youngest director stand in all this? Over the years Ed and I had enjoyed a friendly relationship, but it was based on interest in theatre and stage lighting. I was never under the illusion that we could have worked together in any relationship whatever. Many years ago he referred to me as a "rugged individualist" but I have to declare that I have known an even more rugged example of that species! An appointment was made for the oil tycoon and he enjoyed a cup of Mrs. Ventem's tea with Jack Sheridan. Listening to the 8 o'clock news as usual the following morning we learned that the oil tycoon was no more - he had died in the night, taking with him the takeover and leaving a reprieve behind for me. But for the fact that it was breakfast-time, further glasses of sherry would surely have been in order.

For many of the years to follow, the board meetings were enjoyable occasions and memory says that we found little if anything to quarrel about. I didn't know anything much about finance and they knew little about our kind of R&D by now. Perhaps it was my presence on the board, but it is a fact that the meetings extended in time. May be it was because they were no longer confined to 'official' business. How much other discussion there was before my time it is difficult to tell from the brief minutes. Anyway, before long I suggested that minutes whose main content not infrequently merely declared "The Minutes of the previous Meeting of Directors, held on ... were read and signed as a correct record." inadequately covered what we had in fact done. Another good idea was that Board meetings, where legally we all *had* to be there, but physically need not, should have our names recorded on them in a different order from the normal seniority, to give us a retrospective clue instead of racking our brains to recall a non-existent discussion.

Since I occupied Applebee's vacated chair at Board meetings, I found myself seated opposite the one man around that table with whom I was not on friendly terms. An odd example of his attitude to me turned up years afterwards when Ned Bowman of Pittsburgh University sent me a small book which had been published in 1946. Entitled *Theatre Organ World* he had acquired it second-hand in New York. On page 158 there is an interview with an "expert" about "Music and Colour - Can they blend?" In this, Hugh Cotterill remarks that during the war, in the Opera House at Lisbon "One of our people gave several recitals to full houses, simply by 'playing light' to the accompaniment of gramophone records". Apart from the fact that "full houses" is an overstatement, surely I am entitled to regard "one of our people" rather an understatement! There is no hiding the fact that Cotterill never really became a *member* of Strand and I can recall the general feeling of relief when Jack Sheridan said, after the formal business at a Board meeting early in 1959, "Perhaps you will leave us now, Hugh." and then, as the door shut, "He wants to resign." At this point it is but fair to repeat that Hugh was the creator of *TABS*. It was he who launched it in 1937 and navigated it as editor over the years into the well-loved form that I was only too happy to continue.

First of all, it has to be said that the first Rank offer in Spring 1968 came as a complete surprise. Our shareholders had continued to show their approval of this arcane company and its balance sheet by staying away from the AGM. Nor was there any question of J.S. himself wanting to bail out and retire, as is often the case. Far from it, he still regarded us as the family firm and his son Phillip as taking on his roles one day. Rumour has it that the idea of Rank making an offer for Strand was the result of a muddle of some sort on their part. Anyway they certainly could not have examined the target itself in any detail. Strand Electric Holdings might appear OK to the Stock Exchange, but not to an engineer. Since 1964 Strand Electric had been getting more and more out of its depth in electronics. To put it bluntly, the area of advanced lighting control in which we had become the leaders post-war, was now a disaster area for us. We had been too good for our own good.

Strand's problem can be summed up in a couple of words - Thorn Q-File. In a way the trouble was me. This thought has its origin in Francis Reid choosing me to talk on the "Strand-Bentham Lighting Era" for his 1988 and 1991 British Council courses on Theatre Lighting. He took the title, apparently, from George Izenour's latest book* in which George refers to the time I was at Strand in that way. It so happens that this period of four decades - 1932 through 1972 - was one in which Strand retained a devoted and, each in his own way, suitably talented staff. Into this ambience my own talents fitted very well indeed for the majority of the time. At any rate when I was, officially or unofficially, my own boss. The Board came to take it for granted that R&D, Publicity, Lectures and theatrical presentations could mostly originate in one man. His range was wide, it was not necessary to get an outside

* *Theatre Technology*, pub: McGraw-Hill 1988

consultant to design the new demonstration theatre, showroom or brochure for example. He could even edit *TABS* and write chunks of it at the same time.

Until 1963, except for the pay, whether I was a director or not was irrelevant. Everything happened as necessary and in came the money for J.S. to look after. With the arrival of our first 'sixth' director that Autumn, things began slowly to go sour. I alone had opposed his election, not the way to popularity with most fathers! The trouble was that although Phillip had studied full time at Imperial College and passed out with a good engineering degree, his practical work had been limited to vacation part time *inside Strand*. What I believed and said he should do first, was to spend a couple of years with a large engineering firm and return to us full of ideas and reform.

"In full control of our control market"

Up to 1964, the year of Strand's Golden Jubilee, we were in full control of our control market - just. As to my own department, I had attracted to myself, or at any rate to the type of work I did, a number of versatile enthusiasts. It was an ideal team, but suddenly it was torpedoed by the loss of Len Leggett on whom I had relied to cope with the world of electronics and chips. While we were still in the 'steam age' of servos, clutches and relays I had no problem. I could if necessary, devise, draw, specify and *enjoy* circuitry to carry out my ergonomic desires. However *I knew* we had to make the change in technology and Len Leggett of the post-war generation (pioneering away with his eyes open for each new electronic advance) was just the man for me, especially, as with many of my department he had some experience working backstage. He rightly saw that factory methods of the 'steam age' would not suit the 'solid-state era'. Sadly, it has to be said that it was those very people at the Gunnersbury works under Jim Jordan, those who had been so helpful to me in the earlier years, who looked askance at Leggett as he questioned them and their methods.

Looking through my archive, one senses trouble in a tightly typed 3-page foolscap draft of "Departmental Instruction" of March 1963. The ominous opening paragraph, "Technical Department is responsible for Design. It is not responsible for Production or any Production Processes". One year later Leggett, like an ass, drew up a letter which I, like an ass, showed J.S. thinking it would provoke him to see how serious things had become. It did provoke him, but not as I had hoped.

Len Leggett was shown the door with a rapidity unequalled even by Rank on top form. But he soon found himself in G.E.C. working happily ever after, I am glad to say. The situation became desperate and unhappy for me and the likes of 'B', Percy and Woody and, of course Phil Rose in Canada and Denis Irving in Australia, trying to serve our devoted customers. However, after a while an unexpected ally of unanticipated antecedents turned up at Board level. He was there to look after Administration etc now that Henry Myers had retired after a reign of forty years. It was soon to work out that although in age and training the newcomer and I were poles apart, we increasingly found ourselves forming a minority of two to four.

An extract from something I wrote dated 17th July 1967 conveys the atmosphere. After listing in some detail the range of the things I was recognised as good at, in the eyes of our world, the tirade goes on: "How then does it come about that if Bentham is a success outside the boardroom, he is a continual failure inside it and no words of his ever seem to succeed when it comes to a vote? ...". However, there came a day when a man twenty years younger joined the board. Before many months this handsome debonair man of the world began to show signs of the same frustration. To talk wildly with uplifted voice, prophesying disasters and railing against lack of opportunity to exercise responsibility. To Bentham the sight of another, doing battle just as unsuccessfully as he, was a tonic; for where one lone man might be wrong two could not. The fault obviously lay in the Board of Directors as a body and not with the individual members thereof. Dare one suggest that possibly here is a hint of the old adage, "a committee is as good as its chairman".

That latest arrival on the Strand board had been Jack Hunter, whose father was the Hunter of Rawlinson & Hunter, Strand's accountants for many years no less! Though some years older than Phillip he would obviously take care of the Financial and City side and leave him free to look after the Engineering in a happy future. It is easy to see why the members of our Board took the line they did. Strand had become over fifty years *the name* in stage lighting. It was inconceivable that Thorn, whose only entry into *our* territory had been a misbegotten idea a decade or so earlier (they thought that what theatre needed was fluorescent lamp colour-mixing battens and floats), could be a threat. And this, at the very time when at last theatre had begun to regard the use of spots in a big way as being fundamental.

As for the spotlights themselves, design had presented no particular difficulty provided we could get appropriate lamps. For example, my novel 8-shutter bifocal spot was launched by Richard Pilbrow as the main lighting for *Blitz* at the Adelphi in 1962. In contrast, even after my overnight Rocker switch brainwave at the Royal Opera House in September 1964, the memory control task we had embarked on was to take us years, and lose us, among other things, our mastery of television lighting control.

The design and the ergonomics of a 30-way prototype panel took next to no time, as did the warm welcome for the rocker idea from the likes of 'B' and Francis Reid.

For the storage of cue dimmer levels, we already had a Sperry drum, ready and waiting in R&D. We aimed to launch the system, then known as 'WHZ' because of the high speed rotating memory drum, to our TV lighting directors' 'club' at our King Street theatre in December 1965. There are still members of the club's successor the STLD who think they did see it work then. What they experienced was due to B's drinks and my skill as a lecturer. So there we were with a patent and a prototype which when at last in March 1967 it did work we could not trust it. Enthusiasm for a Memory system with a rotten *memory* was difficult to muster. The BBC had lost faith in our control prowess by now and suggested to Thorn that they had a go and the result in May 1966 was Q-File. Meanwhile Phil Rose had dispatched Fred Lebensold, the architect of the Ottawa Arts Centre, then under construction, to see a demonstration of WHZ. This somehow or other I did manage to give him, and in spite of the fact that the consultants were American, we landed an order for two very large installations and much else besides for the Opera House and Drama theatre respectively. Those consultants were responsible for adding a totally unnecessary vertical extension to each control desk. What all the switches on them were supposed to do, I never knew or cared to find out.

Faced with these orders we simply had to subcontract the WHZ system circuitry to Sperry and that in those days meant a line of expensive racks full of electronics; but it also meant an enthusiastic letter (13/6/69) from Wally Russell, then the Ottawa general manager, reprinted in *TABS* that September. Wally's letter so captures his enthusiasm for the system in action, and he was no stranger to the problems in stage lighting, that it would be sacrilege to quote in part. About a year later I was in Ottawa myself and was greeted by their technical director Andis Celms with the words, "Whatever you do, stick to the Rocker." And that was certainly what I would liked to have done and indeed did in the case of my swansong at Stratford. However long before that, thinking (wrongly) to make things simpler for our own R&D people I devised a memory system around our existing luminous dimmer levers. This was called Instant Dimmer Memory (IDM/DL) while the rocker became IDM/R.

Nothing since Woody's 1948 Electronic Preset so captured our customers, especially the theatre ones. Its full set of normal looking dimmer levers and a 12-page A4 masterpiece of a brochure made it easy to understand. But the fact was that the 120-way prototype would not work

"Nothing since the 1948 Electronic so captured our theatre customers"

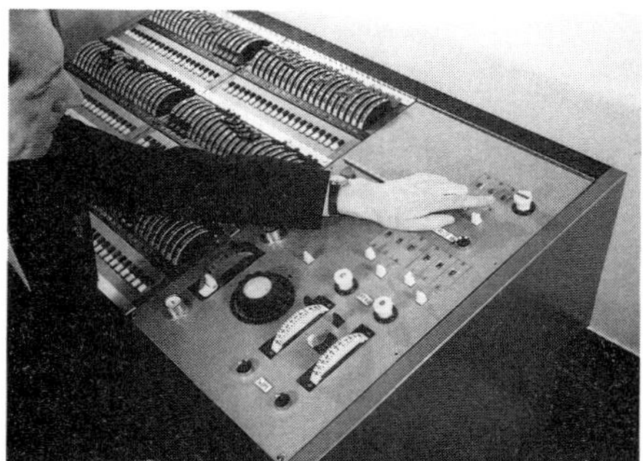

beyond channel no. 19 and those that did were unreliable. So once again my muddled lighting cues technique had to be employed. In this the content of each cue of the series memorised was not itself memorable visually. Nobody could tell whether each cue had come back accurately. One day Stanley came in with his wife Hilda, who had been the Palladium Light Console operator during the war, to show Prince Littler the IDM/DL. She soon spotted my technique and demanded that I set a cue for "down to blues". On that occasion the stage did go all blue. On the other hand at one of our regular house-full technical lectures, I was by then so fed-up that I left the climax, the IDM/DL, to Phillip Sheridan. As I departed down the gangway, I heard him set up a blue cue and describe how the memory would recall it. I could feel, on my back, the full-up everything which followed instead. By then I had pushed the exit door open and did not stop.

In spite of all this we got orders. As at November 17th 1968 there were IDM/DLs installed but not working satisfactorily in Schweinfurt, Budapest, Oslo, Yorkshire TV studios 2 & 3, and the Coliseum. "Lost to Thorn Q-File : BBC TC 3, 4 & 8 and TV Theatre," plus others. A total of 13 jobs representing a loss to Strand *then* of £546,000 nett. Strand had made some attempt to co-operate with Thorn in the second half of 1966; exchange our theatre skills for their technology, but it was not pursued with real enthusiasm by either side and it came to nothing. As Tony Isaacs the genius behind Q-File told me later, they knew they were on a good thing when they saw the sort of money Strand were offering for R&D engineers. So much was happening which involved me in the latter part of the sixties that it is difficult to list exactly what, and it would make tedious reading anyway. What is important is that I drafted a brief for an IDM/R Mk.2 in April 1968 and gave it to Alan Payne an outside consultant with whom we had contact. By that July he had produced his first specification. That we used an outside consultant shows that the seriousness of our position was recognised by the board at last. According to a contemporary schedule of mine on 'progress' of the IDM systems 1964 through 1968, from which these quotes come, "the decision to concentrate on this was made at *Phillip's insistence* that we could not have both IDM/R2 and IDM/DL2." However, at the time the notes were issued, we had just ceased to be Strand Electric and had become Rank Strand.

The fighting off of Rank's first offers was by no means easy. The trouble was that we were a Board of Directors split 4 to 2. It is quite fantastic to look back and see myself allied with our accountants against the others with whom I had enjoyed working and had known for so long. I was even asked by Hunter Snr. at a meeting in his office to allow them to nominate me as Managing Director. Not only was this strange coming from an accountant, but this one was married to Jack Sheridan's sister. Fortunately it did not come to that, though I did meditate on who to get with the extra money I did not want. To add to the confusion Ilse and the boys were holidaying on a hire cruiser on the Fens in East Anglia. Fortunately there was a good train service between Huntingdon and Kings Cross, but blending City demands with equally unfamiliar cruising was to be somewhat out of one's depth at both ends of the journey. We were not the skilled boaters we were to become once we acquired our own boat "Peter Sam" the following Spring; Ilse having wisely declared that I must fall out of love with Strand.

As with anything to do with the Law, to your own specialists you have to add others. Thus we had Hambros as financial advisers we did not need, while Rank had Kleinwort Benson. What we did have and they didn't was the talented editor of *TABS*. He, in conjunction with 'B', produced overnight a special shareholders issue to stress and illustrate how special we were. This I found easy, though how I did it, being on the boat not at home I don't recall. What was not easy was to join in a Hambros statement that the board was unanimous. How could one declare to the shareholders that they were on a good thing to stay with us? The position could be stated that although the great Rank Organisation did not have our arcane expertise, they did have *plenty* of money to spend on the inevitable disasters pending. How could I support policies of which I was so critical? I therefore drafted a dissent which would have had to printed underneath the Board's letter of advice to reject the Rank bid. This was re-drafted when I found Jack Hunter wanted a dissent both of us could sign. Something had to be done right away; especially as Jack Hunter's shareholding amounted to twice that of *all* we other directors added together and these figures had to be published. A last minute compromise was reached in Hambros solemn dark oak boardroom in the heart of the City. Hunter and I accepted, "That in accordance with the advice given by the Company's Solicitors, if the Company remains independent and no arrangements with Berkey Photo are concluded, the Board will urgently seek an additional Director, acceptable to all parties, with responsibility as Finance Director."

The Berkey negotiations came to nothing, as did the solemn promise to appoint another director. Except for an offer to tempt me to leave the firm, which Hunter Snr. counselled me to refuse unless the whole Strand board was behind it, the next few months were just drift at the top. When Rank came back at us, in the Autumn, it was a walkover. Jack Sheridan seemingly had made an arrangement that he would be Managing Director and Phillip a director of the new company. So the rest of us had to negotiate individually. Stanley was of retirement age anyway and the Hunters opted for departure, which left myself, plus Phil Rose and Ken Mould who had become directors in the last months of the old firm. I alone stayed on as a *director* of the moribund Strand Holdings - an untidy nuisance.

As I was to find, staying on is not a custom in the Executive ranks of Rank. Nothing or nobody was left alone for long. Anyway, for the present the new Strand had become a company within Rank Audio Visual, one of the Divisions which made up the Rank Empire. Quite what John Ball's official role was, or rather 'roles were' for he played several topwise ones during the time he survived, I am not sure. Because, while still in the early Rank weeks, J.S. was presented with a deputy Managing Director, Pat Butler by name, who of course took over when J.S. left. After a while Phillip was sent on a Business (or was it Marketing?) course across the Atlantic at Harvard at Rank expense. He returned to find that no job awaited him, apparently a well-known big-company tactic. As to John Ball, what I *do* know is that he took over my King Street second-floor office and I had to move down to ground-floor at the back. I think of him as fun and friction in equal proportions. As to myself, the move had its compensations, it was next to the showroom and theatre. And soon it had the 'Blue Room' in the basement immediately beneath along with 'cellar' and small kitchen. What could be more convenient for the Manager of PR and TL (Technical Liaison) dept? I had been able to get an early insight into Rank thanks to James Twynam, who took me out to lunch with his friend Alec de Jonge - at one time a key figure for many years inside the part of Rank of interest to 'B' and me. From him I learned that Ed Chilton, who ran Audio Visual with undeniable gusto and aplomb if nothing else, was the man to focus on. But all depended in the end absolutely on the will of John Davis. What, or who, he said, went!

I think my new role must have been Chilton's idea and at the age of 57 it suited me as a title, but I was not going to let IDM/R out of my clutches. It was a challenge that had to be seen through to the end. And if that was to be a happy one, the prototype had to stay with Alan Payne working at Kingston. On no account must it be surrendered to the new R&D department which was being set up at Brentford. They could get on with IDM/DL2 and anything else we might dream up. This obsession with my Rocker board soon landed me in the Tower, the top floor of the Vickers one on Millbank. For some reason the Rank finance department was lodged up there and they wanted to get my agreement settled and signed. But what with the fabulous view across the Thames and my preference for putting R&D problems before all, we did not get anywhere. In the end I decided to make Ed Chilton my target and he invited me to lunch at Stones Chop House. Not the real thing which a young 'B' had introduced a young Fred Bentham to long before it got bombed in the war; but it was good enough. In mellow mood I emerged with the belief that Ed would look into things and set them on appropriate paths. The solitary remaining director of the old Strand resigned on Ed's advice that very afternoon. Advice which in retrospect I don't think I should have taken; maybe I should have gone to the top (1st floor actually) at South Street first.

It was to turn out that I got my chance regularly once a year. At a strange annual ritual I was destined to feature as a soloist, not colour music perhaps I should point out. The occasion was Sir John's Rank Executive Day. These ceremonies took place at the Royal Lancaster, flagship of the Rank Hotels. No Royal function was so strict

I imagine - at least in this country. There were rows and rows of us executives facing the platform. Lined up either side of the throne upon the dais were the Managing Directors of the Rank Divisions; nothing so low as a company Managing Director got a look in. Enter Graham Dowson, with the mace bearing the Gong-man emblem across his shoulder, metaphorically speaking, followed by Sir John himself whilst we all stood at attention (or did we kneel?) No one dare be late. That's not quite true. In our very first year, Sir John was well into his opening tirade when down the gangway with relaxed smiles on their faces strode Lorcan and Kevin Bourke, of our Dublin branch of course. Half-way through the morning Sir John would announce a 5-minute interval but declare that he himself did *not* intend to leave the room. Whereupon only a desperate few made the humiliating trip to the relieving regions below. Sir John went on all morning and picked out his managing directors on the platform and chastised them one by one. Only Ed Chilton used to get off lightly with a dose of sympathy in spite of Audio Visual's poor figures. Precision Industries got the figures right, but their MD could do no right nevertheless.

There was a half-hour before lunch for questions. This I couldn't resist. I know I got warm laughter on each occasion - but one. I think the first related to a proving of a new theatre seat at Brentford by Sir John, and Graham Dowson; a man of a size to provide an ample test. My basic theme each time was a plea that things be let alone to mature. Get the R&D right, all Administrative re-shuffles were a waste of time till then. The occasion I do remember well was when I went on to quote the late lamented Pat Butler, "..who turned to me and said as he mounted the scaffold 'I inherited a c—- budget and my mistake was that I went on to create another c—- budget.'" The drop in temperature and silence as I sat down need not be described. We were ordered off to lunch and the executives hastily put as much distance between them and Fred as possible. The stairway down to and up from the loos had a rail down the centre. As I descended I became aware those on the other side of the rail were literally hugging the wall. Suddenly one man put his hand out across the rail to shake mine, declaring in a loud voice, "Well done Fred, that wanted saying." Who he was I never knew. (By the way, Butler, a quiet man, really had used that adjective). We were allocated our places at a series of round tables for the usual excellent lunch and drinks. I don't think my companions, by tradition strangers, enjoyed theirs. Some notable guest from the world outside always made a speech at brandy time. On one occasion it was Ted Heath, for example, and very good he was too. On this occasion it was the Dean of St. Pauls Cathedral - a New Zealander, a man very much in the news at the time. Strangely, his opening remarks were more like a sermon; he rambled on about *forgiveness* and people speaking from the heart and having different ways of expressing themselves. It gradually dawned on me that he must have heard my contribution!

Another year I made the point that surely there was a level below which it cost more to send out the bill than Rank got back. In particular this related to an idiotic proposal to charge for *TABS* with its world-wide circulation then of around 24,000. This was prevented, at any rate as far as UK was concerned, until I had departed and it had become A4. But at the time South Street sent an expert, named Paskins, to consult with me. He was taken off his stride when I immediately switched on my desk cassette; recorders not being all that common in 1970. But here was yet another consultant to waste a morning discussing something that seemed pure common-sense. In contrast discussions with Alan Payne were productive indeed. We got on fine and fast. So fast as to stagger me by some modifications happening overnight. Yet at other times a simple idea might take a week or so. What I had not realised was that Alan was using a secret ingredient - Software. It takes quite a mental effort to go back to the days before this word became common currency, when one's every move was disciplined by the habits of the hardware. Mind you, Alan had to get precise specification from me as to what should happen on touching this or that. The longer mod delays were caused by the need to purchase extra memory capacity.

"An Appropriate Swansong"

It really is dramatic that my very first stage lighting control should introduce the cinema organ techniques, relays and jig-wiring to theatre; while the very last with the Rocker and, unwittingly, Software was a similar giant step to end forty years in the 'same' firm. Called system DDM (Digital Dimmer Memory) it was an appropriate swansong indeed; especially as the intended destination was the Royal Shakespeare Stratford-upon-Avon. The 100-way prototype worked fine and was demonstrated to the likes of David Brierley and 'Brad' (John Bradley) from the RSC one morning followed by lunch in the Blue Room with Chilton as host. He played a decisive role by saying that Rank Strand would design and make a 240-channel control specifically for them; and when made the RSC could decide whether they wanted it. A new much larger capacity installation to replace their 1951 Electronic Preset was overdue anyway, especially as the auditorium was being altered at the same time. Except that DDM/R was put in charge of the new R&D chief David Baker at Brentford instead of being given to Alan at Kingston, something which caused me much anxiety, all went well. In December 1971 Ilse and I were able to see the DDM in action for the D'Oyly Carte company. Not many lighting changes for *Iolanthe* on tour. Seemingly there were also not many cues on the opening night of the RSC 1972 season with *Titus Andronicus*. Indeed I thought the 'Lovable Computer', as it was known by then, had failed and they had gone over to standby. As we all filed out 'Brad' stood by the gangway to direct us to our drinks. Anxiously I caught his eye interrogatively; "It's fine, perfect." or enthusiastic words to that effect. The truth was that the RSC had fallen for *gas* of all things in that production. What with fires, torches, flares all with real flames to catch the eye in every scene, our brand new 240-channel installation was completely upstaged. However the season included three other Roman plays for us all to have some chance later on.

The three Stratford controls (1932, 1951 and 1972) made such an interesting contrast in technology that "A Tale of Three Switchboards" was told in *TABS* (Vol. 30 No.1) at the time. It might be thought that the Mansell clutch never had got a look in there, but in fact it did. It was used in 1932 out-front to give an automatic wave taking out the house lights cove by cove towards the stage. By chance, Francis Reid did not see the completed DDM in Stratford for a year or so, but when he did, he hastily sent off a scrawl with the memorable words, "There it was waiting to be played!" Memorable too was a visit of a small party of Germans to examine it. This David Brierley arranged after the show plus ample drinks and buffet in his office; but they could be not prised away from the DDM out in the deserted house. They were like children with a new toy, while the rest of us did justice to the hospitality into the small hours. Not unnaturally, back in the hotel, our guests wanted a good breakfast so we recommended kippers with the same confidence as we had the DDM. Alas, they were a withered soggy mess dredged from a pan of salt water. However, some fourteen or so DDMs were sold but no others in UK. Neither was the rocker itself pursued as it could have been. As soon as I was out of the way, Brentford R&D substituted triple close-mounted pushes to each channel. By no means the same thing. The rocker was of key/stopkey descent and made, as intended by its inventor, the DDM an instrument: pushes are for digital punch-ups.

Important though the rockers were, it is the word "kippers" that provides an essential prompt. If they had been served in our Blue Room they would not have been that soggy mess. Our cuisine and the venue in which it was served was perfect, as much appreciated in its way by those entertained there, as *TABS* or our lecture-demonstrations. That it was, is yet another tribute to the versatility that our Strand R&D tradition unconsciously engendered. If we could, we did; if we couldn't, we could at least have a go and see if we could! It is a strange thought that for our last four years, we had a small reasonably equipped kitchen designed to look after our special customers, yet we never employed anyone to man or run it. To 'man' is, of course, the wrong verb. It became part of my last secretary's duties. No, "duty" is another wrong word. She, Barbara, found herself doing it in much the same way as her 'boss' found himself doing the decor for the showrooms, Blue Room and so on. Nobody told me to. Nor did I expect Barbara Jameson, when I took her on in 1967, to cook. A cup of tea maybe; but a luncheon in the B. Bear flat tradition, never.

But it happened, as did her articles for *TABS*. By which time, she Barbara Berrington, had become my "PA". This was not due to her marriage, but my status as a Rank "Executive". I was also supposed to have a black-formica topped desk and a Rover car - both of which I turned down. Apparently it did not matter to Rank that at 58 I have never really driven a car and therefore could not use it for business, it was an executive perk.

Another 'happening' was the catering for our Saturday lectures. These were staged in the main for the out-of-towners. The idea being that they could make a really worthwhile journey, spend all day with us and then go on to a 5 o'clock 'matinee' at a West End theatre. And come they certainly did. We were staggered at some of the distances they came. The problem on Saturdays in Covent Garden in those days was where our eighty or so visitors could find a quick lunch; after all, our timing could not allow a long break for that purpose. The solution was to serve them with the basics for a good 'picnic' lunch. There were nowhere near enough chairs in the lower showroom but some happily sat on the floor - it was a real picnic. The last of these was held on Saturday October 13th 1973 at 10.45am. Entitled "Basic Stage Lighting" I was joined by Francis Reid and Brian Legge. The *TABS* programme for that Autumn shows nine lectures including three on "My Kind of Colour" described as "likely to be the last performances of this very personal art." I have played an odd item here and there since. Indeed a touring date on the 20th of that very November at Rank Strand's demonstration theatre in Lowton near Haydock for "the shadow setting which has been featured in London on and off since 1935!" formed part of the Northern programme.

For our 'grander' lunches 'B' would sometimes provide an item which was beyond the capability of the Blue Room's basic kitchen equipment to cook. The most memorable of these was the steak and kidney pudding. This he would cook in his flat and turn up with it in a taxi shortly before apéritif time. It was then a matter of keeping it warm until its turn came. Another speciality of his was an enormous fresh salmon cooked and transported in a like manner. Superb smoked-trout was available from the, improbably named, "Hamburger Products" in Berwick Street. Also very useful were the new quick-frozen pre-cooked items, such as duck a l'orange, by Alverstone Kitchens. These dishes became commonplace long since but not so then. 'B' along with the rest of us thoroughly enjoyed the duck; but the fact that it had been deep-frozen might well have put him off and I can still see Barbara and Lyn Wright feverishly cramming the portions into a saucepan while looking apprehensively around to make sure 'B' couldn't see what they were at. One could do a lot of visitor name dropping in this Blue Room context; but it must be stressed that no matter who they were, these were relaxed 'family' affairs, there was none of the being waited upon of *that* South Street lunch.

X: SHAFTESBURY AVENUE & QUEEN SQUARE -
Life After Strand

The day of departure at the end of December 1973 after 41½ years in the same firm was not memorable. There were no ceremonies. I suppose they were deemed to have taken place at the time of the 100th issue of *TABS* in the previous September. Anyway, this was not a case of my leaving for good as far as the building was concerned. I had asked Sir John Davis to let the ABTT, of which I was then chairman, have the lower showroom, theatre and Blue Room at a peppercorn rent. In consequence I was able to retain my office and had access to the familiar 'workplace', colour music and all, for another four years. The remainder of the building was looked after by Rank City Wall, ie. that part of the Rank Organisation whose balance sheet now bore the burden (or asset?) instead of Strand or Rank Audio Visual. Somehow or other the building package was inclusive of Len Jordan ('Maestro'* himself) for there he was seated as usual at his desk at the bottom of the 29 King Street staircase or the top of the theatre steps, depending on your destination. It remained homely - if lonely.

The Association of British Theatre Technicians was a dozen years old by then. Right from the start I had identified myself with it and saw it as more of an Art Workers Guild than an Illuminating Engineering Society. Theatre proper was hardly a place for engineers or the training of them. The prime aim of the little group that Richard Pilbrow had invited to his tiny office in Goodwins Court, off Garrick Street, was to avert the mistakes pending in the new theatre boom about to take off. Equally, some of us, like him, had been to the 1960 Berlin ITI Colloquium in the previous November and were unhappy at the lack of a knowledgeable technical group from UK to compete with the vast team from the USA. A body of French origin called the AITT had asked Richard Southern to see if he could arrange a conference in June in London, so here was something even more urgent.

* 'Maestro': This title I bestowed on Len Jordan in 1935 and it stuck. I had to demonstrate that someone other than the inventor could operate my Light Console. His party piece was AD 1620 by MacDowell. This he used to play on black drapes with care, rather than inspiration, using my score (lighting plot).

The group became an interim committee of six or so and on March 3rd about a hundred people turned up in Strand's King Street theatre. Under Norman Marshall as chairman we discussed and decided on the formation of the ABTT, there and then. The ABTT grew very quickly but it has to be said that hardly anyone bothered to cross the Thames from the West End to attend our conference that June. But we had a good turnout from those who had to make a real journey to get there.

The National Film Theatre on the South Bank under Waterloo Bridge made an ideal and exciting venue, laced as it was with a couple of 'B's ideas - 15-minutes of 'backstage' extracts from the NFT archive, before the morning and afternoon sessions. The other stroke of genius was to charter a boat to collect us at the jetty close-by and take us on a lunchtime trip. Disley Jones did an excellent report under the title "Adaptable Stages and Inflexible Minds"† which well conveys the atmosphere. As can be gleaned therefrom, supervising of theatre planning was particularly difficult at that time. It was not merely a matter of ensuring that proper backstage space, access, provision for suspension and lighting and so on was made appropriate to the size of the place, but a hectic argument was going on as to what form a theatre and its stage should take. For some, for example, changeable scenery had become a dirty word. To hint at a need for a grid was to provoke a scornful glance. The two *new* theatres, Belgrade Coventry and the Mermaid Puddledock sum it up. Pros. stage versus Stage-sans-everything. Yet this comparison is in fact of like with like, because in both cases the audience *confronts* the stage. There were also stages thrust into the audience or surrounded by them. An adaptable theatre which would take shape as any of these formats, at the touch of a button so to speak, was claimed to exist in the shape of George Izenour's Loeb Harvard. Over here, in the plans for the Questors Theatre Ealing there seemed promise of a more modest way of achieving adaptability. A couple of decades were to elapse before technology in the shape of *air castors* would provide the solution to the 'lug and push' problem posed by large adaptable theatres or halls.

The Belgrade Coventry was the really important post-war theatre because it was our first purpose-built civic repertory house of some style and size. Opened in 1958 and seating 910 with decent foyers and a restaurant front of house, it gave a theatre the facilities that we used to expect of the super-cinemas between the wars. Of course thanks to the LCC and, one gathers, Herbert Morrison, we had learned in 1951 how exciting a Civic building for live entertainment can be, given the right architects. But the Royal Festival Hall was a concert hall and the town hall tradition had accustomed these islanders to great concert halls with a grand facade of show-pipes probably in organ builders' gothic to set the scene. Where the Belgrade most obviously failed was backstage. Space and facilities were minimal - the stage proper was only 27ft deep, for example.

* *TABS* September 1961

Stage-sans-everything, except atmosphere

There was no lack of expertise in the ABTT right from the start. Even the original founders who met in that office in Goodwins Court represented a wide range of talents. There was Sean Kenny who, thanks to *Oliver*, was all the rage and had unmasked the spot-bars seemingly for ever. Though Sean never had his cheque book handy when it came to subscription time, he was a valuable member none the less in those early years. If the word Sean suggests wayward talent then discipline was surely represented by our first treasurer - Eric Jordan - from his high position in County Hall, at the helm of the good ship LCC Regs., was an asset indeed. Then again there was Norman Marshall, our chairman for the first 12-years, whose career not only went right back to Terence Gray's Cambridge Festival theatre and Peter Godfrey's Gate theatre in Floral Street; but covered such mysteries as the British Council, Arts Council, British Drama League and even joint-chairmanship, with Sir Laurence Olivier, of the committee which was going to build us a National Theatre at last! At the other end of the scale our first vice-chairman, Stephen Joseph, functioned in-the-round in the Library Scarborough during the summer seasons. There were no stick-in-the-muds. It is ridiculous to try to name-drop all those who were around and really *worked* for the ABTT then. From architects and consultants right up to the managers and stage managers whose job it would be to make their 'masterpieces' work as theatre. It should be noted that the word 'Technician' did not include Actor. We all got to know each other so well. Was it the fine wines at our meetings?

One evening some of the members assembled in the lower showroom for the noble purpose of wine tasting. Some bottles of red identified only by Strand Electric labels bearing large numbers had been arranged - by 'B' of course. We took our job seriously, but not enough to spit the stuff out. On registering our votes, we found that the cheapest, a vin indeed ordinaire, was the victor. One of the very first theatres to receive attention from the ABTT's Architectural & Planning committee, to nil effect it must be added, was the Prince Charles Theatre off Leicester Square. There was very little that could be suggested, let alone done, at that late stage. The site was terribly tight to cram 420 seats in and the planning showed little appreciation of the needs of anything else. It ended up by earning a living as a cinema. The real worry was the press exaggeration it got maybe because of the name. The advance claims were nonsense. It was one of the three new theatres I reviewed in *TABS* of April 1963. Of the other two, Ashcroft Croydon and the Hampstead Civic, only the latter could and did get an enthusiastic review. It was a smaller version of London's Mermaid theatre, brand new without the atmospheric advantage of the ancient Puddledock warehouse walls running down either side. Incidentally this dramatic asset was chucked overboard thirty years later when the side walls of the front stalls were rebuilt as a fan. The result is a pros-look-alike in spite of the fact that there is no wing space whatever stage left. If ever theatre

"No lack of expertise in the A.B.T.T."

re-planning showed how easy it can be to ruin the character of an auditorium it is the poor old Mermaid.

Thanks largely to the Arts Council, examination of plans over a glass or two of red wine became a fairly frequent irregular evening feature of my life. First in Peter Moro's offices looking across the river appropriately to the Royal Festival Hall; then later at the very top of flights of stairs in Rathbone Street, overlooking nothing in particular, and overlooking it very well. After the meeting we few, we happy few, we band of members, would descend and adjourn to the cosy pub almost next door. Until one evening it was packed out so that we could not get inside. Thereupon we set out to find another. We combed the neighbourhood with little result. It was not that there were no pubs; but that there were no pubs without loud 'Musak'. After all it was conversation that we were really after. As Rod Ham remarked as we were noisily thrown out of yet another door, it was indeed an odd kind of pub crawl.

The procedure was that application to the Arts Council for a Housing the Arts grant to build or reconstruct a theatre meant that the plans had to be submitted to our committee for technical discussion, at which the clients could of course be present. A short report followed. Its recommendations were not mandatory; but only a very conceited architect would ignore such a report. It was like a 3-dimensional proof-reading by several expert readers simultaneously. A very early example, poor sightlines in the circle, had to be remedied very late in the day, but not too late, by making the circle steeper. A very recent example, showed a nice Circle bar with that rather rare luxury, a lift to ensure easy entry for the drinks and easy exit for the empties; but there was no emergency fire exit for the two-legged vessels it was the purpose of the bar to fill. The truth is one can get too used to gazing at the wonders of one's own drawings. Of course, most theatre people make things work somehow. We had proof of this in our own two-hundredth set of plans.

This was a special occasion, the committee had been asked to comment on the scheme for the Robert Gordon Menzies Memorial Theatre in Perth, Australia. It was to be situated in the basement beneath a huge restaurant on one side of a large and very busy square. The plans for the tight site aroused much criticism right away. Indeed many details were hopelessly impractical seen in terms of a working theatre. But that is just what it was. Except for Ian Albery, who had loaned me the plans to get traced, nobody knew it was the Criterion theatre in Piccadilly Circus. A theatre which was designed by Thomas Verity and built in 1874 to seat 645 and stage "plays and musicals". This latter in spite of no height whatever above the pros. opening and an orchestra pit for five. But it was, above all, the scenery get-in over the stalls seating which had inspired my practical joke. Nobody rumbled it and the secret was revealed only when we adjourned for drinks in the Blue Room prior to dinner. Since the 'Perth' plans would not be accompanied by its architect 'he' sent a description of the project and its intent. This used extracts culled from a contemporary account of the Criterion as quoted in Mander & Mitchenson's *Theatres of London*. To conclude my 'moral' tale, it must be revealed that unwittingly I had dropped a clanger; but nobody picked it up. In 1975 it was decidedly premature for Menzies to have a memorial theatre project on any agenda!

As with other ABTT committees, like Materials or Safety, our Architectural & Planning (or Theatre Planning as it became) had a number of members on call. Some projects produced a fantastic turnout of talent. One such was the array for the new Birmingham Rep. of which some of us had to be highly critical. We were meeting in King Street by that time and as I showed the architect to the door I could not help asking whether he would prefer the Thames or Euston, which he took in good part. Timing is all important in this kind of survey. The project must have been drawn out in some detail; but the building itself must not, as so often and certainly was in this case, be in an advanced state of construction. Further we may sit there, with more than one job to look at that evening and the chairman Peter Moro and now Roderick Ham, has to sum each up as a brief report. Obviously this, though useful as an eye-opener, was insufficient in many cases. Stephen Joseph had an idea for a Society of Theatre Consultants and summoned a meeting of the interested at the Arts Council one afternoon in April 1964. I remember it well and have two good reasons for doing so. Travelling to the meeting, then at St. James Square, in a taxi with Sean Kenny, he remarked, apropos of goodness knows what, that he found *TABS* difficult to use for reference because the covers were all the same. I adopted the photo cover idea there and then for June and thereafter. There had in fact been one example earlier when in 1959 I had found a photo of some Patt. 23s parked in the snow during a get-out in Norway irresistible for our December issue. But Sean was the real trigger, *TABS* had become a work of reference.

Stephen's ideas formed the agenda. One of the points he made was:- "though architects had often consulted experts, the buildings had been poor none the less; because (a) the advice had often been given free of charge and had therefore been freely ignored and (b) the expert had not been particularly qualified to give the sort of advice required." After discussion the meeting agreed that there was a gap to be filled and I got up to depart with the others and leave the few embryonic professionals to discuss the detail of their new society. I had just reached the door when Stephen called out, "Where are *you* going?" My recall was a great compliment. For me as a director and member of the best-known commercial firm in our side of theatre, which is exactly what Strand Electric was, I not only became a founder member of the STC but in due course reigned a while as chairman. The truth is that one gets into the habit of playing any role in wider terms than any contract. As with some others it was 'my' theatre I was working for. It was certainly never the money. Thus it was perfectly possible to be described as a professional. Indeed, the likes of me, cushioned by their firm to some extent, could take a more detached approach than a professional consultant whose livelihood depended on what he did in that specific role. Anyway like it or not, that it how it was; but certainly could not be in the 1980s where the target was money first and last.

I did do some work as a paid consultant after I left Rank. But as I had found doing odd jobs on the side when at the GEC at the beginning of my working life, I hit a snag. I detested making out the bills. As in tipping, I suffer from a working-it-out phobia. Quite crazy, but there it is. Maybe it is why I am relaxed when sitting on committees - there is no fee to work out.

One thing led to another. Soon delegates from the various bodies and unions associated with the theatre and music came together regularly for two monthly meetings as the Theatres Advisory Council. That in turn was represented on the Standing Advisory Committee on Local Authorities and the Theatre. The person holding the ABTT, TAC and STC in close embrace has been Ethel Langstreth. That she playing her role as Executive Secretary to each, surrounded by stacks of reports & minutes, has been the linchpin is beyond doubt. For myself, service on all these over the decades has made committee-going a habit. And arising from them are conferences and seminars; some of which one attends to get something done and some just to meet people and have some fun. The older one gets, the more what one wants to get done becomes concerned with the past, with archive, rather than the future, and the less time there is to do it. Inevitably in looking back certain individuals stick out above the rest. An obvious case is that encounter with Bernard Shaw in 1936, even though my work at Strand in the mid-1930s had made me accustomed to legendary characters like C.B. Cochran, Julian Wylie or George Black dropping into 'my' theatre for advice. Stephen Joseph was another matter. At the time he turned up in my life, in Pilbrow's office he was a name in a very small arcane circle - in the round, if one wants to be precise.

The fact that Stephen was Hermione Gingold's son, was surely enough to ensure him fame! But no, it was his own warm personality exuding great enthusiasms, coupled with tireless energy which got things done. It was that energy of his which got me my first real secretary. At the first ABTT committee upstairs in my office, Stephen brought along his secretary Ann Daly to take the minutes. She sat on the other side of him and I found myself thinking that she was the kind of secretary I would choose instead of allowing myself to be 'landed' with one as hitherto. Misinterpreting the intent of my gaze (?!!) she pulled her blouse closer together and that was that. Time passed, and my then secretary who was about to leave to have a baby was declaring in her robust cockney that, "she didn't know what I would do without my Aud," when exit Audrey and enter Ann, who finding Stephen's pace too exhausting applied to Strand at that very time. Her unflappable quality was just what my department needed.

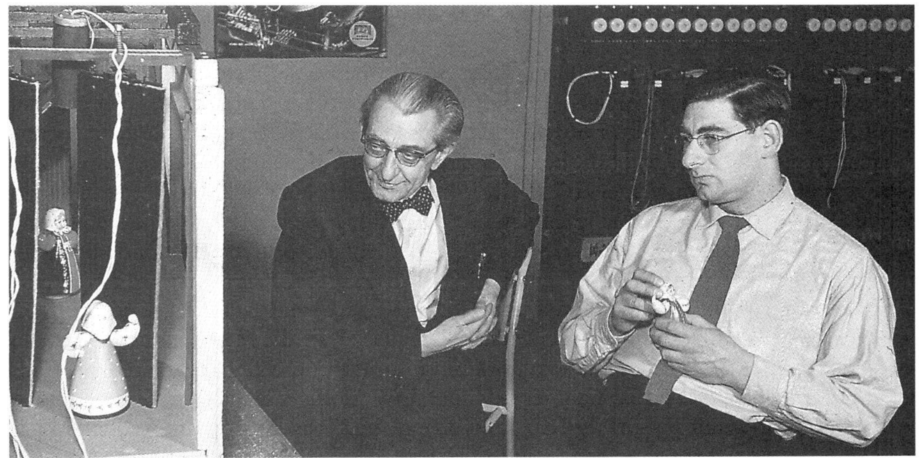

Percy Corry and Stephen Joseph making a Strand "Recorded Lecture"

Alas, there came a day, or rather an evening, when she informed me while dancing sedately across the floor at some function in Strand's Golden Jubilee year, that she and the husband who had acquired her were off to Kenya for a couple of years. Since he, Bob Bryan, was a stage lighting enthusiast, it seemed an odd place to go. Fortunately they did return four years later and from the immediate neighbourhood of Glyndebourne he was able to practice his art and Ilse and I were able to enjoy for some years a house-seat evening-out each season; with the added advantage of a backstage retreat if the weather did not invite a lawn dinner picnic.

Ilse and I have been particularly lucky with 'briefs' for opera. Purchase of tickets has tended to be a rather rare phenomenon. Prior to Ann and Bob, Francis Reid was a source of dress-rehearsal tickets for Glyndebourne during his backstage reign there. His invitations were rather different. It was a case of, "Fred, you must see *Macbeth*" or whatever. Formality was the rule on all occasions at Glyndebourne, but we did attend on one outstanding occasion when the manager came out in front of the house tabs and announced that we gentlemen could remove our dinner-jackets. So there we sat, think of it, some of us actually showing their braces - in the stalls at Glyndebourne! It must have been the hot summer of 1979. Charlie Bristow when electrician at Sadlers Wells in Rosebury Avenue was an intro to less traditional opera; the Weill/Brecht *Rise & Fall of the City of Mahagonny*, Bartok's *Bluebeard's Castle* and the like. Use of the Sadlers Wells small cramped stage in those pre-Coliseum days was ingenious indeed. And the amount of lighting equipment was equally limited. Any Bentham award of that time would have had to go to the Dennis Arundell production of Wagner's *The Flying Dutchman* with sets by Timothy O'Brien. I got Bristow himself to do a description of his lighting of it for *TABS* and reprinted it in each edition of my *Art of Stage Lighting* until its demise in 1980.

Another opera production which has to receive notice here was Jonathan Miller's Mafia version of *Rigoletto* at the Coliseum of 1982. Pat Robertson's clever sets, which gave a complete change from Act 1 scene-l to Act 1 scene-2 in but 2-mins, represented a masterpiece of stagecraft. Furthermore it was from a 'real' interior to a 'real' exterior: the audience was not called upon to deduce or imagine anything. The Zeffirelli production at Covent Garden took around 30-mins to do that change. Between the two scenes we the audience were expected to adjourn to the bars and this after rather less than 20-minutes into the show itself. Unhappily, when Channel-4 televised the Miller *Rigoletto*, they used that 2-minute interval as an advert break, which made it seem like Covent Garden's half-hour. The reader may have gathered that although I like big changes of scene I do not like elaborate special machinery to do it. Certain mechanics are legitimate stagecraft; but I simply cannot come to terms with the mass of engineering represented by a show like *Metropolis* at the Piccadilly or *Time* at the Dominion, for example. The fact that the words and music in each were feeble is not relevant. The fault lay in the expenditure of vast sums on mechanical structures whose real creative wonder needs an ABTT lecture and visit backstage to appreciate. Basic machinery to help changes of scene or playing in repertoire is quite another matter.

This brings us back to Covent Garden Opera House itself where such machinery has been so minimal in potential as to be virtually non-existent during the long time I have known its cramped backstage. The presence of Bill Bundy during the time of Sir David Webster enabled us to enjoy much opera and some ballet. Our locale in the auditorium rose from stalls-circle back-row centre block to the equivalent in the grand-tier above with Bundy's own rise in status. One should remark that as there were only four rows in the first and three in the latter, these were fine seats indeed. The peak has to be the *Tosca* of January 1964 with Callas and Gobbi. Apparently, "They had six weeks in which to mount the opera," which provides all the more reason to admire the decor by Renzo Mongiardino for this Zeffirelli production. The sets were rich indeed and were of the kind of scenery I admire - a combination of painted perspective cloths and cutouts together with cunningly foreshortened 3-dimensional built stuff. Only Puccini's dawn in Act III did not receive full justice. It lacked a cyclorama for the dawn; but at least the parapet did not fall down when Tosca threw herself over it - as had happened at the Stoll some years earlier, the night we were there!

Accidents will happen of course, especially in these computer-controlled days. What is totally unreasonable is the sending home of an audience simply because a

Tosca at the Royal Opera House, 1963

director wants more time to rehearse a new production in preparation. I should have been very annoyed when, as happened at the National the audience turned up to see something already in the repertoire, only to be refused entry because Zeffirelli wanted more time to rehearse *his* new show. We must be true to tradition and the show must go on. Even when, as fairly recently at Covent Garden, a member of the backstage staff was killed in an accident before the performance. It would have been a real tribute to him as a theatre-worker if that show had gone on. Another Bentham black mark goes to those who sanction occupancy of the best seats in the house by *stage lighting* or *sound equipment*. Covent Garden's 1971 *The Knot Garden* was a good example of the first, and *42nd Street* at Drury Lane of the second. Think of it, the whole of the left block front-row dress-circle for *sound* controls. For *The Knot Garden,* 24 seats dead centre grand-tier were replaced by a temporary projection room. Thus it was that the best view of O'Brien's ingenious sets was enjoyed by the pair of projectors producing the slide images on the lines of vertical ropes on-stage which acted as the screen*. Which reminds me that at one time a veritable free-

* *TABS* Vol.29 No.1

standing bungalow occupying the whole of the right half of the rear stalls was built in the King's Edinburgh for lighting and sound controls. Combine this with the removal of the front rows for opera orchestra, the reduction in seating capacity at the critical time of the Edinburgh Festivals was remarkable.

Our attendance at the 'Lane' to see *42nd Street* on August 1st 1984 was due to the sudden death of Joe Davis who had begun to light it. Thanks to David Merrick a benefit matinee took place in Joe's memory. Afterwards we all assembled in the dress circle bar for a wake. A marvellous tribute to this man of the theatre - the Doyen of stage lighting - a real pioneer. The contrast with the requiem mass in Shoreham three weeks earlier, which with Ann Bryan I had attended, could not have been greater. We had good seats for that too. The priest kept on referring to "Joseph" which puzzled some of us. What had St. Joseph got to do with this time of year? Eventually one rumbled it; "Joseph" was Joe. Mercifully the same mistake was not made in St. Paul's Covent Garden when a "Joe Davis lighting designer 1912-1984" took its rightful place among the tablets which adorn the walls of the actors' church. Talking of Doyens, I have noticed a tendency since then on the part of some to pass on this title to me. This is most improper. Joe Davis was unique. His whole career was based on *doing* stage lighting, ie. lighting shows. In my own case, while it would be false modesty to deny that I did exercise considerable influence over stage lighting, in U.K. at any rate once upon a time; it was over the equipment itself, not the use of it. No matter what I preached or wrote, and I did a lot of both as I hardly need to point out, Richard Pilbrow's expression "a multi-lantern complexity" became more and more a reality. What is odd is that while designing controls in terms of large numbers of dimmers from the start of my career, nevertheless I always saw the lanterns themselves, as relatively few and each decisively decisive in what it did.

As earlier chapters show, in Strand Electric I soon became aware that as far as electrical or illuminating engineering were concerned theatre was staffed from top to bottom with the ignorant. They had to be informed and converted somehow and to have attempted this straight from school or university would have been out of the question. But after nearly three years in the GEC with Basil Davis it was quite another matter. I could write specifications and draw wiring diagrams, do electrical or lighting layouts and so forth. There was also a good idea of the kind of money around for new cinema-theatre installations and why not for *theatre* one day? Further, the GEC range of catalogues and other technical literature had led me to expect a high standard in the layout and printing for that. At the other end of the scale, making the minimum do the maximum, there was the experience as an amateur. All in all I was lucky, there could have been no better training for a jack of some thespian trades - Doyen of none.

Antiques and Archive

1984 was also memorable for my first and only visit to Buckingham Palace. It was no merit of mine which got me there that Autumn. In fact I had turned down an earlier opportunity. No sooner had M. Thatcher ascended the throne at No.10 for the first time, than she got her Principal Private Secretary to write to me to say that she had "it in mind, on the occasion of the forthcoming list of Birthday Honours to submit [my] name to The Queen with a recommendation that Her Majesty may be graciously pleased to approve [I] be appointed a Member of the Order of the British Empire." Two days later I turned down the honour. It was particularly irritating coming, as it did supposedly, from Mrs Thatcher; but the real trigger was the form attached which in effect asked me to fill in why they were awarding me the MBE. I had just wasted much time on my Tax Return and this was one form I need not fill up! One can't help wondering now if my response would have been the same if the award had been a bit higher in rank. But no, to have to guess what conceivable "voluntary service" I had done was too great a task. If they didn't know, neither did I. Be that as it may, November 7th five years later did find me descending from

Roderick Ham's Volvo in the famous inner courtyard and having 'porte-cochéred' and entered, about to ascend the grand staircase inside. As I did so my companion muttered "Granada Tooting".

Thank goodness he, Richard Greenough, was there because he echoed just what I was thinking. There it all was: concealed cornice lighting, crystal chandeliers and all; what we were both doing was climbing the grand staircase of a picture palace in times long past. So, those super-cinemas accessible to all at such a modest price between the wars, really had been palaces. We were each greeted by HRH Duke of Edinburgh and there in the 155ft long Picture Gallery where the reception took place a shock awaited me. Up above the grand ornamental doorway, we had entered by, screwed to a bit of 2 x 1 inch whitewood was a lone very old Patt.23 spot. Its target was the great Van Dyck of Charles I on horseback. My tale has been told in usual detail elsewhere*. The Patt.23's presence there was so incongruous as to savour of a practical joke.

It was quite something that my 'double' brother Phil and I were present at both the Art Workers Guild's golden jubilee and the centenary celebrations. This was especially so as he died suddenly the following year. He had been elected in 1947 and was Master in 1981. His "was a year notable for the fact that the Master was the son of an important Guildsman and the brother of a Past-Master, a combination unique in the annals of the Guild," to quote the 98th Annual Report.

On my departure from Rank Strand I became a "Theatre Consultant". After all I was a founder member ('perforce'), of that society and its chairman about that time. Anyway I became nominally, and *nominal* was the word, associated with the partnership of Carr & Angier. The Liverpool Everyman came into my life about this time because they were considering a change of venue from their converted chapel in Hope Street to a disused Midland railway goods depot and warehouse in Victoria Street. This was, true to its period, a building of some architectural merit and size. The latter meant that it had to be shared with some other enterprise. I found myself sketching out several projects as the proposed theatre site moved from one part and level of the building to another. It was all very enjoyable. Being the Everyman they didn't want an orthodox theatre anyway and there was a Liverpool firm of architects† to attend to the practical side of any conversion. My last scheme I really fell in love with. It was an asymmetric thrust stage, backed by an inner stage, with an auditorium of a different asymmetry around it. This had a real logic since it was based on the maximum use of the fine brickwork and cast-iron columns of the

* *CUE* no. 35

† "He and I have been working hand in glove," Norman Kingham (Kingham Knight Assoc.)

existing structure. Some inspiration may have come from the use of the Puddledock brick walls for the Mermaid theatre of 1959. However this building was vast in comparison and asymmetric in plan anyway. This latter had resulted in some superb examples of skew brickwork, part of which I was able to use as a feature on one side of the stage. When desired, thrust shows could have been staged by simply filling in the 'pros.' opening with false brickwork. Alas, none of this came to anything and thoughts had to turn to improving the theatre in Hope Street. I was able to make one useful suggestion; but for the rest they knew their own theatre and it was much better to let them get on with its improvement.

Anyway I had to get off to America and conduct some Master classes at various universities, at the behest of Joel Rubin and USITT. The previous year the Master had been Josef Svoboda. It was possible to talk to the same group on theatre design and stage lighting as two distinct subjects instead of focusing on an audience interested in one or the other. Each stopover was of 4 or 5 days, which meant that I was able to look around a bit in addition to my work. Lunch, even breakfast on occasion, with students and dinner with some of the staff. It was a happy chance that it was one year later than my one and only Australian trip and one year before the United States Bicentennial celebrations. This meant that there was considerable refurbishment of the buildings of that time going on. Since Master dates were scattered right across the sub-continent, places like Lexington Mass. on the one side and Sacramento Calif. on the other were taken in my winged stride. Rightly or wrongly I associate the latter with the gold rush. In which case it was odd to find myself there exactly one year later than my visit to Ballarat, down-under. The Sacramento visit was due to its proximity to Davis. That university turned out to be great fun. I was having breakfast in my motel just beyond the campus, when I was told that my taxi was waiting. I denied ordering any such, as I intended to enjoy a walk there. However they were insistent, so breakfast finished, out I strode somewhat indignantly, there to discover a London black-cab ready and waiting!

Much the same thing happened at the other end of the day. Would I make sure the class ended at 4pm? On going outside, there it was - a red London double-decker. The real thing, not the automatic-door 'economic' substitutes we have been compelled to get used to, no matter how inappropriate they are to Central London traffic. Needless to say this Londoner had to pose on the rear platform while cameras clicked. The taxis and buses were run by the students to provide transport over the enormous Davis campus. Goodness knows whose good idea it was that they should acquire our London cast-offs for the purpose. At another of my stopovers I happened to remark as I opened my diary to begin the class "Good gracious it's my 64th birthday," and thought no more about it. At 'tea-time' the classroom lights suddenly blacked-out and through the doorway there was borne in triumph a large square iced cake with the requisite number of lighted candles! Everyone, tutors and all gathered around and that was the end of the class for that day. My last date was in a college of Technology in the heart of Los Angeles. Fortunately the hotel was not downtown but high on a hillside so I could enjoy some fresh air. It belonged very positively to the age of trans-continental rail travel tycoons for whom it had been built. There were archive photos everywhere and villas in the grounds. It was just as well that I slept out there, for I developed a sore throat and realised when I went on stage to give the lecture (an open one which usually ended each date), that once I paused, my voice would not restart. The result was unique. Words followed upon words and the audience, I hope, were unaware of any strain. But when I sat down at last and the chairman asked for questions, there was nothing for it but to shake my head and point to my throat from which nothing emerged. By chance, it was the last of all the dates and next day it was off home across the Pole. We had hardly taken-off when my nose started bleeding. Luckily there was no-one in the adjacent seats and I was able to tear up bits of paper serviette and stuff them up my left nostril; later to be discreetly stowed on my food trays. Back home an appointment to have the wayward veins cauterised, a more civilised process than dentistry, solved that problem.

Apropos of body troubles, speaking could carry something of a threat; namely how to keep clear of the need to cough. My TB troubles might be over, but my body no longer permitted a coughing cadenza. Too much of a tickle meant stop until, thanks to cold water, linctus or lozenge my body allowed me to speak again. My plight resembled that of any 'star' who has to take the stage, except there would be an understudy on hand. In my Strand years I used to comfort myself that thanks to a tape, sometimes a special one made in case, accompanied by someone to answer questions the *show* would go on. Infection could germinate in the immobilised regions of my chest much spittle. That nice polite word cannot disguise the task of getting rid of it in front of an audience *politely*.

My lecturing 'talents' achieved their peak in 1974 when without any effort on my part my name received Star-billing outside a real theatre in the West End for fourteen weeks or so. The idea of me giving a "Theatre Teach-In" as the Tuesday matinee attraction was Ian Albery's and the theatre was the Wyndhams. Could any much more distinguished theatrical family name be found, or a finer venue for the purpose than that theatre of theirs, which had just been carefully restored. So here was the 1899 Sprague auditorium ready to play its part in *my* show! The permanent set on stage for the evening performances of *Godspell* was another matter. It resembled, in so far as it resembled anything, a prison-camp exercise yard surrounded by metal posts and chicken-wire. Why I do not recall, although of course I saw the show. Anyway, there it was and there was certainly no question of dismantling it each Tuesday afternoon for my matinee. So I not only made myself use it and its Joe Davis lights for my demonstrations but also for a flourish of colour-music as the finale. The music for that purpose being the end of Tchaikovsky's *Manfred* symphony.

Since the CD-console was in a small room at the rear of the Dress Circle and I was on stage my role was limited to composition and the all important execution was delegated to the theatre's own switchboard operator. She - Marilyn James - played it very well and I never had a moment's anxiety. Indeed the co-operation of everyone was simply marvellous. They all entered into the fun of these unusual matinees. After the show proper, all those that wanted to were welcomed on stage, backstage, up in the flys and so on. With its 27-ft pros. and 51-ft high grid mainly of hemp-lines it was ideal for visitors. When the run ceased I was presented, much to my surprise, with a tape of my ad-lib lecture for my archive.

Since the object was to introduce the public to the technicians' side of theatre, the tabs were flown out and the working lights glared away on stage and auditorium alike before members of the audience drifted into the stalls. They had been issued with numbered seat tickets, which meant they were spread out to give the right feel no matter how many or few they were. The box-office skill in producing a half-full effect rather than a half-empty one never ceased to amaze me - no computer can be so human. There was one occasion when a large, Kohl-sized, German couple got up and left halfway into my Act 1. It turned out that it had taken them that long to realise I was not "Godspell". Not being an actor I thought it improper to enter via the wings, so I used the pass door and up the temporary forestage steps. The first thing was to tell my audience about the prompt corner and play a bit of tape of the SM in action at the start of a performance. Next the safety-curtain was introduced and how it had to 'hit' the stage in 30-seconds explained. Then down it came with the eyes of the entire house on it for once. It was then flown out to reveal that the house-tabs had been dropped in, and at the same time the house lights were raised. There Wyndhams was, dressed for a show. These tabs were something very special. They were brand new, beautifully made to the original swagged design. So good were they that I suggested interested members of the audience might like to use the forestage steps during the interval and enjoy them close-up. This some did. Relaxing over my cup of tea on stage behind the tabs I would see them move as they were felt and examined. The onset of this interval had to be exactly on time; otherwise the ice-creams sold in the auditorium would be too soft or too hard to 'spoon' out - more theatre technology!

The beauty of lecturing in a modest sized traditional theatre like this was the way its devices could be used, and explained at the same time because they were simple. Thus the screen, onto which slides were back-projected from time to time, was motorised and could be seen to fly in and out with a purpose - using push-buttons held in full view as I stood downstage. Likewise when slides were shown of the

'Lane', Covent Garden or something modern in its architecture or plan, it could be made to register strongly by direct comparison with the theatre in which they were sitting. The role of traditional scenery and the equipment to change and store it could be *understood.* This applies even to big sets and changes whereas the one-off star-role playing machinery of *Time* or *Miss Saigon*, for example, need the background of an engineer to appreciate. Conducted visits around the National on the South Bank and the like have become common since my time; but I have a feeling that like visitors to cathedrals and much else of our heritage, they are on a gawp-trip.

End of November 1974 found me listening to members of the Australian Opera, singing in wine cellars beneath my feet while another Aussie refilled this Pommie's glass by squirting champagne at it with a petrol pump hosepipe - for that is what the trigger-operated gadget resembled. It was Spring down-under and I had just enjoyed a lone stride along a sandy beach while the Aussies shunned its sunlight. The place was a large vineyard area not far from Adelaide. The reason I was able to do this was that I still had my summer tan whereas they hadn't developed theirs yet. The picture was the exact reverse of what I had expected - a lone pale Pom dwarfed by beach of muscular tanned Aussies. A bit later we were to hear that Opera company do *Tosca* and *Magic Flute* in the new Adelaide Festival theatre opera house. This Sunday they were relaxing!

The fact that I was there in South Australia was due to my role as the then chairman of the ABTT and organiser of the overseas speakers for the "Building Theatres for Communities" symposium in the new Adelaide Festival Centre. My own experience, particularly at the 1960 Berlin Colloquium, had taught me that I must keep the USA out of it or we would be swamped with delegates. So acting on the advice of Gerd Ohlmer, Wally Russell and other 'locals' known to me, I was able to field a team of seven speakers - two each from Germany, Canada and England, and one from the Netherlands. The Aussies did us proud and by flying us to various venues in a pair of small Cessnas, we were able to get the feel of the kind of Communities which were to be under discussion. These stopovers involved stowing our luggage in the plane behind the rear pair of seats. Helmut Grosser watched our untidy attempts until he could stand it no longer; he said, "Here let me." or something of the sort and slung the stuff out to pack it back systematically. A perfect job resulted, as might be expected from the then Technical Director of the Cologne Opera, and we were more than content to leave it in his expert hands each time. In these towns a 1920s middle-class feeling seemed to prevail socially. It took me back to my Aeschylus amateur years. At Mildura I was so moved that I sought out backstage the chap who did a soft-shoe shuffle act. There he was helping do the washing-up. Another piquant effect, particularly apparent at Whyalla, was the approach of Christmas. The contrast between the tinsel decorated town and the blazing hot sunshine can be imagined. Apparently Christmas pudding on *the day* is de rigueur.

It was our first visit down-under and I know we were all equally struck by this civilisation still living on the edges of the vast empty continent. To me there was not the usual feeling as a stranger visiting a foreign country; *they* didn't seem to me really to belong *there* either - nonsense, of course. My own visit was extended by arriving at Perth in the far West before and going to Melbourne via Ballarat after the Colloquium. This was to fulfil the non-Adelaide lecture dates at Denis Irving's behest. As he was then both general-manager Strand Electric Australia and chairman of the IES there, this was appropriate. Perth was a mixture of the mature and the new. The new concert hall evoked something of the feel of our 1930s Bournemouth Pavilion, although the Swan river had to replace the Solent. Perhaps it was the sort of people using it. It certainly was not the architectural style. Also the 1904 His Majesty's Theatre ("The Maj.") on the edge of threatening high-rise development made a lasting impression. Fortunately it also lasted to be splendidly restored and improved in 1980*; but I imagine there is now a mass of the usual high-rise office blocks beyond. Indeed I fear that a return visit if made in this year of 1992 might show a much less attractive Australia than that of 1974. The real charm of the Australian variants of Victorian and Edwardian architecture was as big a surprise as the mosaic paving and other wonders of Lisbon on that first visit in 1940. The practical corrugated iron roofs really did fit and with the cast-iron railings, veranda and balcony fronts - and the purely decorative use as brackets and valences made a great impression. Masses of ironwork had been shipped out as ballast and, as I was to find, it was not peculiar to Perth. I was so overcome that I had to give a talk about it at the Art Workers Guild when I got home. Happily there were Rod Ham's fine slides, taken then, to confirm what their PM Fred said.

To return to the real purpose of the visit: I quote from a contemporary account by Richard Pilbrow, who managed to join us, as part of a circumnavigation of the globe he was doing at the time:-

> *The conference begins. We move into the smallest auditorium, the adaptable studio theatre. Problem; it is a black box 80-ft square with bleacher seating across one end. Fred Bentham kicks off in splendid and caustic style. Irreverent introductions of the foreign visitors are intermingled with even more pungent remarks on unadaptable adaptability. At lunch one begins to meet the other delegates. It's apparently a quite unique assembly of*

* *Sightline* Vol.14 No.2 Autumn 1980

> *people from right across Australia, many of whom are meeting for the first time. That in itself, like the foundation of our ABTT in 1961, is sort of special.*
>
> *Even more special is Fred's luncheon partner. We were expecting the afternoon session to be opened by the Premier of South Australia, the Hon. Don Dunstan, who is to make a speech on radio and television about his policy for the arts. Fred I discover, talking to a young, somewhat extravagantly dressed, long-haired character. A white linen bell-bottomed shirtless suit with plunging neckline and gold medallion. Thinking to rescue Fred from a possibly 'not-his-scene' conversation with the principal dancer of the Australian Ballet, I sidle up. 'Ah, Richard,' says Fred, 'I don't believe you've met the Premier.' The writer, not used to such political confrontation, simply gawped.*
>
> *The gawping soon turned to envy and enthusiasm. By the end of the lunch break the adaptable theatre had been rejigged by Bentham, Russell and Pilbrow into some resemblance of intimacy and our youthful but distinguished guest spoke on the Arts and his determination to provoke a renaissance...*

Our conference was not there to discuss the likes of the Sydney Opera House or the Adelaide Festival Centre itself, both of which had not long opened then. Speaking of likes, I must say that Adelaide has a practical building to work in whereas Sydney - but there is no need to go on about that 'opera house'. What was especially charming about Adelaide was the costume, white blouse and long red skirt, worn by the attendants. This style eventually turned up on our South Bank; but the National chose a muddy mauve for the same skirts. Adelaide had been doing Festivals for years before the Centre was built and I had been invited over there several times; but as I have hinted the Aussies and their continent had intimidated me. How wrong I was. I really fell in love with the place and could imagine myself living there and working in their very varied theatres. Above all, the way nobody expected or wanted tips made it the only civilised society that I have encountered. Denis Irving warned me not to tip and he as an Aussie knew; I wonder whether it still applies? Conversation with head waiters and so on was between equals, instead of giving the diner the usual sense of inferiority. Particularly they liked it if you knew that part of England they or their families had come from. The head waiter at the Windsor in Melbourne was delighted to find that I had recently visited Stamford in Lincolnshire and could assure him that it was well looked after.

Not everything was dictated by thespian duty or interest on this trip, and my ever abiding memory must be of the vividly coloured bird life. Nothing had prepared me for the shock of budgies and parakeets flying or perching among the rather drab foliage. One simply does not expect to be accosted by vivid red, blue and green birds outside a cage. Not even our "most remarkable bird" Willie* had prepared me for this. They might talk fluently, but saturated hues flying around, certainly not. Denis drove Richard Pilbrow and I from Adelaide to Melbourne via Ballarat in his new Range Rover and we were able to experience what it is like to leave the car and walk out into The Bush. At the point he chose, at any rate, there was a complete lack of landmarks. Nothing distinctive to home in on; to get lost would be second nature to me there - in spite of the "bump of locality" Father always claimed he and I were born with. Another surprise was the narrowness of the tarmac on this important trunk highway, to pass or overtake seemed almost always to involve raising a cloud of dust by swerving onto the un-made up border. Then again there were the run-over kangaroos, where in England we might encounter rabbits or sadly a badger.

My last night was in Sydney, where our group had the run of a wine store, and the fine full moon outside decided to total eclipse and thereby take Helmut and I off our guard when we emerged. Habitually used to checking lighting effects, we could swear that there was a moon, except that there wasn't. The flight home to England with but a short stop in Perth for refuelling and an hour only at Bombay airport, seemed to be designed to ensure complete darkness outside for 90% of the journey. After 20, or was it 24, hours of this I arrived back with the reasoning part of my brain inert. That my companions on the two gangway seats had been a Civil Servant type and his son, with whom I found it difficult to exchange any real conversation, hadn't been any help either. In contrast on the outward journey my neighbour had chanced to be a Dane who was great fun; especially as the breakfast taken on at Bombay claimed to be *Danish* pastries. Seizing my case as soon as it landed on the carousel at Heathrow I was passed through Customs without having to open it. Ilse picked me up outside and when we got home I proudly opened-up my case to give her *the* present - a black opal. There on the top of everything was spread out a very much second hand pair of lacy cami-knickers!! Plunging into the depths there was other evidence - this was not my own case. Curiously it was of the same rather uncommon type, colour and size. I then remembered that when picking up it had looked much more elderly than mine; but the brain had been in no condition to veto this action. So what to do? Ringing the baggage hall, they told me to bring it back to them there and then. How do I get past the Customs? Just come back the same way

* Our resident verbose Budgie's description of himself. One did not have to prompt him, but a favourite of his; "Strand Electric Lighting for 'Tainment" got as far as "Temple Bar four" and then he became incoherent in his excitement.

as you went out. So in due course there am I walking contra-flow with a nervous shifty-look and nobody took any notice. I went up to a sort of foreman's counter and the chap behind it simply told me to dump it down and look for mine among the others dumped here and there on the floor. Having found it, I walked out again unchallenged by anyone. Of course, that was 1974. All the same, such lax supervision was rather asking for trouble one fine day, was it not?

Back home, there was writing to do for Francis Reid as *TABS* (Vol.33 No2) and for myself as *Sightline* (Vol.8 No.2) about the Australian adventure - many words but few photographs. Cameras have never been a love of mine. I have possessed some, including 8mm-film ones in the clockwork and battery eras; but systematic labelling and filing for access has never been me. Writing is another matter, I enjoy taking trouble over that. And have to confess I also enjoy reading my stuff if I got it right and it looks inviting on paper.

I think the word "Sightline" evokes the decade which immediately followed my departure from Rank Strand. It provided a discipline among my varied free-lance roles as author, lecturer, consultant, committee member or whatever. In Spring and Autumn each year this new ABTT journal had to appear. Being ABTT it had to be produced as inexpensively as possible. Since none of today's computer composition and printing aids were around, it meant that one had to rely on oneself and other enthusiastic amateurs for everything except the actual process of printing. Any resort to the Twynam organisation, on whom I had automatically relied in the case of *TABS*, was out of the question. 'B' found our first printer, at that time based nearby in Garrick Street. I am sure "The Lamb and Flag" had much to do with the making of this convenient contact. Needless to say 'B' also had a lot to do with the successful production of those early issues. Hardly had we got our Spring 1974 issue of *Sightline* under way, when Andrew Taylor, who had stopped *TABS**, was prevailed upon by Strand reps. to restart *TABS,* which he did with Francis Reid as editor. The first, in its large A4 format and in colour, came out that April. After 14 issues that came to an end in 1978. One year later, Twynam launched *CUE* (Rank having retained the *TABS* title) with six issues a year. Although I wrote a number of articles for both over the years, my first duty was to *Sightline* for the time I was its editor. I disliked the large A4 format so kept to A5. This granted, in effect, ten years further life for the old *TABS* with its 'anon' editorials etc as a handy reference book to *read* rather than look at.

Piquantly, the reign of Reid began with a full page article, "Thank You, Fred" and ended with a full page, "Thank You, Francis". The first bears the initials F.R. and the latter F.P.B. There was to be a complete change of character when after a gap of two

* This, plus the closing of King Street, was the reason I decided to retire.

years a Vol. 37 No. 1 appeared under Richard Harris as editor. The change in style was so great that I used to think of it as the *Strand Sun.* Photographs not least of the editor, and of the ever changing managers and executives, joined the latest equipment to be promoted in a news journal which did ultimately become what suited the style of the time - a commercial handout to push the goods for sale - *Strandlight.* As soon as I gave up *Sightline* it in its turn became A4 under Ian Herbert, and before long a quarterly. It is these that I regard as of true *TABS* descent. Other technical journals, have come and gone, and did certainly pay their authors better, do not belong here. At this point I was intrigued to find out from my aged youthful press book, that in 1935 there were *eleven* technical journals who considered my Light Console of interest to their readers around the time of its launch.

Nothing in marketing or company promotion stays for long nowadays even if the Company or Organisation manages to avoid its sell-off or its takeover. So it was hardly surprising to find a new journal from Strand under the title of *LIGHTS!* with the opening of the new decade of the 90s. Both Vol .1 Issue 1 and 2 have large female faces in full colour on the cover. A long way from the demure damsel cowering within the protective embrace of the young hero while a middle-aged threat enters actors right complete with top hat. Issue 2 page 3 presented us with, for the first time ever, a real *page 3* blonde with garters, thighs and bulging Bs. Contrast that with the trouble to get my fellow directors to accept, "and it wasn't 'F' for Frank or Flame either" for the 1964 Golden Jubilee *TABS*. That *LIGHTS!* is "Edited, designed and produced" by a Communications Group" may explain the photographic slant. Or it could be the fact that one of the two "Editorial advisers" in 1990 was at one time a Royal Artillery officer?

"...the demure damsel cowering..."

On an ABTT visit to see and hear the special effects for Ayckbourne's *Henceforward* and go behind scenes afterwards, I was waiting in the foyer of the Vaudeville while members assembled. Among them entered Bill

Crisp (then part-time at Strand Lighting) with his lovely young daughter. Sitting together in the stalls during the demonstration I remembered that Bill hadn't got a daughter; son yes, daughter no. So who was this alongside all agog for any wise words I might drop? When the time came to depart, still puzzled, as we exited together through the main doors I contrived to linger a moment frantically to ask Paul Weston - who is she? She was the aforesaid ex-Artillery officer, no less. What's more, I had been introduced to her a few months earlier playing her marketing manager role at the Rank Strand 'New Year do' in the Grand Saloon at Drury Lane! A few months later she, Camilla, departed from Rank Strand for Unipart and all likelihood of her consulting me on anything was thereby removed. Opting for such a great change of scene is difficult to understand for the likes of me. In the Strand-Bentham era one had a love of stage lighting or whatever, which led one automatically into the various areas to foster and expand it. Now you go in for marketing, admin. or whatever as a career and the material objects you handle is of little personal concern. It could be filing-cabinets, potato-crisps, carpets or computers. Any satisfaction is obtained from figures on your own and the firm's balance sheets. Can there be a bigger contrast than the art of theatrical lights and that of car-parts? I wonder if this lament would have taken shape on paper here if the marketing executive in question had been a man? Many of them have come and gone in the Rank reign without remark. If anyone had told me back in the 1930s that in my eightieth year my heart would still beat somewhat faster at the sight of an attractive woman, I would not have believed them. Yet, come to think of it, Grandpa Bentham told Phil and I so on one of our rare visits to Clacton and it couldn't have been The Mater he was referring to!

Eighty: I received a warning from the DHSS* in January that this event was in sight. From October 23rd they told me I would receive an extra *25p* per week pension. I well recall the occasion in 1974 when Percy Corry and I 'celebrated' his extra 25p. We thought this increase dotty then; but after all the inflation since what was one to think in 1991? There can be no doubt that while in government, ministers simply do not inhabit the real world. They only see the things they do as totals in budgets or on balance sheets, they don't *feel* them. Add to this the fact that nowadays the minister spends even less time 'in charge' of a particular department than a Managing Director at Rank Strand. There is no need to go on to labour (or rather to Tory) the point; it has all been so well expressed in BBC TV's "Yes, Minister" programmes. How can one face up to voting in the over-heralded next election? During the last decade or so it was easy, the aim had to be to get rid of Margaret Thatcher. This in spite of her good work (aided by Arthur Scargill!) with

* Department of Heath and Social Security

the unions. In much the same way back in July 1945, Churchill notwithstanding, the Conservatives *had* to go. All in all it is a disillusioned Fred who writes this particular paragraph. It is so easy to go on and on in this mode. In hasty glance around for the real achievements during my eighty years, medicine and surgery must surely come top. It may be difficult of access but it is there; one looks back with horror at what they could not do in Father's lifetime; he died from a simple minor operation in hospital. My sister would still be more likely to die prematurely at the age of 32 from the cancer she had, but she would have stood some chance. Let the imagination roam further back in history and I find the singing of plainchant gives me the creeps - think of what they could not do in those distant centuries. In other fields we could do without most developments of my own time, except of course washing-up liquid. We certainly did without television very easily in the days before it existed, much as I have enjoyed certain programmes and have had pleasure in playing a tiny part in its development.

It was television which prompted a real celebration of my *eightieth* on the very day itself. My 70th and 75th birthdays by chance (or design!) each coincided with a meeting of a committee known to me as E3192. It began by representing theatre and film lighting for the CIE† in Paris. Officially its object is to collect reports and present them at an international conference held every four years. I know Fred wrote our part of the report for the Eindhoven conference before the Hitler War and L.G. Applebee presented it. Anyway, we have the UK committee, meeting every six months for business and lunch. The venues vary depending whose turn it is to host the occasion. On October 23rd 1991 is was appropriately Strand Lighting. Thanks to connivance between Ken Ackerman and Andy Collier, many were the familiar faces when we adjourned for lunch in today's equivalent of the Seecol demonstration theatre of far-off days.

Somehow we have become more detached from the filing cabinets in Paris. Television was added and soon became the leading component from Riverside time and our chairman now for decades has been Ken Ackerman. He it was who invented the *Showlight* conference amid grave doubts of many of us, including myself. The first was held in June 1981. It was also notable for being the first event, other than the laying of the foundation concrete-block, to be held in the Barbican Centre. It was a great and friendly success, *Showlight* that is!

An early E3192 secretary was Phil Berkeley of ABC Television down by the Thames in Teddington. He was a very energetic pioneer, whose contribution must not be forgotten. In 1965 there was a mini-conference in Prague at the invitation of their CIE branch. So having just landed, there we were about to go through

† Commission International d'Eclairage

customs. The focus was on Ilse and I. Would they open her case and, if so, would they regard me as *superman*? Although our party was only staying for a week or so, Ilse was going to see her sister in Leipzig and she had lots of packets of a romantic commodity difficult to obtain there. Both Ken and Johnny Johnson were in the know and watched expectantly. But we were all waved through. That evening we had a real problem. We had started to walk to the National Theatre but realising we would be late, summoned a taxi. But how to get the driver to take us to the theatre on time for the Svoboda *Romeo & Juliet*? None of the variants on the word "theatre" we thought up produced any response. Eventually we found that we were almost there anyway. The word we needed, as we found inside, was "Divadlo". We were in the "Narodni Divadlo", across the frontier in Russia it would have been "Narodni Teatr" or something of that sort. With Ilse's fluent German we thought we would get on fine. Not so, not unnaturally they had 'sworn' not to use German. Their second language was the Russian of their liberators. Once home (via Leipzig!) Ilse set about learning Russian. Our next visit to see and write an article for *TABS* about the theatre we had equipped in Usti, gave Ilse no chance to use her Russian. Thanks to the invasion shortly before, their second language was German! We also revisited some friends we had made in Prague on our first visit. In fact their daughter Leda had been with us on 'Peter Sam' canalling at the time of that invasion. Prague was a wonderful city to see and had a fabulous range of theatres*. It has of course become with the co-operation of John Bury the HQ of scene designers (or scenographers as they prefer to call them) worldwide.

It was the craft of television design which introduced me to Richard Greenough, when he was head of it for ATV. Since his retirement he, the AWG's only "television designer", has been promoted to become my only assistant in the only department left to me at 80 to call my own. This, the Guild Sherry bar, uses his talents (or some of them at any rate) deployed as pouring-out and as change-giving. That we have this bar to warm up our meetings as they assemble is due to Bentham nagging over very many years. Eventually it was agreed upon, provided we ran it. This Phil and I did originally and Richard is his worthy successor. It is great fun and ensures my attendance at each fortnightly meeting whether I like the subject or not. It often turns out that the latter provide the really interesting evenings. I owe a lot to the Guild especially in the later part of my life. It was even responsible in 1988 for my return to the Midhurst King Edward VII sanatorium and what is more, my nurse went along with me!

* see *TABS* Vol.23 No.2 and Vol. 30 No.4

The visit arose from the choice of Haselmere (not unnaturally as Carl Dolmetsch was master that year) for the Summer Outing. So on the 16th of July, Ilse and I found ourselves passing through the Blue Lounge of "another bod" memory and being shown round. For me, although a resident for so long, it was an eye-opening tour, as I had never been outside in all that time because my body never managed to qualify as an up-patient for long enough. Why would the AWG want to visit the scene of my confinement? The answer is that I had discovered that this building of 1903 was designed by Charles Holden and is therefore of architectural interest. The party was not taken around the wards; but Ilse and I, as a very special couple, were conducted on a sentimental journey up there afterwards by the administrator. The history of this sanatorium has a lesson for us at a time when opting-out has become a key word for NHS hospitals.

"At the turn of the century tuberculosis was widespread in Britain. At least a quarter of a million people suffered from it and 40,000 died every year, many of them in their youth or in the prime of their life." This quote and those that follow, are from the history of "The King's Sanatorium" published in 1986*, a copy of which was presented to the two of us. One gathers that King Edward VII really did get much involved in this enterprise. It was not just a matter of lending his name and in due course, declaring the building open, to the applause of the multitude. Consumption, as it was then known, was no respecter of class. Obviously, the rich could languish in their estates or travel abroad to kinder climates. For the poor there was charity maybe; but what of the gap between the two? This Midhurst was intended to cover. Thus, "The social status of patients was an important factor in deciding whether they should or should not be accepted for admission.... "the King and his Advisory Committee had indicated quite clearly for whom the Institution was intended: the educated but less well off, middle class, professional people who were neither able to pay full private fees nor were the proper recipients of public charity." This certainly sums up that Fred Bentham of Strand Electric. But in "1906 Count Albert Mensdoff's valet was refused admission because he did not belong to the class of patient ... And in 1910 the future Lord Dawson of Penn "reported that one or two of the women patients were below the social standard which he felt was 'desirable to keep the tone of the sanatorium good' ".

Open Air and Absolute Rest were the rule and patients were not to be encouraged "even to read". What I can't imagine is what you were supposed to do with your mind while stuck in bed on your own, forbidden to read. After all, those were the years long before the coming of the wireless, let alone TV. Having typed these words I realised that is just what hostages, like Terry Waite, have put up with today. With the same uncertainty as to when, if ever, they will be released, and in

* by S.E. Large, pub. by Phillimore & Co. Ltd., Chichester, Sussex.

appalling conditions. The marvellous gardens at the Midhurst sanatorium (now hospital thanks to effective TB chemotherapy) were by Gertrude Jekyll and apparently gardening had been at one time the equivalent for the less ill of the glove-making therapy offered me. Faced as I had been for those many months with an open view in all weathers of the gardens, it was but fair that on this one occasion when I was free to walk and sit in them, the sun came out.

It is all too easy to look back as an elderly, with sixty years of light work behind him, and find satisfaction in the periods he lived in rather than that he now inhabits. Things were better then or is he subconsciously picking out the best bits in the memory? Thus, even the immediate post-war years, when there was rationing still and so much to clear up or rebuild, many of us remember as a happy time of promise. Things were bound to improve one day . On the contrary in New York, the city seemed haunted in the mid-fifties by the certainty that they would be 'nuked sooner or later'. There were notices all over the place telling you where to go to, if! Usually six floors lower down, if I recall aright, than wherever you were, no matter how high the skyscraper. It was as if they felt guilty because they had not been bombed. In London we had our bombing penance behind us and in a very real way the 1951 Festival summed up our feelings, especially if you had some role to play there. Add to that my own recovery from a prolonged 'fatal' illness culminating in marriage and two sons.

The word "sons" prompts the thought that there *is* another achievement of this time to add to my very short list and that is the improved status of women. That our civilised society expected them to retire into the home, maybe for ever as soon as children arrived on scene, is now as incredible as the yashmaks of the Middle East always were. There is no doubt looking back that Ilse should have had the chance to return to her own nursing world a lot earlier than she eventually did. At least she did go back in time to enjoy several years using her many qualifications. To excuse my poor role in this, one has only to look at my upbringing. All middle class wives stayed at home. The better off, who certainly did not include Mother, seemingly doing nothing in particular and doing it very well. In preparing for marriage before the war the man had to pay for everything and took it for granted that the girl he was courting would give up her job the moment the vow was taken, if not some weeks beforehand so she could kit out for the great ceremony. Our registry office wedding was no such grand affair. It was nice and intimate with just three friends invited for lunch afterwards. Then '*my*' wife went off to her Ealing clinic for afternoon duty . As for myself I cannot remember that afternoon; but I do recall that just as lunch was about to start, there was a long urgent call from the LCC about the Royal Festival Hall. Even more important, that very evening I had to go all on my own to the Art Workers Guild. Why a solo visit on that night of all nights? The answer was that the subject was the Pipe Organ, an all time first for the Guild and this was not a Ladies' night. Women visitors were not allowed; not even on their wedding night!

This true tale I could not relate for 41 years - until May 30th 1991 to be precise, at the Guild's very next meeting on this particular subject. It took the form of a visit to the organ works of N.P. Mander Ltd in Bethnal Green. There has been no sex discrimination since 1964; but Ilse was not there, she was pursuing her addictive hobby of the last decade - bell-ringing! As can be imagined walking round a real pipe organ works revived many varied distant memories. Overall hung the same perfume of woodworking as at North Acton and to prime the pump, my walk there from the station actually took me along "Pollard Row" - an evocation of dear old Jim of Comptons indeed. Strangely, the last active outing he and I did was to St. Paul's Cathedral to hear George Thalben Ball give one of the inaugural recitals on the Mander rebuild of the Willis organ. On which nostalgic note it would not seem inappropriate to bring this coda of mine to a close. I wonder what might have happened if as a schoolboy I *had* learned to play the real organ and not had to invent one of my own I *could* play to express myself.

APPENDIX : STRAND - BENTHAM CONTROL SYSTEMS 1935-72

Edited extracts from my 1976 edition of The Art of Stage Lighting.

Electro-Mechanical Dimmer Bank

The extensive use of these prior to 1964 by Strand Electric had no parallel anywhere else. Based on the Mansell clutch, in which pairs of 15 - 17 volt electro-magnets gripped either side of an iron wheel and were linked to a dimmer crank above and below the pivot to obtain reversal. The dimmer wheels were mounted on horizontal shafts and driven, sometimes as many as 120, as a single bank by one variable-speed motor. The dimmers were resistances or double-commutator 5 kW transformers. From 1955 a polarized relay servo was used. When the dimmer lever potentiometer was moved, DC current in the centre line causes the sensitive relay to switch in the appropriate clutch and drive the dimmer and its slave potentiometer until they balanced. Current ceased to flow and the relay cut out. Time taken was determined by the motor speed - usually variable between 3 and 45 sec. Contactor switches in series with the dimmer, and in the case of the Light Console (q.v.) in parallel as well, were used for instantaneous changes.

Light Console

Each channel was selected by a stopkey to be "played" on a master keyboard. When off, the dimmer stayed where it was last driven. Each master consisted of twelve keys, three of each colour - white, red, blue, and green. The stopkeys were coloured similarly. Dimmers could be moved against their colour master by using "Reverse" and "General Move". Master keys were double-touch giving in fours from the left: Blackout/Dim, Raise/Dim, Full-on/Raise. Dimmers had both series and short-circuiting contactors. Speed of dimmer movement was by balanced (swell) pedal usually one per keyboard. Each keyboard had a left master and a right master with a centre set of keys to operate both at once. Where there was more than one keyboard they also coupled together. There were usually between thirty-two and forty channels per master of four colours. Stopkeys were subject to organ-type memory combination action from pistons in the keyslip. Second touch on a stopkey read the position of the dimmer on a dial, one per colour, which at other times read a dummy dimmer ("setter") to measure the amount of movement imparted. The groups

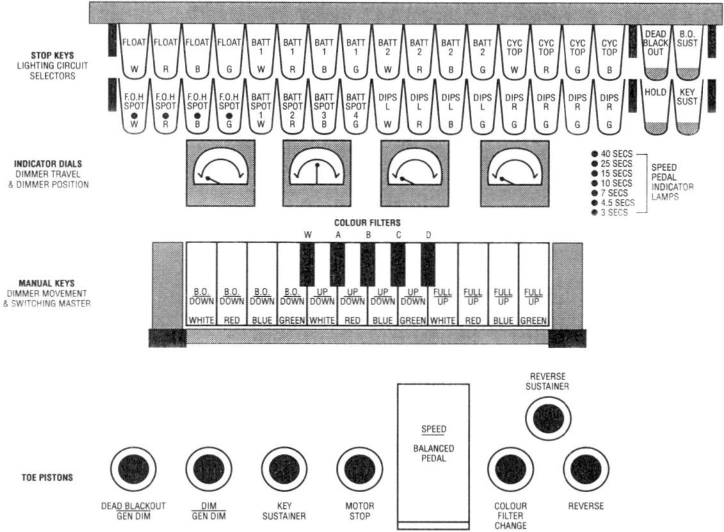

Basic Controls for Light Console

of five black notes gave colour filters, A, B, C, D and white on any channels whose lanterns were so fitted and whose stopkeys were selected.

Polarized Relay Servo (System PR)

Originally an attempt to reproduce with electro-mechanical servo the facilities of the "Electronic" preset (q.v.). Being electro mechanical, inertia gave a two preset ahead effect. This was further exploited in later models housed in vertical control cabinets where dimmer grouping and contactor switching was given separate three-position amber tablet switches so that three groups could be formed for movement within the presets.

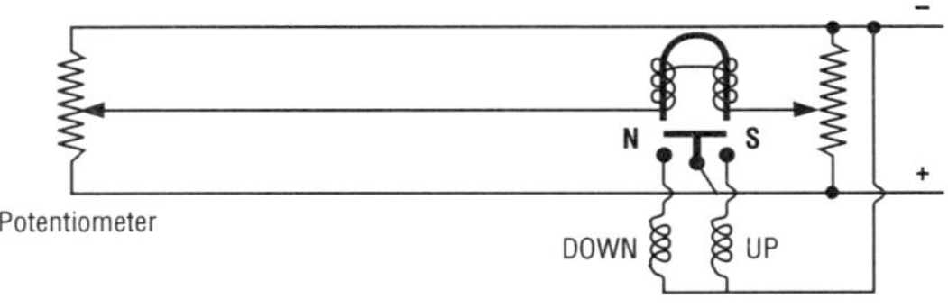

Polarized Relay Servo

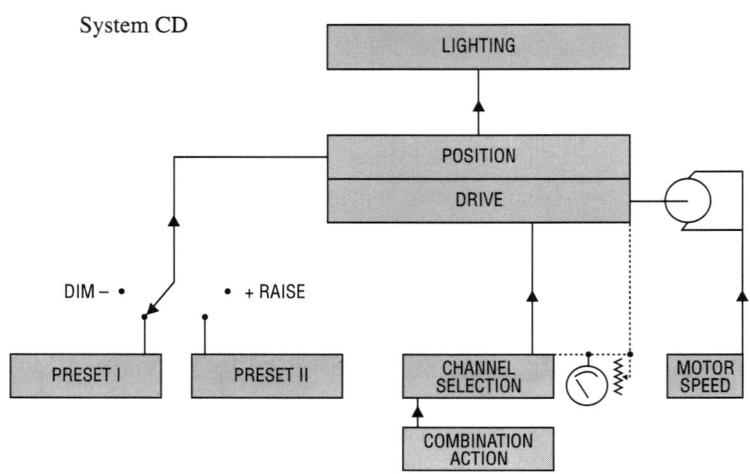

System CD
A combination of the polarized relay servo and the Light Console designed to exploit fully the "inertia" possibilities of electro-mechanical servo.

One or two sets of dimmer levers as presets was usual and, in addition, each channel had a stopkey as a selector. Combinations of these could be captured and moved whenever required by memory action, fourteen or twenty memories being usual. Normally only the dimmers of the channels selected moved, no matter what the position of the levers on the preset, the speed of movement being governed by a balanced foot pedal. A full-on and a dim push could be used to raise or lower them without need to reset their preset levers. "Remainder Dim" took out all channels not selected and when used with a preset provided a very easy cross-fade. Individual dimmer positions could be read on a dial by second touching each channel stopkey.

System C
This was a variant of CD with a further extension of facilities for television, and there principally by the BBC for Grade I studios. It used a luminous stophead selector adjacent to each pair of preset levers in the earlier versions and in the later a touch contact illuminated scale integral with the dimmer levers.

All-electric Dimmer Systems
There were seven main forms of these dimmers : Saturable Reactor, Thyratron-controlled Reactor, Transistor-controlled Reactor, Magnetic Amplifier, Two-valve Thyratron, Three-valve Thyratron, and Thyristor. The main distinction was that in the first four the load-carrying unit is an iron-cored reactor whose impedance is

varied, whereas the other three function by chopping the a.c. wave to allow a varying part to be transmitted directly through them. In its simplest and least expensive form the reactor was not suitable for presetting.

Saturable Reactor Dimmers

Limited load variation of two to one requiring tap changing at dimmer to achieve best performance. Dimmer sizes were commonly 1 kW and 2 kW but also 500 watt, 3 kW and 5 kW. Weight considerable. Control by saturation of iron core with d.c. winding fed through metal rectifier from a.c. potentiometer network. Contactor to each channel to discount load line was essential.

Simple Reactor Control

Single dimmer level per channel with, in Strand Electric (System SR) examples, twenty-one steps covered by reactor time lag. Grouping switches to select on master X or master Y. In smaller models combined with contactor feed to give "off" at mid position. When separate contactor switches were fitted, centre position of dimmer switch (coloured amber) became independent live allowing cross-fade between two groups with a third remaining stationary. Channel contactor switches then connected a Blackout A or B off.

Preset Reactor Control system LC

Transistor amplifiers with feedback in control line which gave presetting and improve variable load performance within the same curve. Four to one possible in good examples but pronounced time-lag at quarter load.

Two presets standard with amber tablet switches to form groups X, Y, and Z on rotary masters three per reset. Switches to couple together to any one preset master. Second set of switches connected channel contactor to either master blackout, A or B or off. Maximum number of possible channels was ninety-six but forty-eight or seventy-two was usual.

Luminous Preset (LP and Lightset)

Three presets in horizontal rows. Touch contact dimmer scales would light in red and white to form and display group X and Y separately or together or off. Cross-fades within presets with third group stationary were therefore possible. Further, while different groups could be set on each preset, they can be instantly matched for cross-fade at the touch of the appropriate push when required.

IDM

Introduced by Strand Electric in 1967 and superseded four years later by Rank Strand's system MSR with improved electronics. Complete set of luminous mimic micro-switch levers with A and B manual masters. Mechanical numerical selectors (IDM) or keyboard type (MSR) for Record and Playback. C and D faders and crossfader for playback. For IDM/R see under WHZ.

MEMO-Q

This was the version of the IDM memory system made in the United States for Century Strand and Strand Century in Canada. The keyboard call-up represented an improvement.

Multi-group Preset (C/AE MGP)

Two or three preset solid state switching version of what was known in its relay form a C/AE. Each preset had a set of touch-contact dimmer scales lit in red and white, corresponding to a red (active) master and a white (park) master. Memory action could record the red combination in use as on or off for recall (hence MG = multi group). Transfer from the red master to the white or vice versa took place at any time these are approximately lined up. The white master is mainly intended to hold a channel in use but not active, said to be "parked". Cross-fades could take place within a preset by using both masters. This is the nearest all-electric equivalent to System CD.

DDM

This system was based on a computer software and using rockers for channel control was the last to be devised and made under my immediate direction. It was installed at Stratford-upon-Avon in the winter of 1971. If the Light Console is the alpha then this was the omega of that side of my Strand Electric career. Subsequently Rank Strand engineers slightly altered the ergonomic basis of the master panel and in the revised form a good number were installed of which the largest was 320 channels.

System WHZ

This Strand control managed to stagger through its demonstration in February 1966 to become "the world's first stage lighting control to record dimmer positions instantly by magnetic means, access for playback or modification being immediate also". The first such system to work reliably was, however, Thorn's Q-File (with numerical call-up) four months later. The spirit of what WHZ should have done was captured in the rockers of DDM.

A large proportion of this equipment both lanterns and controls, survive in the Museum in Southbourne, Hants, run by David Sandham, or can be hired from Jim Laws Lighting, Wrentham, Suffolk.

INDEX